ADOLESCENT PREGNANCY AND PARENTHOOD

REFERENCE BOOKS
ON FAMILY ISSUES
(VOL. 16)

GARLAND REFERENCE LIBRARY
OF SOCIAL SCIENCE
(VOL. 523)

Reference Books
On Family Issues

ADOLESCENT PREGNANCY AND PARENTHOOD
An Annotated Guide

Ann Creighton-Zollar

GARLAND PUBLISHING, INC. • NEW YORK & LONDON
1990

Library of Congress Cataloging-in-Publication Data

Zollar, Ann Creighton
    Adolescent pregnancy and parenthood: an annotated guide / Ann
Creighton-Zollar.
        p. cm. — (Reference books on family issues; vol. 16)
(Garland reference library of social science; vol. 523)
    Includes bibliographical references.
    ISBN 0–8240–4295–6 (alk. paper)
    1. Teenage parents—United States—Bibliography. 2. Teenagers—
United States—Sexual behaviors—Bibliography. 3. Teenage
pregnancy—United States—Bibliography. I. Title. II. Series:
Reference books on family issues ; v. 16. III. Series: Garland
reference library of social science; v. 523.
Z7164.Y8Z64   1990
[HQ759.64]
016.30685'6—dc20   89–25596
                                                                    CIP

Printed on acid-free, 250-year-life paper
Manufactured in the United States of America

To
Nicai Quinn Zollar

CONTENTS

PREFACE

This bibliography is selective rather than exhaustive. It emphasizes the research literature available in the social and behavioral sciences. It is limited to English language publications. The initial search was limited to *Sociological Abstracts* and *Psychological Abstracts*. After the original search an attempt was made to locate the most frequently referenced items. The bibliography does not contain items that are difficult to obtain (like some government documents) or those which are expensive to obtain (like dissertations). The majority of the items were published in the 1970s and 1980s, though a few from the 1960s have also been included. I read each of the items and wrote each of the annotations myself. The items published in 1988 and 1989 were obtained by searching the current periodicals reading rooms in both James Branch Cabell Library at the Academic Campus and Tompkins-McCaw Library at the Medical College of Virginia Campus of Virginia Commonwealth University.

I tried to include items that were reflective of the entire range of research interests in the area of adolescent pregnancy and parenthood in the United States. Since I plan to use many of these items in graduate seminars where the students will be called upon to evaluate existing research, I did not critique but rather summarized them. Where the limitations of time and space allowed, I wrote annotations that I thought would be helpful to researchers and to those interested in the nature as well as the results of research. These annotations include information about sample size and data collection techniques as well as information about the research problems and findings.

Every social scientist who examines this volume will recognize that I was not successful in identifying mutually exclusive and exhaustive categories. Nevertheless, I resisted the temptation to list items in more than one place. Where the item dealt with more than one of the subject categories I made a judgement about its emphasis and placed it accordingly.

I have provided a more detailed breakdown on the literature concerned with the social consequences of adolescent pregnancy and parenthood and the services designed to ameliorate those consequences than I have in the other subject areas. This is reflective of both my area of research interest and my professional training.

I selected the reference format that I thought I would feel most comfortable working with. This lead to at least two problems which I was not completely able to overcome. Every journal does not use every element required by the format. Some journals use all the elements but only on the title page. In the last case I was not able to supply those elements for articles that I obtained through interlibrary loan. Journals also use different conventions in regard to names. In the body of the text I have attempted to use the form of the name which appeared on the first page of the article, chapter or book itself. In the author index, however, I have tried to use only one form for each name.

ACKNOWLEDGMENTS

This material is based upon work supported by the National Science Foundation under Grant No. 8714031. The Government has certain rights in this material. Any opinions, findings, and conclusions or recommendations expressed in this material are those of the author and do not necessarily reflect the views of the National Science Foundation.
The students both undergraduate and graduate who worked for me as paid assistants during the period that I was working on the volume all made some contribution. These include: Brian Bowles, Georgiana Ball, Crystal Overton, Eileen Gilheany and Nancy Brady.

For most of the time that I was working on this project I either could not walk or could only walk with great pain and difficulty. This put me in the position of having to depend on other people to actually go to the library and obtain materials for me to read and annotate. My most important assistant has been my adolescent daughter Nicai Quinn Zollar. And that is why this work is dedicated to her. Her success in helping me is certainly related to generational differences in the willingness to deal with computers, her artistic eye, and the fact that she has spent her entire life on the campus of large urban universities. Nicai was not intimidated by ALIS, the online computer cataloging system used by Virginia Commonwealth University Library Services, but rather "played" her with great skill. She figured out all by her artistic self that the most readable copies from microfilm were those which used white on black. She managed to get to the MCV campus and locate and use its library. What she demonstrated above all else, however, was the willingness and the ability to do dull, tedious, and boring work with some degree of efficiency. This means that I can never again refer to this young poet, dancer, and actress as a "space cadet."

I must also acknowledge the invaluable assistance of Sue Bass and her staff in the interlibrary loan department of James Branch Cabell Library. I must thank Susan Howell, secretary in the Department of Sociology, for entering some of the annotations and for her willingness to do more. All of the errors and omissions are mine.

INTRODUCTION

This work was initiated and organized with my own needs in mind. As a sociologist, however, I am sensitive to the idea that my needs and purposes are not unique. This bibliography is being published because it will assist other researchers and professors with similar needs, as well as their students.

First of all I am a researcher who made a conscious decision to conduct research in the area of adolescent family formation but had to admit that while I had a great deal of personal experience I had only the vaguest knowledge of the findings of prior research. This bibliography then should be quite useful for the novice in this area.

Secondly, I am a professor who needed to make the diverse literature more accessible to students. I teach two undergraduate courses concerned with the family in the United States and have grown extremely bored with term papers which either rely on the same few sources over and over again, employ references only from the popular press, or which begin, "very little has been written about adolescent fathers."

The students who participate in a graduate level seminar on the sociology of the family also needed some idea of how various disciplines deal with the subject matter. The students who take part in this seminar come not only from the Department of Sociology and other departments within the College of Humanities and Sciences, but also from the School of Social Work, the School of Nursing, and the School of Community and Public Affairs. Each of them seems to be familiar with what type of article is published in the major journals in their own field but are unfamiliar with the others. While this bibliography is not exhaustive it does provide an idea of how broad is the array of journals publishing articles in this area.

One of my long term goals in this area is to participate in moving the study of adolescent pregnancy and parenthood from the periphery to the center of my discipline. In order for this shift to occur it is important to separate the reality of the phenomena from the myths about them.

The many myths exist because adolescent pregnancy and parenthood in American society *are* social problems. They can be termed social problems because they are widely perceived as norm violating and evaluated negatively. But perhaps even more importantly, they are problems that have clearly been socially constructed. To suggest that adolescent pregnancy and parenthood in American society are socially constructed problems is not to deny their existence or the problematic nature of them. For, to paraphrase one of the founding fathers of American sociology, when American society decides that a problem is real it is real in its consequences. It is, in fact, the very suspicion that, a "self fulfilling prophecy" is implicated in the nature of the consequences of adolescent pregnancy and parenthood in United States society, which impels me to study the phenomenon of adolescent family formation.

In this area there are several ideologies implicated in the creation of the myths. Murcott (303) has argued that in order to understand the construction of adolescent pregnancy as a social problem one must understand that it is situated at the intersection of the ideologies of reproduction and the ideologies of childhood. I submit that in order to understand the myths which have developed around these issues in American society, one must also be aware of the ideologies about race and the ideologies about poverty.

The first requirement in attempting to objectively study adolescent fertility and family formation in the United States is an accurate description of the phenomenon. The items presented in the first chapter are those which will allow one to begin constructing an accurate picture of the fertility behavior of adolescents in the United States. Taken together they describe what is known about adolescent fertility rates in the United States from the late 1940s through the mid 1980s. They describe the variations in adolescent fertility by race, age and marital status. They also give some idea of how the fertility of adolescents in this country compares to that of adolescents in the rest of the world. You cannot understand what is going on in the United States in isolation from what is going on in the rest of the world.

The crossnational studies highlight two important facts. First of all, black adolescents in the United States have higher fertility rates than any other group in the developed world. But they also point out that white adolescents in the United States have fertility rates that are significantly higher than their counterparts in Canada and in Western Europe. The items concerned with trends in the United States alone, however, make it quite clear that the "real" problem in this area has not been an unprecedented "epidemic" of births to adolescents in the very recent past. Several things are clearly problematic here. One of these is the fact that the adolescent birth rate has not declined as rapidly as the rate of births to older women so that births to adolescents constitute a larger proportion of all births. The items in this section also indicate that a larger proportion of the births to adolescents occur while they remain unmarried and that the rate of births has decreased even slower in the youngest age category.

The next five chapters are concerned with the etiology of adolescent pregnancy and parenthood in this society. It is a truism that adolescents become pregnant because they engage in sexual intercourse without utilizing effective contraception. They become adolescent parents because even with legalized abortion many of them choose to carry to term and the vast majority are no longer willing to give up their children for other people to rear. The third chapter includes items which describe the sexuality, that is, the sexual attitudes and behaviors of adolescents in this country. What do they do? What do they think and feel about what they do? What do they think other adolescents do? How are their sexual attitudes and behaviors related to race, class, religiosity, family structure, level of individual development and various attributes of personaliy? Are their behaviors and attitudes indicative of an adolescent sexual revolution? Chapter four includes items that are primarily concerned with the contraceptive behavior of adolescents. What are the correlates of effective contraception among adolescents? Why don't more of them contracept effectively?

The fifth chapter contains items concerned with sex education: What forms does it take? What effects does it have? How do parents feel about it? How much of it do they provide? While the literature distinguishes counseling in regard to sexuality from sex education, I have included items that treat both topics in this chapter.

Chapter six includes items which deal with the differential risk of experiencing adolescent pregnancy and parenthood beyond the clearly most proximate causes. Here concern is not with the frequency of intercourse or the correlates of effective contraception but with race, class, neighborhood status, self concept, locus of control and knowledge of risk.

Chapter seven presents items concerned with how adolescents in contemporary American society arrive at their decisions about how to resolve their pregnancies as well as those which deal with their later adaptation to and satisfaction with their resolution decisions.

The next two chapters are concerned with the consequences of adolescent pregnancy and parenthood. Chapter eight contains those items that deal primarily with the social and/or psychological consequences. Chapter nine includes items basically concerned with the medical or physiological repercussions of adolescent childbearing. The items included here are those which did not appear to require that one have a medical education in order to understand. There is some overlap between the two chapters in the area of the intellectual and social development of the children who are born to adolescent mothers.

What the research reports in these two chapters suggest, as they have become more sophisticated, is that the consequences are not nearly as monolithically negative as originally conceived. They suggest that there is variance to be explained. It is the existence of this variance which requires that the phenomena be examined as sociological and not only as social problems. Nowhere is this made clearer than in the items which report on a longitudinal study in which women who became mothers in their midteens have been followed over 17 years.

The popular belief that early childbearing almost certainly leads to school dropout, subsequent unwanted births and economic dependendence is greatly oversimplified if not seriously distorted (313, p.1).

Still there are many items in this section which reflect the great amount of concern about the costs of early childbearing to society, as well as to the young parents, their families and their offspring.

In terms of medical and physiological consequences the more recent reports suggest that, from the midteens on, at least some of the negative outcomes associated with adolescent childbearing may be more attributable to social factors such as race, class, and quantity and quality of health care than to some simple biological factor which can be measured in terms of chronological age. Because the medical and physiological consequences are presented as being so strongly related to medical care, items which discuss the management of pregnancy in adolescence which are written in a language understandable to educated persons outside of the health care professions are also included in this chapter.

Chapter ten demonstrates that while little may be known about adolescent fathers as compared to adolescent mothers, there is not a total lack of research and writings on the subject. Most of the items in this chapter present an image of the adolescent father which runs counter to the stereotypical view. The items in this chapter deal not only with the personality attributes of young males who father, but also their needs. Also included in this chapter are items which present the bleak economic outlook for young fathers whether they marry or not.

Chapter 11 describes the various services that exist in this society to serve the family planning needs of adolescents, those which are directed at preventing adolescent pregnancy and parenthood, and those which are concerned with providing services to pregnant and parenting adolescents. The research concerned with evaluating these services is also presented here. It is worth noting that while in the recent past the programs for pregnant and parenting teens were seen as having little or only very short term positive effects, several newer efforts report more optimistic findings.

Chapter 12 presents those articles concerned with the legislation and legal issues which have a bearing on adolescent pregnancy and parenthood. This introduction is written as the Supreme Court is considering the most serious challenge to Roe versus Wade since that decision was handed down. Whatever the exact wording of the decision in the current case, it can be expected to complicate this area and lead to more literature. As a researcher I intend to carry out some secondary data analysis in this field. The existence of the Data Archive on Adolescent Pregnancy and Pregnancy Prevention (DAAPPP) makes this a very feasible goal. As a teacher I would like to interest graduate students in this process. It is one thing for students to simply read and critique an article. It is a much richer experience when they can critique the article, the original instrument, the codebook and then attempt to analyze the data themselves. That is why the DAAPPP holdings list is included here. The Data Archive on Adolescent Pregnancy and Pregnancy Prevention is sponsored by the U.S. Office of Population Affairs. For more information about DAAPPP write to Sociometrics Corporation, 685 High Street, Suite 2E, Palo Alto, California 94301, (415) 321-7946.

Adolescent Pregnancy
and Parenthood

I. FERTILITY BEHAVIOR - THE DEMOGRAPHIC PICTURE

A. Articles

001. Baldwin, Wendy. "The Fertility of Young Adolescents." JOURNAL OF ADOLESCENT HEALTH CARE I (1980): 54-59.

Offers a demographic analysis of trends and patterns of fertility behavior of adolescents under age 16 in the United States. Points out that while childbearing is not a new phenomenon for teenagers, the likelihood of entering into reproductive behavior as a young adolescent has visibly increased. Trends in numbers and rates of births are presented with particular attention to parity, race and marital status. Black/white differences are found; with the birth rates being higher among blacks, as well as the likelihood of having additional pregnancies while still a teen, along with a higher illegitimacy rate. The sexual and contraceptive behavior of these women is discussed along with abortion behavior. Increasingly, these young adolescents begin having intercourse without using proper contraceptive methods thereby placing themselves in a situation where the likelihood of becoming pregnant is high. Suggests that programs offering services to teens must do more than simply wait for them to show up.

002. Baldwin, Wendy. "Adolescent Pregnancy and Childbearing Growing Concerns for Americans." POPULATION BULLETIN 32 (1976): 3-21.

Presents a demographic picture of the fertility behavior of American adolescents. Examines both the rates that were current in 1974-75 and change over time in childbearing, sexual behavior, contraceptive practices and abortion. Briefly compares the U.S. situation to the experience in other developed countries. When possible differentiates births occurring within marriage from those happening out of wedlock. Looks at differences by age and race. The limited information on men is presented.

003. Deschamps, J.B., and G. Valentin. "Pregnancy in Adolescence: Incidence and Outcome in European Countries." JOURNAL OF BIOSOCIAL SCIENCE SUPPLEMENT 5 (1978): 101-116.

Presents the adolescent fertility rates for 22 European countries breaking the data down into those occurring in the under 15 and the 15-19 year old groups. Finds that there is a great deal of variation in the rates for these two groups in the countries studied and that the variation is not easy to explain. The variables considered include religious tradition and availability of abortion. Gives trend data for France. Decomposes adolescent fertility in these countries into its married and unmarried components and discusses the medical and social consequences.

004. Digest. "Out-of-Wedlock Birthrate Rising Among Whites, Falling Among Blacks: Overall Fertility Declining." FAMILY PLANNING PERSPECTIVES 16 (March/April 1984): 90-91.

Summarizes some of the major findings of a report issued by the National Center for Health Statistics. Included among these findings is the fact that the overall fertility rate declined in the United States in 1981. This was the first decline in the fertility rate since 1978. The only age group to register a rise in fertility was women aged 35-39. There was a small increase in out of wedlock fertility which was exclusive to whites as black nonmarital fertility declined. The fertility rate of adolescents decreased in 1981, but the out of wedlock fertility of teenagers grew slightly. This rise was also confined to whites.

005. Engstrom, Lars. "Teenage Pregnancy in Developing Countries." JOURNAL OF BIOSOCIAL SCIENCE SUPPLEMENT 5 (1978): 117-126.

Takes the position that reviewing the problems of teenage pregnancies in developing countries is difficult because they: (1) do not constitute a sociocultural entity; (2) lack resources in both health and social services and reliable vital statistics; and (3) accept adolescent pregnancy as long as it takes place within marriage. Presents the legal minimum age of marriage in selected countries as well as the percentage of births by birth order occurring to women under the age of 20. Argues that the prevailing pattern in many developing countries seems to be an early reproductive debut in the midteens with repeated pregnancies before age 20. This is seen as a general health problem related to higher maternal and infant mortality.

006. Jones, Elise F.; Forrest, Jacqueline Darroch; Goldman, Noreen; Henshaw, Stanley K.; Lincoln, Richard; Rosoff, Jeannie I.; Westoff, Charles F.; and Deidre Wulf. "Teenage Pregnancy in Developed Countries: Determinants and Policy." FAMILY PLANNING PERSPECTIVES 17 (March/April 1985): 53-63.

Uses both a quantitative analysis of the factors associated with adolescent fertility in 37 developed countries and case studies of teenage pregnancy in five countries and the United States to address two major questions: Why are teenage fertility rates so much higher in this country? And what can be learned from these other countries to lower the U.S. rates? Argues that American teenagers appear to be no more sexually active than their counterparts in these other countries and explains the differences in fertility in terms of the mixed messages that U.S. teens get about sex, their lack of knowledge about and access to contraception.

007. Klerman, L.V., and J.F. Jekel. "Teenage Pregnancy."
SCIENCE 199 (1978): 1390.
Argues in a letter to the editor that adolescent pregnancy is an important social problem, one which deserves to be carefully studied. Points out that there has been no epidemic of adolescent pregnancy. Explains that attention must be paid to age specific rates including the fact that in 1975, 42 percent of the births to adolescents were to married 18 and 19 year olds -- which is not by the current standards of American society immoral, illegal or deviant.

008. Pittman, Karen, and Gina Adams. TEENAGE PREGNANCY: AN ADVOCATE'S GUIDE TO THE NUMBERS.
Washington, D.C: Children's Defense Fund's Adolescent Pregnancy Prevention Clearinghouse (January/March 1988).
Presents an impressive amount of data on the sexual and fertility behavior of American teenagers through 1985. Explains how many of the most important measures of sexuality and fertility are calculated and provides brief definitions of many of the most important terms. With an emphasis on prevention, discusses such topics as trends, racial and ethnic differences, adolescent males and their reproductive behavior, geographic differences, and finding and using the data.

009. Robinson, Walter W., and Donald W. Hastings. "A Strategy for Obtaining Estimates of Premarital Pregnancy Using a 1970 Census Public Use Sample." PUBLIC USE DATA 2 (July 1974): 30-34.
Reports a strategy for obtaining estimates of premarital pregnancy using the 1/1000 Public Use Sample (PUS) of basic records from the 1970 Census for the United States Population.

Examines the child spacing performance for all once married women (currently living with their husband) with all children currently in the household. Shows that for this population roughly 14 percent of all first births are premarital conceptions.

010. Tietze, Christopher. "Teenage Pregnancies: Looking Ahead to 1984." FAMILY PLANNING PERSPECTIVES 10 (July/August 1978): 205-207.

Uses data for 1976 to estimate how many of those females who were currently 14 years old would probably experience one or more pregnancies, births, abortions and miscarriages before they reach age 20. Assuming that there would be no change in the level of sexual activity or contraceptive use, it was predicted that by age 20, about 21 percent would have experienced at least one live birth; fifteen percent would have obtained at least one abortion, and 6 percent would have had at least one miscarriage.

011. Sklar, June, and Beth Berkov. "The Effects of Legal Abortion on Legitimate and Illegitimate Birth Rates: The California Experience." STUDIES IN FAMILY PLANNING 4 (November 1973): 281-292.

Utilizes vital statistics data to describe the impact of the legalization of abortion on the marital and unmarried components of the fertility rate in California. Notes that in 1971 California experienced a dramatic decline in fertility which can be associated with the widespread availability of legal abortions. Since the fertility decline was especially marked for illegitimate births, this seemed to reflect a significant reversal in the upward trend of the illegitimate fertility rate. However, analysis of the data for 1972 demonstrated that while the legitimate fertility rates continued to decline as much as they had the year before, the decline in illegitimacy slowed. This phenomenon is interpreted to signal that even with legal abortions many women are choosing motherhood without marriage.

012. Sklar, June, and Beth Berkov. "Teenage Family Formation in Postwar America." FAMILY PLANNING PERSPECTIVES 6 (Spring 1974): 80-90.

Describes the massive demographic shifts and fundamental social changes experienced by "baby boomers" as they moved into and through adolescence. Uses data from a number of sources to describe teenage family formation from 1900 to 1971. Describes the marriage and delay of births trends after 1960 and the subsequent decline in marital fertlity and rise in unmarried fertility. Discusses the impact of the legalization of abortion and offers explanations for why when effective contraception is available and abortion legal, U.S. adolescents still tend to have such high relative fertility.

013. Vinovskis, Maris A. "An 'Epidemic' of Adolescent Pregnancy? Some Historical Considerations." JOURNAL OF FAMILY HISTORY 6 (Summer 1981): 205-230.
Argues that historians should include adolescent pregnancy on their research agendas. Begins by reviewing the debate over adolescent pregnancy in the 95th Congress which resulted in the passage of the Adolescent Health Services and Pregnancy Prevention Act of 1978. Points out that contrary to the viewpoint presented in the popular media and promulgated by special interest groups, such as the Guttmacher Institute, there had not been a dramatic and/or unprecedented increase in -- therefore no epidemic of -- adolescent pregnancy. In fact a consideration of just the recent history of adolescent fertility revealed that teenage childbearing increased sharply after World War II, peaked in 1957, and then decreased sharply over the next twenty years. Here, the real contemporary issues are seen as the increase in births to females under 15, the dramatic rise in the proportion of births to unmarried women, and the high social costs associated with the increase in the proportion of adolescent mothers who decide to keep and rear their children. Briefly critiques existing research with a strong emphasis on the extent to which it is cross sectional and ahistorical and ends with some specific suggestions about how the issues could and should be explored historically.

014. Westoff, Charles F.; Calot, Gerard; and Andrew D. Foster. "Teenage Fertility in Developed Nations." FAMILY PLANNING PERSPECTIVES 15 (May/June 1983): 105-110.
Presents a demographic analysis of adolescent fertility in 30 developed countries as well as two subpopulations: blacks in the United States and Arabs in Israel. Finds that teenage fertility is fairly low to moderate in western and northern Europe and rates have declined over the 1970s. Eastern and southern European countries on the other hand have experienced increasing rates of teenage childbearing. The highest rate of adolescent childbearing among the countries considered is that which characterizes blacks in the United States. The rate for this segment of the American population was 37 percent higher than the next highest rate which

was that for Israeli Arabs. However, even though the rate of adolescent fertility among black Americans is twice as high as that for whites, white Americans have rates that are higher than those found in most of western Europe, Australia and Canada. The lowest rate of adolescent fertility was found in Japan.

015. Zelnik, Melvin, and John F. Kantner. "First Pregnancies to Women Aged 15-19: 1976 and 1971." FAMILY PLANNING PERSPECTIVES 10 (January/February 1978): 11-20.

Focuses on the prevalence, resolution, intendedness, and contraceptive behavior associated with premarital first pregnancies to women aged 15-19 in 1971 and 1976. Over the five year period there was an increase in the proportion of 15-19 year old white women who had ever experienced sexual intercourse, but the proportion experiencing a premarital pregnancy remained about the same. Less than a quarter of these pregnancies were intended even though more than 80 percent of those not intending to get pregnant failed to practice contraception at both survey dates. There was a substantial reduction in the number of whites who married before the outcome of the pregnancy and a small decline in the percentage who married after a live birth. Among whites there was an increase in the proportion of pregnancies which were terminated through abortion and a decrease in the percentage of live births where the child was put up for adoption. For blacks there was also an increase in the percentage of 15-19 year olds who had ever experienced sexual intercourse, but the increase was smaller than the one among whites. The proportion of all black women who had ever experienced a premarital pregnancy remained about the same, as did the proportion who married before outcome. Blacks remained much less likely than whites to marry between conception and birth. Blacks, at both survey dates, were more likely than whites to say that their pregnancies were intended and less likely to practice contraception even where the pregnancy was not intended. The data show blacks to be much less likely to terminate pregnancies with abortion, but the researchers question the validity of these data arguing that the rate of abortion among blacks is severely underestimated. Blacks are still less likely than whites to put babies born premaritally up for adoption.

B. Chapters in Books

016. Baldwin, Wendy. "Trends in Adolescent Contraception and Childbearing." PREMATURE ADOLESCENT PREGNANCY AND PARENTHOOD. Edited by Elizabeth McAnarney. New York: Grune and Stratton, 1983, pp. 3-20.
Presents the demographic data for single years of age for women under 20 broken down by race.

017. Campbell, Arthur A. "Trends in Teenage Childbearing in the United States." ADOLESCENT PREGNANCY AND CHILDBEARING: FINDINGS FROM RESEARCH. Edited by Catherine S. Chilman. U. S. Department of Health and Human Services, 1980, pp. 3-14.
Describes trends in adolescent childbearing for single years of age from 1920-1977. Decomposes the rates into their marital and nonmarital components.

018. Dryfoos, Joy. "The Epidemiology of Adolescent Pregnancy: Incidence, Outcomes and Interventions." PREGNANCY IN ADOLESCENCE: NEEDS, PROBLEMS, AND MANAGEMENT. Edited by Irving R. Stuart and Carl F. Wells. New York: Van Nostrand Reinhold Company, 1982, pp. 27-47.
Describes the trends in adolescent fertility over the 1970s. Introduces factors implicated in the creation of the problem and makes recommendations for intervention strategies.

019. Scott, Keith G. "Epidemiologic Aspects of Teenage Pregnancy." TEENAGE PARENTS AND THEIR OFFSPRING. Edited by Keith G. Scott, Tiffany Field and Euan G. Robertson. New York: Grune and Stratton, 1981, pp. 3-14.
Charts trends in adolescent pregnancy to arrive at the conclusion that births to adolescents have in fact been decreasing and do not represent an epidemic.

020. Vinovskis, Maris. "Adolescent Sexuality, Pregnancy and Childbearing in Early America." SCHOOL-AGE PREGNANCY: BIOSOCIAL DIMENSIONS. Edited by Jane B. Lancaster and Beatrix A. Hamburg. New York: Aldine De Gruyter, 1986, pp. 303-322.

C. Books

021. Dryfoos, Joy. FACTBOOK ON TEENAGE PREGNANCY.
New York: Alan Guttmacher Institute, 1981.
Presents 114 tables containing detailed information on the
sexual behavior, reproductive knowledge, contraceptive use,
pregnancy rates and pregnancy consequences for adolescents.
Also covers parental attitudes and knowledge and a wide range
of needs and services.

022. Jones, Elise; Forrest, Jacqueline Darroch; Goldman, Noreen;
Henshaw, Stanley; Lincoln, Richard; Rosoff, Jeannie I.;
Westoff, Charles F. and Deidre Wulf. TEENAGE
PREGNANCY IN INDUSTRIALIZED COUNTRIES: A
STUDY SPONSORED BY THE ALAN GUTTMACHER
INSTITUTE. New Haven: Yale University Press, 1986.
Presents in book length form the study carried out by the
Guttmacher Institute and described in item 006.

II. REVIEWS OF THE LITERATURE

A. Articles

023. Baizerman, Michael; Sheehan, Cynthia; Ellison, David L.; and Edward Schlesinger. "A Critique of the Research Literature Concerning Pregnant Adolescents, 1960-1970." JOURNAL OF YOUTH AND ADOLESCENCE 3 (1974): 61-75.

Actually critiques rather than reviews the literature concerned with pregnant adolescents. Begins by pointing out that most of the research initially reviewed is not definitive due to methodological and/or theoretical flaws. Then offers suggestions for content and methodologies which are more congruent with the requirements of the scientific approach. These suggestions include, but are not limited to, the recommendations that: (1) researchers must develop a level of consensus on what are the concepts and variables to be studied; (2) researchers need to employ explicit theoretical and research models; (3) studies in this area need to be longitudinal and prospective, beginning at a point in the life cycle of the adolescent before the sexual debut; (4) research on medical and health outcomes needs improved methodology; and (5) prenatal care must be addressed as a sociomedical process. Also presented is a discussion of three assumptions underlying much of the research in this area. These are the assumptions of difference, homogeneity, and special need. Finally, a discussion of the risk concept and how it needs to be clarified is presented.

024. Chilman, Catherine S. "Social and Psychological Research Concerning Adolescent Childbearing: 1970-1980." JOURNAL OF MARRIAGE AND THE FAMILY 42 (November 1980): 793-805.

Begins by pointing out that prior to the late 1960s there was almost no research on the sexual development and behaviors of adolescents but that by 1980 at least 15 important studies had been reported which were concerned with either the sexual behavior of adolescents or its consequences. Reviews studies which deal with recent trends in adolescent childbearing and points out that there was no rampant increase in the birth rate of adolescents but that the widespread view that this phenomenon had reached epidemic proportions had positive as well as negative consequences. The major positive consequence was the stimulation of additional research. Also reviews studies which deal with the causes of adolescent pregnancy as well as those which look at the consequences of early childbearing for both the young mother and her child. Points out that while there was a great improvement in statistical methodology during the 1970s, more limited progress was made in the area of conceptualization. Among the problems found in this area are: (1) a simplistic search for single explanatory factors; (2) an insufficient consideration of the confounding effects of such factors as developmental level, socioeconomic status, region, ethnicity and race; (3) insufficient attention to male attitudes and behaviors; (4) a confusion of correlation with causation in the area of outcomes; and (5) the predominance of personalistic design and interpretation.

025. Fielding, Jonathan E. "Adolescent Pregnancy Revisited." NEW ENGLAND JOURNAL OF MEDICINE 299 (October 1978): 893-896.
      Reviews briefly the trends in American fertility rates with an emphasis on how the rate for adolescents has fallen more slowly than those for other women. Reviews the results of studies pointing to the health risks for mothers and children as well as several of those which highlight the negative consequences in social, educational and vocational outcomes. Discusses the nature and effectiveness of current prevention and intervention strategies.

026. McKenry, Patrick C.; Walters, Lynda H.; and Carolyn Johnson. "Adolescent Pregnancy: A Review of the Literature." THE FAMILY COORDINATOR (January 1979): 17-28.
      Reviews the literature on adolescent pregnancy written in the 1960s and 1970s in order to help professionals make use of the research in making public policy. Points out the troublesome nature of much of this literature including the fact that much of it: (1) is descriptive and advocatory; (2) employs a limited range of variables which are used inconsistently; and (3) uses small samples from clinical populations and employs unsophisticated methodologies without proper controls. Also points out that the atheoretical approach to the issue fails to contribute to cumulative findings. Looks first at research concerned with the physical, psychological, and social factors implicated in the etiology of adolescent pregnancy, contraception and abortion. Attention is then turned to the literature which deals with medical and physiological consequences for both the young mother and her

child.   Finally   the   literature   concerned   with   lost   social
opportunities is presented.

027. Newberger, Carolyn M.; Melnicoe, Lora H.; and Eli H.
      Newberger. "The American Family in Crises: Implications for
      Children." CURRENT PROBLEMS IN PEDIATRICS 16
      (December 1986): 677-684.
      Presents, in this special issue of the journal, a section on
      adolescent pregnancy which covers the demographic trends in
      adolescent pregnancy, adolescent childbearing and marital status,
      sexual activity and contraceptive use and the outcomes and
      economic implications for adolescent parents and their children.

028. Simkins, Lawrence. "Consequences of Teenage Pregnancy and
      Motherhood." ADOLESCENCE 19 (Spring 1984): 39-54.
      Reviews the literature concerned with adolescent sexual
      behavior with a focus on adolescent pregnancy and its
      consequences for both mother and child.

029. Trussell, James. "Teenage Pregnancy in the United States."
      FAMILY PLANNING PERSPECTIVES 20
      (November/December 1988): 263-272.
      Summarizes the recent literature concerned with the frequency
      of adolescent pregnancy in the United States; how the U.S.
      experience compares to that of other industrialized nations; the
      causes of adolescent pregnancy and the consequences of early
      childbearing; and examines the potential impact of various
      intervention strategies.   Argues that without a fundamental
      restructuring of American society in such a way as to eliminate
      the underclass, adolescent pregnancy and parenthood will never
      be completely eliminated. Concludes that while it may be most
      desirable to eliminate sexual activity among adolescents, practical
      considerations demand that the first priority be to reduce early
      childbearing.

030. Wallis, Claudia. "Children Having Children: Teen Pregnancies
      Are Corroding America's Social Fabric." TIME (December
      1985): 78-90.
      Is included here primarily because it provides such an excellent
      example of how the issues surrounding adolescent pregnancy and
      parenthood are treated in the popular press. While on one of its
      interior pages it is pointed out that the adolescent birthrate was
      higher in 1957 than in 1985 and that current concern is actually

addressed to the problem of births to unmarried women and to younger adolescents, the title is clearly sensational. The subtitle certainly continues the trend of suggesting that we are dealing with an unprecedented epidemic of deviant behavior on the part of adolescents. If the reader can get past the stimulating opening, however, the article does provide a good nontechnical overview suitable for the general reader.

B. Chapters in Books

031. Jones, Audrey E., and Paul J. Placek. "Teenage Women in the United States: Sex, Contraception, Pregnancy, Fertility and Maternal and Infant Health." TEENAGE PREGNANCY IN A FAMILY CONTEXT. Edited by Theodora Ooms. Philadelphia: Temple University Press, 1981, pp. 49-72. Reviews the available data on the areas listed in the title.

032. McAnarney, Elizabeth R., and Henry A. Thiede. "Adolescent Pregnancy and Childbearing: What We Learned during the 1970s and What Remains to be Learned." PREMATURE ADOLESCENT PREGNANCY AND PARENTHOOD. Edited by Elizabeth McAnarney. New York: Grune and Stratton, 1983, pp. 375-396.

C. Books

033. Chilman, Catherine S. ADOLESCENT PREGNANCY AND CHILDBEARING: FINDINGS FROM RESEARCH. Washington, D.C.: U.S. Department of Health and Human Services, 1980. Consists mainly of papers presented at two conferences sponsored by the Center for Population Research. The first conference was concerned with consequences of adolescent childbearing and was co-sponsored with the Alan Guttmacher Institute. The second conference was concerned with the determinant of adolescent fertility. Includes the responses of discussants to each paper. Contains items 017, 085, 093, 272, 409, 424, 503, 645, 647, 652, and 653.

034. Chilman, Catherine S. ADOLESCENT SEXUALITY IN A
CHANGING SOCIETY: SOCIAL AND
PSYCHOLOGICAL PERSPECTIVES FOR THE HUMAN
SERVICE PROFESSIONAL. New York: John Wiley and
Sons, 1983.
Offers to human service professionals encouragement toward a
comprehensive and humane understanding of adolescent sexuality.
Blends the rational-scientific with the humanistic-individualistic.
Includes an analytical overview of the available research
concerned with the social and psychological aspects of sexuality,
discussions of adolescent sexual education, counseling of
adolescents about their sexuality, family planning programs,
programs for adolescent parents and their children and
suggestions for programs and policies needed in the future.
Contains items 643, 654 and 669.

035. Chilman, Catherine S. ADOLESCENT SEXUALITY IN A
CHANGING AMERICAN SOCIETY. Washington, D.C.,
U.S. Government Printing Office, 1983.
Reviews and critiques the research related to adolescent
sexuality in the United States. Offers suggestions for future
research and makes recommendations for policy. Includes an
annotated bibliography which evaluates the research reports listed.

036. Gordon, Sol; Scales, Peter; and Kathleen Everly. THE
SEXUAL ADOLESCENT: COMMUNICATING WITH
ADOLESCENTS ABOUT SEX. North Scituate, MA
Duxbury Press, 1979.
Presents a supplementary text for all professionals w io work
with young people. Based upon the belief that it is best for
adolescents not to impregnate, become pregnant or have children,
it describes the steps necessary to foster sexual health. Also
outlines the contributions which can be made by parents,
educators, legislators, religious leaders and the media.

037. Guttmacher Institute. 11 MILLION TEENAGERS: WHAT
CAN BE DONE ABOUT THE EPIDEMIC OF
ADOLESCENT PREGNANCIES IN THE UNITED
STATES. New York: Alan F. Guttmacher Institute, 1976.
Presents a statistical compilation in chart form of what was then
known about adolescent sexuality, contraceptive use, pregnancy,
childbirth, abortion and the health and social consequences of
adolescent childbearing. Specifies services available to prevent

adolescent births and to help pregnant teenagers and teenage
parents to cope with the serious problems that they face.

038. Hayes, Cheryl D. RISKING THE FUTURE: ADOLESCENT
    SEXUALITY, PREGNANCY, AND CHILDBEARING
    VOLUME 1. Washington, D.C.: National Academy Press,
    1987.
    Presents the findings, conclusions, and recommendations of a 15
    person multidisciplinary panel which undertook three important
    tasks: (1) to assemble, integrate, and assess data on trends in
    teenage sexual and fertility behavior; (2) to review and synthesize
    research on the antecedents and consequences of early pregnancy
    and childbearing; and (3) to review alternative preventive and
    ameliorative policies and programs.

039. Lancaster, Jane B., and Beatrix A. Hamburg. SCHOOL-AGE
    PREGNANCY AND PARENTHOOD: BIOSOCIAL
    DIMENSIONS. New York: Aldine De Gruyter, 1986.
    Contains items 202, 084, 087, 091, 165, 273, 275, 277, 397, 403,
    404, 406, 408, 417, 423, 495, and 560.

040. McAnarney, Elizabeth R. (Ed.) PREMATURE
    ADOLESCENT PREGNANCY AND PARENTHOOD.
    New York: Grune and Stratton, 1983.
    Combines a clinical and an investigative approach to adolescent
    pregnancy and parenthood primarily geared toward the
    professional in perinatology.

041. Semens, James P., and Kermit E. Krantz. THE
    ADOLESCENT EXPERIENCE: A COUNSELING GUIDE
    TO SOCIAL AND SEXUAL BEHAVIOR. New York: The
    Macmillan Co., 1970.

042. Stuart, Irving R., and Carl F. Wells. (Eds.) PREGNANCY IN
    ADOLESCENCE: NEEDS, PROBLEMS, AND
    MANAGEMENT. New York: Van Nostrand Reinhold
    Company, 1982.
    Presents in textbook format an overview of the field which
    includes chapters devoted to how many adolescents get pregnant
    which adolescents get pregnant, and the nature of adolescent
    contraceptive behavior. Also includes chapters concerned with
    the legal aspects of adolescent pregnancy and parenting, programs
    that attempts to serve young mothers and family involvement.

Contains items 018, 089, 157, 168, 169, 170, 296, 298, 394, 396, 398, 493, 507, 655, 657, 670, and 696.

043. Zackler, Jack, and Wayne Brandstadt. (Eds.) THE TEENAGE PREGNANT GIRL. Springfield, Illinois: Charles C. Thomas, 1975.
Contains chapters presented as comprising a comprehensive view of the subject of the pregnant adolescent. Contains items 172, 271, 420, 501, 510, 511, 651, 665, 667, 673, 677, 697.

III. ADOLESCENT SEXUALITY

A. Articles

044. Baker, Sharon A.; Thalberg, Stanton P.; and Diane M. Morrison. "Parents' Behavioral Norms as Predictors of Adolescent Sexual Activity and Contraceptive Use." ADOLESCENCE 23 (Summer 1988): 265-282.

Investigates the relationship between the behavioral norms of parents and the sexual activity and contraceptive use in a sample of 329 high school students. The findings indicate that there is a significant relationship between the parents' behavioral norms that indicate approval or disapproval of adolescent sexual activity and the sexual activity and contraceptive usage of high school students. Parents who are more liberal or approving of adolescent sexual activity have children who are slightly more likely to be sexually active and substantially more likely to use contraception if they are sexually active.

045. Bernache-Baker, Barbara. "The Sexual Attitudes and Behavior of Private and Public School Students: A Comparative Study." ADOLESCENCE 22 (Summer 1987) 259-269.

Compares the sexual attitudes and behaviors of recent graduates of the sixteen top ranked New England college preparatory schools to college bound graduates of public high schools. The areas measured were: virginity, orgasm, oral-genital sex, masturbation, birth control, abortion, pregnancy, homosexuality, sexually transmitted diseases, sexual variation, drugs and sex and politics and gender. Significant differences were found in virginity, sexual variation, drugs and sex and politics and gender. Concludes that despite enormous amounts of energy expended to prevent it, the sexual activity of the preparatory school student, in both amount and sophistication, is significantly greater than that of the public school student.

046. Billy, John O.G., and J. Richard Udry. "Patterns of Adolescent Friendship and Effects on Sexual Behavior." SOCIAL PSYCHOLOGICAL QUARTERLY 48 (March 1985): 27-41.

Uses data from a panel study of junior high school students in an urban area of Florida to examine the influence of both same sex and opposite sex friends on the sexual behavior of adolescents. In this analysis the sample was limited to those who were virgins in the first round of data collection and the strategy was to assess the relationship between the sexual behavior of their same sex and opposite sex friend and their being non-virgins at the time of the second round. In an earlier study, the only race sex group whose sexual behavior was influenced by that of their same sex friends was white females. This analysis found them to be the only group whose behavior was also influenced by that of their opposite sex friends.

047. Billy, John O.G., and J. Richard Udry. "The Influence of Male and Female Best Friends on Adolescent Sexual Behavior." ADOLESCENCE 20 (Spring 1985): 21-32.

Uses data from a panel study of junior high school students in urban Florida to separate empirically the three sources of homogeneity bias in same sex friendships and to assess which factors are significant in terms of friendship similarity in sexual intercourse experience. Three models of friendship structure are utilized; influence, deselection and acquisition. The deselection process was found not to be operative for any of the race-sex groups. The only group for which the influence process was found to be operative was white females. The acquisition process was found to be operative for both white females and white males, but not for blacks of either sex. The data did not allow for appropriate tests of the influence and deselection processes for blacks. Whites, both male and female, acquire friends who are similar to themselves in sexual behavior but only white females appear to be influenced by the behavior of their friends.

048. Clayton, Richard, and Janet L. Bokemeier. "Premarital Sex in the Seventies." JOURNAL OF MARRIAGE AND THE FAMILY 42 (September 1980): 759-775.

Reviews the research literature on premarital sexuality published during the 1970s, including several studies which are specifically concerned with the sexuality of pre-college age adolescents. Argues that though the literature in this area shows a great improvement in conceptual clarity and methodological rigor, the glass is still only half full and proposes a research and theory agenda for the 1980s.

049. Cvetkovich, George; Grote, Barbara; Lieberman, James E.; and Warren Miller. "Sex Role Development and Teenage Fertility Behavior." ADOLESCENCE 13 (Summer 1978): 231-236.

Uses data on 369 adolescent females (16-18) to examine the relationship between sex role attitudes, sexual behavior and contraceptive use. Found that it was illuminating to separate virgins into those who were considering premarital sex and those who were not. When attitudes on sexual permissiveness were controlled, it was found that the non virgins held relatively stereotypical sex role attitudes or were sexually liberal but not necessarily liberated. The virgins who were not willing to consider engaging in premarital intercourse held more extremely stereotypical sex role attitudes than the sexually active. Those who were not currently sexually active but were considering premarital intercourse held the least stereotypical sex role attitudes. It is conjectured that this last group is at a higher level of psychological maturity than either of the other two. It was also found that those who begin sexual activity after age 16 were more likely to be users of contraceptives than those who made their sexual debut at an earlier age.

050. Diepold, John, Jr., and Richard D. Young. "Empirical Studies of Adolescent Sexual Behavior: A Critical Review." ADOLESCENCE 14 (Spring 1979): 45-64.
Reviews twenty studies of adolescent sexual behavior conducted in the U.S. since 1940. The areas of adolescent sexuality which are treated include dating, kissing, petting, masturbation, premarital intercourse, homosexual contact and contraception. The major conclusion reached is that there has been no adolescent sexual revolution. Instead, there has been a gradual evolution which among other things, has included a closing of the gap in the sexual behaviors reported by males and females. The authors are extremely critical of both the atheoretical nature of the existing literature and its methodological flaws. They make suggestions for future research which could overcome these problems.

051. Eberhardt, Carolyn, and Thomas Schill. "Differences in Sexual Attitudes and Likeliness of Sexual Behaviors of Black Lower Socioeconomic Father Present vs. Father Absent Female Adolescents." ADOLESCENCE 19 (Spring 1984): 99-105.
Employs data on 90 female adolescents, all black, lower class and from a small midwestern town, to study the relationship between the presence or absence of the father and sexually permissive attitudes and behaviors. Overall, the findings do not

support the hypothesis that in this population father absent girls are more sexually permissive than father present girls.

052. Elias, James E. "Adolescents and Sex." THE HUMANIST (March/April 1978): 29-31.

Argues that there are three categories of questions about adolescent sexuality and reviews the findings of four studies that explore them. The first set of questions ask, is there a sexual "revolution" among teenagers. Interprets study findings to indicate that there is no sexual revolution among U.S. adolescents. They are more permissive in their attitudes and talk more openly about sexual matters but in terms of behavior do not differ radically from their parents. The second category of questions are those which ask about the influence of erotic stimuli and pornography on adolescent sex life. Points out that the role of erotic stimuli varies both by social class and sex. The final question category includes those that ask about the relationship between sex education and sexual activity. Points out that the most frequently cited source of information about sex is the peer group, that sex education begins before formal education does and that the "innocence" of youth is a myth.

053. Faulkenberry, J. Ron; Vincent, Murray; James, Arnold; and Wayne Johnson. "Coital Behaviors, Attitudes, and Knowledge of Students who Experience Early Coitus." ADOLESCENCE 22 (Summer 1987): 321-332.

Uses data on 929 students enrolled in personal health courses at 14 South Carolina colleges and universities to assess sexually related differences in those students who made an early sexual debut (age 16 or younger) and those who experienced their first intercourse at an older age. Found that both groups of students had little knowledge of the basic facts about fertility, contraception and sexually transmitted diseases. Also found four significant differences between early and late coital initiators. Those who initiated intercourse at age 17 or older: (1) used more effective methods of contraception at first intercourse; (2) had more committed relationships with their first sexual partner; (3) engaged in more discussion and planning about contraception; and (4) used more reliable sources for information about contraception.

054. Fisher, Terri D. "Parent Child Communication About Sex and Young Adolescents' Sexual Knowledge and Attitudes." ADOLESCENCE 21 (Fall 1986): 517-527.

Uses data from 22 families in order to determine if there are differences in the sexual knowledge, attitudes and contraceptive choices between young adolescents whose parents discuss sexual topics with them frequently (high communication) and those whose parents rarely discuss such topics (low communication). No significant differences were found between the children in the high and low communications groups. What was found was a greater correlation between the attitudes of parents and children in the high communication group.

055. Hajcak, Frank, and Patricia Garwood. "What Parents Can Do To Prevent Pseudo-Hypersexuality in Adolescents." FAMILY THERAPY 15 (1988): 99-105.

Focuses on how nonsexual needs drive sexual behavior and produce an artificially high sex drive. Argues that adolescents engage in intercourse to: confirm masculinity/femininity; gain affection; rebel against authority, parents, or social norms; build self-esteem and feel important; acquire or avoid intimacy; revenge, or to hurt or degrade others; alleviate anger; ensure fidelity; alleviate boredom; and express jealousy. Suggests that parents and therapists can alleviate hypersexuality by teaching adolescents to use nonsexual techniques to satisfy nonsexual needs.

056. Hanson, Robert O.; O'Connor, Mary E.; Jones, Warren H.; and T. Jean Blocker. "Maternal Employment and Adolescent Sexual Behavior." JOURNAL OF YOUTH AND ADOLESCENCE 10 (1981): 55-60.

Employs data on 64 unmarried female college students, 21 or under, to assess the nature of the relationship between maternal employment and sexual activity, contraceptive knowledge, and the willingness to risk conception. Found that those with employed mothers were more likely to have initiated sexual activity as adolescents, were less knowledgeable about contraception and expressed a willingness to accept a higher risk of pregnancy.

057. Hofferth, Sandra L.; Kahn, Joan R.; and Wendy Baldwin. "Premarital Sexual Activity Among U.S. Teenage Women over the Past Three Decades." FAMILY PLANNING PERSPECTIVES 19 (March/April 1987): 46-53.

Utilizes data from the National Surveys of Young Women to describe changes in the premarital sexuality of female adolescents in the United States over the past 30 years. Argues that there was a sexual revolution in the late 1960s and the 1970s as the level of sexual experience increased among both black and white young women. Older teenagers were in the vanguard of the increase and now are at the forefront of a stabilization in rates of sexual activity. Young adolescents, however, continue to begin sexual activity at earlier ages and in larger proportions.

058. Jessor, Shirley, and Richard Jessor. "Transition from Virginity to Nonvirginity Among Youth: A Social-Psychological Study over Time." DEVELOPMENTAL PSYCHOLOGY 11 (1975): 473-484.

Uses data collected in four waves from high school and college aged adolescents to explore the utility of a social psychology of problem behavior for understanding the transition from virginity to non-virginity. It was found that a pattern of attributes appears to be associated with virgin and non-virgin status. Among the non-virgins, these patterns reflected less conventionality. The non virgins had environments that were less controlling and less involved with conventional behavior and institutions. The parental and peer environments of the non virgins offered both more opportunity and more support for transition behavior. The non virgins see independence as important, have loosened their family ties in the direction of more reliance upon friends. They have also engaged more frequently in other unconventional behavior such as marijuana smoking and alcohol drinking. Concludes that the theoretical approach taken has in fact empirically demonstrated the relevance of a social psychology of problem behavior to studies of youthful development.

059. Juhasz, Anne McCreary, and Mary Sonnenshein-Schneider. "Adolescent Sexuality: Values Morality and Decision Making." ADOLESCENCE 22 (Fall 1987): 579-590.

Attempts to understand the factors which underlie the value structures which motivate the sexual activity of adolescents. The six factors which were extrapolated in an earlier study were: (1) family establishment competence; (2) external morality; (3) consequences of childbearing; (4) self enhancement through sexual intercourse; (5) intimacy considerations regarding sexual intercourse; and (6) consequences of marriage. In this analysis gender, age, race, socioeconomic status, religiosity, intelligence, locus of control and personality characteristics all had varying degrees of influence on the factors. Gender differences emerged on all six factors.

060. Kantner, John, and Melvin Zelnik. "Sexual Experiences of Young Unmarried Women in the U.S." FAMILY PLANNING PERSPECTIVES 4 (October 1972): 9-17.
Employs data on 4,240 never married women between 15 and 19 to elaborate upon aspects of their sexuality and their knowledge of the risk of conception. Young black women are twice as likely as young white women to be sexually active even when social class is taken into account. There is in both race groups an inverse relationship between social class and coital experience. Region of the country is not related to the proportion of young women with sexual experience. The relationship between family structure and dynamics is complicated with differences by race and age. The amount of misinformation about the risk of conception is substantial.

061. Kinnaird, Keri. "Premarital Sexual Behavior and Attitudes Toward Marriage and Divorce among Young Women as a Function of Their Mothers' Marital Status." JOURNAL OF MARRIAGE AND THE FAMILY 48 (November 1986): 757-765.
Uses data from 875 females enrolled in introductory psychology courses at a large midwestern university: (1) to test the hypothesis that those from divorced and reconstituted families would have more dating and sexual experience than those from intact families and (2) to determine what variables predict their attitudes toward dating, sexual activity, marriage and divorce. Subjects in the divorced and reconstituted groups were less likely to be virgins and were sexually active at an earlier age than those from intact families. A very large majority of those in each group reported wanting to marry, but those from the divorced and reconstituted families were more skeptical about marriage and had attitudes that were more accepting of divorce. Those who had experienced their mother's remarriage were the most accepting of divorce.

062. Kornfield, Ruth. "Who's to Blame: Adolescent Sexual Activity." JOURNAL OF ADOLESCENCE 8 (March 1985): 17-31.
Uses data from in-depth interviews with 59 adolescent females (13-17) in order to examine the relationship between the availability of contraceptive services and the young women's

decision to become and remain sexually active. The data suggest that there is no direct relationship between the availability of contraceptive services and the decision to become sexually active. The continuation of sexual activity may, on the other hand, be influenced by the availability of such services once the young woman decides that though she does not want to become pregnant she does want to continue sexual activity

063. Miller, Brent C.; McCoy, J. Kelly; Olson, Terrance D.; and Christopher M. Wallace. "Parental Discipline and Control Attempts in Relation to Adolescent Sexual Attitudes and Behavior." JOURNAL OF MARRIAGE AND THE FAMILY 48 (August 1986): 503-512.
Reports on a research project designed to test for the existence of a curvilinear relationship between parental control and adolescent sexual experience. The data were collected from a non random sample of 836 students in 1983 and 1,587 students in 1984. Most of the students (95%) were between 15 and 18 and about one-third of the students were associated with the Mormon Church. The data confirmed the existence of a curvilinear relationship. The highest level of sexually permissive attitudes and experience in sexual intercourse among adolescents were associated with a lack of parental rules. Those adolescents who perceived parental discipline as very strict with many dating rules held more permissive attitudes and had more intercourse activities than those with moderate parental strictness and rules. Plausible explanations for the findings are discussed as well as the limitations on interpretation due to the nature of the sample.

064. Mishne, Judith Marks. "Adolescent Sexuality." CHILD AND ADOLESCENT SOCIAL WORK 5 (Fall 1988): 187-204.
Discusses how adolescent sexuality has, in contemporary society, evolved in response to shifts in societal values and realities. Examines the trends in adolescent pregnancy and parenthood and discusses sexually transmitted diseases. Also introduces the recent views that clinicians have about homosexuality and heterosexuality. Finally presents a case study of a thoughtful young upper middle class male adolescent dealing with his current developmental task.

065. Moore, Kristin; Peterson, James L.; and Frank F. Furstenberg. "Parental Attitudes and the Occurrence of Early Sexual

Activity." JOURNAL OF MARRIAGE AND THE FAMILY 48 (November 1986): 777-782.

Analyzes data on the 15 and 16 year olds interviewed in the National Survey of Children (and data from a parent, usually the mother) to test for the hypothesis that a combination of both traditional attitudes and effective communication practices is required to produce low rates of sexual activity among adolescents. The results indicate that parental discussion is associated with a lower frequency of the initiation of sexual activity only for the daughters of parents with traditional family values.

066. Mott, Frank L., and R. Jean Haurin. "Linkages Between Sexual Activity and Alcohol and Drug Use Among American Adolescents." FAMILY PLANNING PERSPECTIVES 20 (May/June 1988): 128-136.

Analyzes data from the National Longitudinal Survey of Youth Labor Market Experience to describe the relationship between early substance use and early sexual activity. Found that approximately two-thirds of the females under 16 and 50 percent of the males have neither engaged in intercourse nor used alcohol or marijuana. It is only by age 19 that one third of the young women have engaged in all three behaviors. Even though younger blacks are more likely than whites or Hispanics to have initiated sexual activity, young minority women are less likely to have begun substance use than young white women. Discusses the time lapse which tends to occur between one behavior and the other two.

067. Newcomer, Susan, and J. Richard Udry. "Parental Marital Status Effects on Adolescent Sexual Behavior." JOURNAL OF MARRIAGE AND THE FAMILY 49 (May 1987): 235-240.

Uses data from 286 young white adolescents to examine the relationship between changes in their parents' marital status and their coital behavior. For girls, the transition to a mother-only household increases the probability of transition from virgin to non-virgin status. For boys it is the disruption of the two parent household between interviews which predicts the transition. The findings suggests that the important factor is loss of parental control over the entire spectrum of age graded delinquent behaviors rather than a specific sex related behavior.

068. Newcomer, Susan F., and J. Richard Udry. "Parent-Child
     Communication and Adolescent Sexual Behavior." FAMILY
     PLANNING PERSPECTIVES 17 (July/August 1985):
     169-174.
     Uses data on more than 500 adolescents and their mothers to
     examine the relationship between parental attitudes and
     communication about sex and contraceptive behavior and the
     sexual and contraceptive behavior of their adolescent children.
     Often the adolescents were not even aware of their parents'
     attitudes. A significant relationship was found between
     communication and adolescent sexual behavior in only two areas
     and these relationships disappeared when who reported the
     discussion was controlled. In one case, when mothers reported
     discussing sex with their daughters the girls were less likely to
     initiate intercourse; but when the daughter reported the
     discussion, there was no relationship. In the other case, when the
     girls reported discussing contraception with their mothers, they
     were more likely to use effective birth control; however, the
     relationship disappeared when the mothers reported the
     discussion.

069. Newcomer, Susan F., and J. Richard Udry. "Mothers' Influence
     on the Sexual Behavior of Their Teenage Children."
     JOURNAL OF MARRIAGE AND THE FAMILY 46 (May
     1984): 477-485.
     Analyzes the data on a subset of junior and senior high school
     students who were interviewed and whose mothers also filled out
     questionnaires in order to examine the influence that mothers
     have on the sexual behavior of their adolescent children. Finds
     that the differential attitudes or communication patterns of
     mothers with various early sexual experience have little direct
     effect on the sexual behavior of their adolescent children. The
     data do suggest that what mothers may pass on to their daughters
     is early physical maturation, which, in turn, leads to early sexual
     behavior.

070. Pestrak, Victor, and Don Martin. "Cognitive Development and
     Aspects of Adolescent Sexuality." ADOLESCENCE 20
     (Winter 1985): 981-987.
     Points out that adolescents are becoming sexually active at
     earlier ages partially as a response to earlier physical maturation
     and greater social acceptance. Earlier physical maturation,
     however, is not necessarily coupled with earlier cognitive or moral

development. This disjuncture between level of physical development and level of cognitive development may account for the fact that simply giving adolescents information about contraception may not lead them to use it effectively. Suggests that when adolescents have not reached cognitive maturity, the most effective contraceptive method for them may be the IUD.

071. Roche, John P. "Premarital Sex: Attitudes and Behavior by Dating Stage." ADOLESCENCE 21 (Spring 1986): 107-121.
Uses data from 196 females and 84 males to assess what the respondents think is proper sexual behavior, what they do themselves, and what they think others are doing in various stages of the dating process. Found that both males and females tend to be more permissive in their behavior than in their attitudes and that they are even more permissive in terms of what they think others are doing. Males are more permissive than females but only in the early stages of dating.

072. Rodgers, Joseph L. "Family Configuration and Adolescent Sexual Behavior." POPULATION AND ENVIRONMENT 6 (Summer 1983): 73-83.
Utilizes questionnaire data from 504 junior high students in North Carolina to examine the relationship between family configuration and intercourse behavior among adolescents. Several of the family configuration variables were significantly related to intercourse behavior at the zero-order level. When controlling for variables that may confound the relationship, however, the strongest relationship was that between number of brothers and sexual behavior. Argues that three mechanisms may operate together to account for the existence of this relationship: (1) the masculinization of the environment; (2) brothers bringing friends into the family environment; and (3) brothers acting as role models.

073. Seltzer, Vicki L.; Rabin, Jill and Fred Benjamin. "Teenagers' Awareness of the Acquired Immunodeficiency Syndrome and the Impact on Their Sexual Behavior." OBSTETRICS AND GYNECOLOGY 74 (July 1989): 55-58.

074. Smith, Edward A.; Udry, Richard J.; and Naomi M. Morris. "Pubertal Development and Friends: A Biosocial Explanation of Adolescent Sexual Behavior." JOURNAL OF HEALTH AND SOCIAL BEHAVIOR 26 (September 1985): 183-192.

Analyzes data from interviews with 433 female and 370 male adolescents to assess the simultaneous impact of pubertal development and friendship patterns on the sexual behavior of adolescents. Argues that the level of the biologically determined sexual drive associated with pubertal maturation interacts with friend's sexual activity to influence the sexual behavior of adolescents. Among the females in the study the impact of friend's behavior is contingent upon level of pubertal development. An adolescent girl with a low level of sexual motivation is less likely to initiate sexual involvement regardless of friend's level of sexual involvement. For females with high levels of libidinal development, friend's sexual behavior is more important. The effect of friend's sexual involvement on adolescent males is not contingent upon their own level of development. At higher levels of development the effect of friend's behavior does not become stronger for males.

075. Smith, Edward, and J. Richard Udry. "Coital and Non-Coital Sexual Behaviors of White and Black Adolescents." AMERICAN JOURNAL OF PUBLIC HEALTH 75 (October 1985): 1200-1203.
Employs longitudinal data on junior and senior high school students to determine the sequence of sexual behaviors. Found that whites are more likely than blacks to engage in a predictable succession of noncoital behaviors over a period of time before engaging in intercourse. The sequence for blacks was much less ordered and often involved intercourse preceded only by necking. Argues that this difference may offer a partial explanation for the differences in pregnancy rates and has implications for sex education and contraceptive services.

076. Udry, J. Richard; Bauman, Karl E.; and Naomi M. Morris. "Changes in Premarital Coital Experience of Recent Decades of Birth Cohorts of Urban America." JOURNAL OF MARRIAGE AND THE FAMILY 37 (1975): 783-787.
Uses data on samples of 100 black and 100 white never married women age 15-44 selected through area sample surveys of low income neighborhoods in each of 16 selected U.S. cities who were interviewed in 1969-70 and in 1973-74 to estimate changes in the prevalence of premartial sexual experience by cohort. The data indicate a clear increase in sexual intercourse among women 15 to 19 from the cohort born in the 1920s to the cohort born in the 1950s.

077. Vadies, Eugene, and Darryl Hale. "Attitudes of Adolescent Males Towards Abortion, Contraception, and Sexuality." SOCIAL WORK IN HEALTH CARE 3 (Winter 1977): 169-174.

Uses data on 1,017 adolescent males in order to measure their attitudes toward pregnancy, family planning and sexuality. Black and white male adolescents differed in terms of their attitudes toward abortion, with blacks having very strong negative views. Nearly half of these males believed that females are responsible for contraception. Found that a majority of young males were willing to lie about love in order to have sex and that peer pressure was an important influence on their sexual activity.

078. Vener, Arthur M., and Cyrus S. Steward. "Adolescent Sexual Behavior in Middle America Revisited: 1970-1973." JOURNAL OF MARRIAGE AND THE FAMILY 36 (November 1974): 728-735.

Reports on a resurvey of junior and senior high school students in three anonymous Michigan communities thought to be representative of that 40 percent of U.S. society termed "middle America." The communities, and therefore the respondents, were white, ranged in socioeconomic status from upper working to upper middle and were not a part of a metropolitan complex. Using the same measure of sexual activity in 1973 as was used in 1970, changes in the sexual activity of the adolescents were gauged. The data indicate significant increases in the coital experience of both male and female 14 and 15-year-olds. Heavy involvement in intercourse was associated with the use of illicit drugs, alcohol and cigarettes. A high level of sexual activity is also associated with other delinquent behavior. By the age of 17, an equal proportion of males and females have made their sexual debut.

079. Wagner, Carol A. "Sexuality of American Adolescents," ADOLESCENCE 15 (Fall 1980): 567-580.

Attempts to describe the understanding of adolescent sexuality that can be garnered through an examination of the research literature. Describes changing American patterns of sexuality including those aspects of adolescent sexuality which are seen as most problematic, pregnancy and sexually transmitted diseases. Discusses adolescents' knowledge about sexuality as well as their sexual behavior including masturbation and homosexuality as well as heterosexual behavior.

080. Westney, Ouida E.; Jenkins, Renee R.; Butts, June D.; and
     Irving Williams. "Sexual Development and Behavior in Black
     Preadolescents." ADOLESCENCE 19 (Fall 1984): 557-568.
     Utilizes data on a volunteer sample of 46 boys and 55 girls (all
     black) between 8.3 and 11.4 years old to assess the nature of the
     relationship between biological maturation and sexual behavior.
     The subjects in this study evidenced considerable variability in
     physiological maturation as it relates to chronological age. For
     the boys in the sample, there was a positive relationship between
     maturational staging and sociosexual behavior, but no such
     relationship existed for the females.

081. Woodroof, Timothy J. "Premarital Sexual Behavior and
     Religious Adolescents." JOURNAL FOR THE SCIENTIFIC
     STUDY OF RELIGION 24 (December 1985): 343-366.
     Analyzes questionnaire data from 477 freshman attending
     colleges associated with the Churches of Christ to examine the
     relationship between religiosity (treated in terms of both behavior
     and orientation) and premarital sexual activity. In this
     conservative Christian sample the frequently cited relationship
     between religious and sexual behavior is found. A relationship is
     also found between religious orientation and sexual behavior. It
     is also found that while the religious variables identify virgins with
     great precision, they do poorly in identifying nonvirgins.

082. Zabin, Laurie Schwab; Kantner, John F.; and Melvin Zelnik.
     "Risk of Adolescent Pregnancy in the First Months of
     Intercourse." FAMILY PLANNING PERSPECTIVES 11
     (July/August 1979): 215-222.
     Employs data collected in 1981-1982 through questionnaires
     filled out by 3,500 inner city junior and senior high school
     students to examine the relationship between their sexual attitudes
     and behavior. Found that 83 percent of the sexually active believe
     that intercourse should be initiated at an older age than the one
     at which they made their own sexual debut. Also found that 88
     percent of the adolescent mothers in the sample believe that the
     best age to first give birth is older than the age at which they had
     their first child. A very large percentage of the young people
     believe that contraception is the joint responsibility of both sexual
     partners. Concludes that the majority of young people have
     values and attitudes indicative of sexual responsibility, but many
     of them are not able to behave in accord with their own attitudes
     and values.

083. Zelnik, Melvin and Farida K. Shah. "First Intercourse Among Young Americans." FAMILY PLANNING PERSPECTIVES 15 (March/April 1983): 64-70.

Employs data from a national probability sample survey, conducted in 1979, to examine a number of demographic and social factors associated with the first premarital sexual experience of U.S. adolescents of both sexes. Provides the age at first intercourse for the respondents and the age of their partners. The mean age at first intercourse for female respondents was 16.2 and the average age of their partners 19. The mean age of male respondents at first intercourse was 15.7 and that of their partners 16.4. When the relationship with the first partner was examined, the young women were more likely to say that they were engaged or going steady than were the young men. Only 17 percent of the young women and 25 percent of the young men report having planned their first intercourse. A large proportion of both sexes did not use a contraceptive at first intercourse. Racial differences are discussed in each area.

B. Chapters in Books

084. Chilman, Catherine S. "Some Psychosocial Aspects of Adolescent Sexual and Contraceptive Behaviors in a Changing American Society." SCHOOL-AGE PREGNANCY: BIOSOCIAL DIMENSIONS. Edited by Jane B. Lancaster and Beatrix A. Hamburg. New York: Aldine De Gruyter, 1986, pp. 191-217.

085. Chilman, Catherine S. "Toward a Reconceptualization of Adolescent Sexuality." ADOLESCENT PREGNANCY AND CHILDBEARING: FINDINGS FROM RESEARCH. Edited by Catherine S. Chilman. U. S. Department of Health and Human Services, 1980, pp. 101-128.

Elaborates upon the reconceptualization of adolescent sexuality which is required if society is to arrive at a humane and integrated understanding of adolescents both male and female.

086. Fisher, Susan M. "The Psychodynamics of Teenage Pregnancy and Motherhood." ADOLESCENT PARENTHOOD. Edited by Max Sugar. New York: SP Medical and Scientific Books, 1984, pp. 55-64.

Attempts to integrate the psychology of the pregnant teenager into the complex and variegated context of modern American life.

087. Lancaster, Jane B. "Human Adolescence and Reproduction: An Evolutionary Perspective." SCHOOL-AGE PREGNANCY: BIOSOCIAL DIMENSIONS. Edited by Jane B. Lancaster and Beatrix A. Hamburg. New York: Aldine De Gruyter, 1986, pp. 17-38.

088. Lipsitz, Joan. "Adolescent Psychosocial Development." ADOLESCENT PREGNANCY: PERSPECTIVES FOR THE HEALTH CARE PROFESSIONAL. Edited by Peggy B. Smith and David M. Mumford. Boston: G.K. Hall, 1980, pp. 1-13.
Addresses the questions, what aspects of normal adolescent development are related to a teenager's unplanned pregnancy, and how are these characteristics influenced by the family and the rest of society.

089. Scales, Peter, and Douglas Beckstein. "From Macho to Mutuality: Helping Young Men Make Effective Decisions About Sex, Contraception and Pregnancy." PREGNANCY IN ADOLESCENCE: NEEDS, PROBLEMS, AND MANAGEMENT. Edited by Irving R. Stuart and Carl F. Wells. New York: Van Nostrand Reinhold Company, 1982, pp. 264-289.
Reviews the literature on young men's decision making about sexuality, contraception, and pregnancy. Refers to organized efforts to counter the limitations of young men in these areas which results from macho socialization.

090. Sugar, Max. "Adolescent Decision Making Toward Motherhood." ADOLESCENT PARENTHOOD. Edited by Max Sugar. New York: SP Medical and Scientific Books, 1984, pp. 21-34.
Reviews aspects of decision making which lead to adolescent motherhood. Argues that differences in intelligence, nutritional status, socioeconomic, emotional development, culture, dynamics, and psychopathology all contribute at each branch in the decision process which leads to motherhood in adolescents.

091. Whiting, John W.M.; Burbank, Victoria K.; and Mitchell S. Ratner. "The Duration of Maidenhood Across Cultures."

SCHOOL-AGE PREGNANCY: BIOSOCIAL
DIMENSIONS. Edited by Jane B. Lancaster and Beatrix A.
Hamburg. New York: Aldine De Gruyter, 1986, pp. 273-302.

092. Youngs, David D. "Psychiatric Aspects of Adolescent
Pregnancy." ADOLESCENT PREGNANCY:
PERSPECTIVES FOR THE HEALTH CARE
PROFESSIONAL. Edited by Peggy B. Smith and David M.
Mumford. Boston: G.K. Hall, 1980, pp. 23-31.
Questions the more traditional views on adolescent pregnancy
which see such pregnancies as indicators of individual
psychopathology and those which tend to view adolescents as a
homogeneous grouping.

093. Zelnik, Melvin, and John F. Kantner. "Sexual and
Contraceptive Experience of Young Unmarried Women in
the United States, 1976 and 1971." ADOLESCENT
PREGNANCY AND CHILDBEARING: FINDINGS FROM
RESEARCH. Edited by Catherine S. Chilman. U. S.
Department of Health and Human Services, 1980, pp. 43-82.
An overview of the sexual and contraceptive behavior of female
adolescents 15-19 in the United States in 1971 and 1976.

094. Zelnik, Melvin. "Sexual Activity among Adolescents:
Perspective of a Decade." PREMATURE ADOLESCENT
PREGNANCY AND PARENTHOOD. Edited by Elizabeth
McAnarney. New York: Grune and Stratton, 1983, pp. 21-33.
Presents the data from the 1971, 1976, and 1979 surveys.

C. Books

095. Coles, Robert, and Geoffrey Stokes. SEX AND THE
AMERICAN TEENAGER. New York: Harper and Row,
1985.
Uses data from 1,067 questionnaires to address two major
questions about sexuality in the generation referred to as the
"children of the children of Woodstock." What do kids do? How
do they feel about it?

096. DeLameter, John, and Patricia MacCorquodale.
PREMARITAL SEXUALITY: ATTITUDES,

RELATIONSHIPS, BEHAVIOR. Madison: University of
Wisconsin Press, 1979.

097. Zelnik, Melvin, and John F. Kantner. SEX AND
PREGNANCY IN ADOLESCENCE. Beverly Hills: Sage
Publications, 1981.
Attempts to explain the sexual, contraceptive, and pregnancy
experience of U.S. adolescents based on three large scale surveys
the results of which have been described in numerous articles.

IV. CONTRACEPTION

A. Articles

098. Akpom, C. Amechi; Akpom, Kathy L.; and Marianne Davis.
"Prior Sexual Behavior of Teenagers Attending Rap Sessions
for the First Time." FAMILY PLANNING PERSPECTIVES
8 (July/August 1976): 203-208.
Studies the 303 female adolescents (18 and younger) who
attended the rap sessions conducted by a family planning clinic
in a rapidly growing industrial city with a population of more than
130,000. The young women are encouraged to attend the rap
sessions before they receive contraceptive services at the clinic.
It was found that most of the adolescents attending the rap
sessions for the first time between July 1972 and February 1973,
had been sexually active for a year or more before coming to the
clinic. These young people were at high risk of unintended
pregnancy.

099. Arnold, Charles B. "The Sexual Behavior of Inner City
Condom Users." JOURNAL OF SEX RESEARCH 8
(November 1972): 315-325.
Attempts to understand the sexual behavior and condom use
patterns of inner city adolescent males. The sample includes 134
single adolescent males, most of whom have not completed high
school and all of whom have been sexually active for about four
years beginning at age 14. All come from a low socioeconomic
status background. The mean age is 18.2. The data were collected by means of an interview which was administered by three
(3) young males (20-22) in November and December of 1970.
Finds that condoms are acceptable to adolescent males. If given
the chance males will accept a sizeable share of the burden for
pregnancy prevention. Only 17 percent of the young men in the
sample discussed birth control with their sexual partners. They
use condoms regularly despite the fact that on the average they
didn't learn about fertilization and pregnancy until about six
months after they became sexually active.

100. Beck, J. Gayle, and Dana K. Davies. "Teen Contraception: A
Review of Perspectives on Compliance." ARCHIVES OF
SEXUAL BEHAVIOR 16 (August 1987): 337-368.

101. Bergman, Abraham B. "Condoms for Sexually Active
     Adolescents." AMERICAN JOURNAL OF DISEASES OF
     CHILDREN 134 (March 1980): 247-249.
     Argues that physicians should promote the use of condoms in
     their professional activities as a way of reducing both unplanned
     adolescent pregnancies and sexually transmitted diseases.

102. Blake, Judith. "The Teenage Birth Control Dilemma and
     Public Opinion." SCIENCE 180 (May 1973): 708-712.
     Uses data from Gallup Organization National surveys of voting
     age white men and women conducted between January 1969 and
     August 1972 to describe public opinion on the issues surrounding
     making birth control available to adolescents. Concludes that by
     August of 1972 a majority of white Americans favored making
     education about contraception available to adolescent girls but
     were less inclined to actually provide them with birth control
     services. There were no significant differences on these issues
     between Catholics and non-Catholics but younger people were
     more favorable toward both contraceptive education and services
     than older people were. The surveys show that most white
     Americans were not permissive about premarital sexual activity
     for teens but suggests that many are willing to be pragmatic about
     trying to prevent unwanted adolescent pregnancies.

103. Clark, Samuel D. Jr., Zabin, Lauire S.; and Janet B. Hardy.
     "Sex, Contraception and Parenthood: Experience Among
     Urban Black Young Men." FAMILY PLANNING
     PERSPECTIVES 16 (March/April 1984): 77-82.
     Uses data from a self administered questionnaire filled out by
     663 never married black inner city male adolescents who attended
     one junior and one senior high school in Baltimore to review
     their sexual, contraceptive and pregnancy experiences. Examines
     the attitudes that these adolescents have toward birth control and
     parenthood and the relationship between attitudes and experience.
     Eighty percent of the sexually active have used a contraceptive
     and there is strong reliance on male methods. Nine tenths of the
     adolescents have heard of the pill and condom, with two fifths of
     those recognizing the methods and believing that they are
     effective. Nearly four in ten believe that they need parental
     permission to buy nonprescription contraception. While almost
     nine in 10 agree that males share contraceptive responsibility with
     their female partners, more than half are willing to have
     unprotected intercourse. While the majority wish to defer

fatherhood until their early 20s, many hold attitudes that appear
to be favorable to premarital conception. Most of the high school
students recognize that school age parenthood can be problematic
for everyone involved; yet 13 percent would not be upset if they
impregnated a girl and 12 percent would actually be happy.

104. Cobliner, W. Godfrey. "Pregnancy in the Single Adolescent
     Girl: The Role of Cognitive Functioning." JOURNAL OF
     YOUTH AND ADOLESCENCE 3 (1974): 17-29.
     Explores the psychological aspects associated with the abortion
decision using data on 461 adolescents: 211 who elected to abort,
200 who were carrying to term, and 50 who were sexually active
but not pregnant. Three fourths of the pregnancies were
unintended. It is argued that these young women, largely from
very poor backgrounds, certainly have to deal with the external
barriers to contraceptive use which involve lack of access to
affordable services. However, what is emphasized is that since
they have not yet reached the cognitive stage of development
which is characterized by the ability to reason abstractly, they are
unable to convert their knowledge of birth control into effective
contraceptive behavior. Instead psychological mechanisms act as
internal barriers to effective birth control practices.

105. Cohen, Donald D., and Ryda D. Rose. "Male Adolescent Birth
     Control Behavior: The Importance of Developmental Factors
     and Sex Differences." JOURNAL OF YOUTH AND
     ADOLESCENCE 13 (1984): 239-252.
     Examines the birth control behavior of 51 adolescent males (15-
17) and compares their behavior to what is known about that of
females. The findings indicate that in this group of males
contraceptive behavior is primarily self-oriented. The young men
studied are more likely to practice birth control in casual
encounters than with steady girl friends. They are more likely
to communicate about sex and birth control with their similar age
peers than they are with their family. These young men also tend
to view decisions about sex and birth control as female decisions.

106. Cvetkovich, George, and Barbara Grote. "Psychosocial Maturity
     and Teenage Contraceptive Use: An Investigation of
     Decision-making and Communication Skills." POPULATION
     AND ENVIRONMENT 4 (Winter 1981): 211-226.
     Reports the results of a study investigating two aspects of
maturity related to fertility control, the perceived need for

contraception and interpersonal communication skills. The data analyzed were collected on 87 sexually active female high school students. Both the pill users and condom users are distinguishable from those who use no contraceptive method. Pill users perceive a greater risk of becoming pregnant and have more negative attitudes toward becoming premaritally pregnant. Pill users have also had a longer relationship with their partners and trust their partners more. They were also older when they begin having intercourse and engage in it more frequently. Condom users have discussed their initiation of sex with their partner before hand and have had more discussions with male friends about a wider variety of subjects. They also have better role taking skills. The results are interpreted to indicate that contraceptive behavior can be conceptualized as varying on the basis of the psychosocial costs to the young woman.

107. Cvetkovich, George; Grote, Barbara; Bjorseth, Ann, and Julia Sarkissian. "On the Psychology of Adolescent use of Contraceptives." THE JOURNAL OF SEX RESEARCH 11 (August 1975): 256-270.
Attempts to apply existing psychological theory to explain the patterns of contraceptive usage during the first years of sexual activity. Points out that the most consistently cited characteristic of adolescent contraceptive use is its irrationality. Argues that this characteristic needs to be further studied using what is known about the psychology of adolescence. The egocentrism of adolescents must be taken into account including the notions of the imaginary audience and the personal fable. Suggests that effective contraceptive education must involve personalized discussion and cross age tutors. Also suggests that adolescent contraception decisions may be influenced by the perceived aesthetic qualities of the diverse methods.

108. DeLameter, John, and Patricia MacCorquodale. "Premarital Contraceptive Use: A Test of Two Models." JOURNAL OF MARRIAGE AND THE FAMILY 40 (May 1978): 235-247.
Uses data on a large representative sample to test the utility of two models for explaining contraceptive use. The findings suggest that contraceptive behavior is influenced by the types of factors highlighted in both models, cognitive or attitudinal factors as well as interactional/behavioral factors.

109. Evans, Jerome R.; Selstad, Georgiana, and Wayne H. Welcher. "Teenagers: Fertility Control Behavior and Attitudes." FAMILY PLANNING PERSPECTIVES 8 (July/August 1976): 192-200.

Analyzes data on 333 adolescents who sought pregnancy related assistance in Ventura County, California between 1972 and 1974. Thirty-six of the young women thought they were pregnant but had negative pregnancy tests, 68 decided to carry to term and remain single, and 184 chose to terminate by legal abortion. Findings are reported in regard to their education, economic dependence, abortion attitudes, satisfaction with resolution decision, initial attitudes and knowledge about contraception, and attitudes and contraceptive behavior at the time of follow-up. One of the significant findings was that those in the negative pregnancy test group continued to engage in unprotected intercourse.

110. Ewer, Phyllis, and James O. Gibbs. "Relationship with Putative Father and Use of Contraception in a Population of Black Ghetto Adolescent Mothers." PUBLIC HEALTH REPORTS 90 (September/October 1875): 417-423.

Analyzes data on 22 black adolescent mothers in order to ascertain the association between her relationship with her child's father and her contraceptive usage. The findings suggest that among the unmarried adolescents if the relationship was never close or became less close she was more likely to have unprotected intercourse. This is seen as resulting from a tendency to engage in sex infrequently and on an unpredictable basis. Married adolescent mothers, even when they do not express a desire for more children, have rates of contraceptive discontinuation that are higher than those for unmarried ones and the highest rates occur among the divorced and the separated. These latter findings are also explained in terms of the on again-off again nature of the relationship which allows the young mother to define herself as not needing continuous birth control and having a tendency to resume sex before resuming birth control.

111. Finkel, Madelon L., and David J. Finkel. "Sexual and Contraceptive Knowledge, Attitudes, and Behavior of Male Adolescents." FAMILY PLANNING PERSPECTIVES 7 (November/December 1975): 256-260.

Uses data from 421 male high school students to describe their
knowledge of reproduction and contraception, the level of their
sexual activity and contraceptive usage and to gauge the impact
of a sex education course on their knowledge and behavior. The
males in this study made an early sexual debut (mean age at first
intercourse was 12.8). The sexual activity, however was sporadic
and their contraceptive practices haphazard. At last intercourse
55 percent of these boys used no method of contraception or
relied on such unreliable techniques as withdrawal or douching
by their partner. It is argued that sex education given in high
school comes too late to help these boys become effective
contraceptors by the time of their first intercourse.

112. Finkel, Madelon L., and Finkel, David J. "Male Adolescent
     Contraceptive Utilization." ADOLESCENCE 13 (Fall 1978):
     443-451.
     Describes the patterns of contraceptive usage in a sample of
     male urban high school students (106 black, 119 Hispanic, 63
     white). The majority of blacks and Hispanics were classified as
     ineffective contraceptors, while the majority of whites were
     classified as effective contraceptors. The ineffective contraceptors
     failed to use birth control because they were not prepared for
     intercourse   or   were   unconcerned   about   the   possible
     consequences.

113. Freeman, Ellen W.; Rickels, Karl.; Huggins, George R.; and
     Celso-Ramon Garcia. "Urban Black Adolescents Who
     Obtain Contraceptive Services Before or After Their First
     Pregnancy." JOURNAL OF ADOLESCENT HEALTH
     CARE 5 (1984): 183-190.
     Employs data on 263 black female adolescents to identify the
     psychosocial factors which differentiate never pregnant teens
     enrolling in a family planning program (115) from those who
     deliver (86) or abort (62) before getting contraceptive services.
     Also includes data from a one year follow-up. Significant
     differences between the three groups were found on age,
     relationship with partner, and communication from the mother
     about contraception and pregnancy. The never pregnant group
     scored highest on the measure of self-esteem. All three groups
     were within the normal range on personality factors, emotional
     distress and social adjustment. There were no differences
     between the three groups on these measures. At the time of the

follow-up the most consistent contraceptive usage was found in the never pregnant group.

114. Freeman, Ellen; Rickels, Karl; Huggins, George; Mudd, Emily; Garcia, Celso-Ramon; and Helen O. Dickens. "Contraceptive Use: Comparisons of Male and Female Attitudes and AMERICAN JOURNAL OF PUBLIC HEALTH 70 (August 1980):790-797.
   Discusses data obtained from 730 black adolescents, 123 females attending a family planning clinic, 358 females in high school health classes, and 249 male students in the same classes. While the males and the females in the health classes agreed with the principle that both sexes share the responsibility for contraception there were differences in their specific knowledge and attitudes. Males demonstrated less knowledge about the risk of pregnancy and less knowledge about contraception. The males tended to believe that females had more knowledge in this area than they did and therefore had attitudes less supportive of contraception. The two groups of females were very similar but the school group was more likely to have discussed contraception with their male friends and their mothers. The school group also reported receiving more information about contraception from their mothers.

115. Furstenberg, Frank F., Jr. "Birth Control Experience Among Pregnant Adolescents: The Process of Unplanned Parenthood." SOCIAL PROBLEMS 19 (1971): 192-203.
   Utilizes data on 337 pregnant mostly black adolescents to investigate why contraception was not used more often in this group. Argues that overall the pregnancies in this group were not intentional but rather the unanticipated results of unprotected sexual intercourse. A major determinant of nonuse of contraception was lack of knowledge about birth control. Another important determinant was attitudes with many in the sample fearing harm from them or simply not liking the idea of them. Girls from families in which both the mother and daughter report discussing birth control were more likely to have attempted contraception. Contraceptive use was also associated with the nature of the relationship with the sex partner, the more stable the relationship the more likely contraception was used.

116. Furstenberg, Frank F., Jr.; Herceg-Baron, Roberta; Shea, Judy; and David Webb. "Family Communication and Teenagers'

Contraceptive Use." FAMILY PLANNING PERSPECTIVE 16 (July/August 1984): 163-170.

Employs data from 290 adolescents who were family planning clinic clients in southeastern Pennsylvania. The young people were interviewed three times over 15 months about their communication with their parents and their use of contraceptives. Over this time period the percentage of mothers who knew their child was attending a family planning clinic increased but the percentage of adolescents who actually discussed sex or birth control with their parents did not. Overall, family communication about sex and birth control had very little effect on the level of contraceptive use. Those teenagers who communicated well with their parents about these issues and those who communicated little did not differ significantly in the effectiveness of their use of contraception. In fact, better communication appeared to be a consequence rather than a cause of more effective contraception.

117. Garris, Lorie; Steckler, Allan; and J.R. McIntire. "The Relationship Between Oral Contraceptives and Adolescent Sexual Behavior." JOURNAL OF SEX RESEARCH 12 (May 1976): 135-146.

Describes the sexual behavior of 192 female adolescents, (15-20), receiving contraceptive services from the Los Angeles County Department of Health Services. The before group consisted of 96 who were using the services of the clinic for the first time while the after group consisted of 96 girls coming for their follow-up six to eight months after first using clinic services. After oral contraceptives had been taken for six to eight months, there was an increase in the frequency of intercourse but no increase in the number of partners. The respondents in both groups reported positive feelings about their families but were neutral in regard to their peers and religion. They also reported feeling positive about their own sexual experience. Members of the before group reported stronger feelings that their parents would not approve of their sexual behavior.

118. Goldsmith, Sadja; Gabrielson, Mary O.; Gabrielson, Ira; Mathews, Vicki; and Leah Potts. "Teenagers, Sex and Contraception." FAMILY PLANNING PERSPECTIVES 4 (January 1972): 32-38.

Reports the results of a study in which 377 sexually active female adolescents (13-17), mostly white, were interviewed about their knowledge, attitudes and practices in regard to sex and contraception. The young women were divided into three groups: (1) 210 who were never pregnant and seeking contraceptive services; (2) 100 who were seeking abortion; and (3) 67 who were carrying to term and living in two maternity homes. The group seeking contraception was seen as showing more self acceptance and as having less negative attitudes about pregnancy prevention. This group was also seen as having more interest in achievement and education. The groups were similar in that even though a third of them had taken a sex education course in school they were greatly misinformed regarding sex and contraception.

119. Gruber, Enid and Christopher V. Chambers. "Cognitive Development and Adolescent Contraception: Integrating Theory and Practice." ADOLESCENCE 22 (Fall 1987): 661-670.

Elaborates the developmental skills needed for effective contraception among adolescents and discusses how those skills must be integrated with key aspects of medical history in order to provide the most appropriate care, both developmentally and medically.

120. Herceg-Baron, Roberta; Furstenberg, Frank F., Jr.; Shea, Judy; and Kathleen Mullan Harris. "Supporting Teenager's Use of Contraceptives: A Comparison of Clinic Services." FAMILY PLANNING PERSPECTIVES 18 (March/April 1986): 61-66.

121. Hewson, Patricia M. "Research on Adolescent Male Attitudes About Contraceptives." PEDIATRIC NURSING 12 (March/April 1986): 114-116.

Reviews research reports concerned with the attitudes and knowledge that adolescent males have about contraception and their contraceptive behavior. Most of the studies reviewed point out that adolescent males have a great deal of misinformation about reproduction and contraception and that they desire more education about sex. The young males in these studies are not knowledgeable about obtaining nonprescription methods. Fathers and nonfathers do not differ in knowledge, but there are differences by ethnicity in perceptions about the effectiveness of the various methods of birth control.

122. Hofmann, Adele D. "Contraception in Adolescence: A Review." BULLETIN OF THE WORLD HEALTH ORGANIZATION 62 (1984): 331-344.

Discusses the biomedical aspects of adolescent use of the various contraceptive methods. Argues that the risk associated with any existing means of contraception is outweighed by the cost of an unplanned adolescent pregnancy.

123. Hogan, Dennis P.; Astone, Nan Marie and Evelyn M. Kitagawa. "Social and Environmental Factors Influencing Contraceptive Use Among Black Adolescents." FAMILY PLANNING PERSPECTIVES 17 (July/August 1985): 165-169.

Utilizes data from a survey of unmarried black adolescents residing in Chicago to explore the correlates of contraceptive usage. Three social and environmental factors were related to the use of contraceptives at first intercourse. Those young women who were higher in socioeconomic status, lived in higher status neighborhoods and had parents with intact marriages were the most likely to use contraception at first intercourse. Under each of these conditions, however, less than 50 percent made their sexual and contraceptive debut at the same time. For the males in the sample only social class was significantly related to use of contraception at first intercourse.

124. Jones, Judith B., and Susan G. Philliber. "Sexually Active, But Not Pregnant: A Comparison of Teens Who Risk and Teens Who Plan." JOURNAL OF YOUTH AND ADOLESCENCE 12 (1983): 235-251.

Employs data on 119 women aged 21 or younger who visited a hospital based clinic in New York City in the summer of 1981. The goal of the study was to describe the characteristics of a mostly minority group sample of women who have been sexually active for at least a year but who have never been pregnant. Even though all of the young women came to the clinic for contraceptive services, only 36 percent could be described as consistent contraceptors. The remainder either used birth control sporadically or did not use it at all. The consistent users, however, were more similar to the others than different. The two groups even had very similar motivations for not yet having a baby. It is concluded that adolescents may not have cognitive consistency in this area. Clinic counselors are warned that they cannot interpret a young woman's motivation not to become pregnant as an indication that she will consistently use available contraceptives.

125. Jorgensen, Stephen R. and Janet S. Sonstegard. "Predicting Adolescent Sexual and Contraceptive Behavior: An Application and Test of the Fishbein Model." JOURNAL OF MARRIAGE AND THE FAMILY 46 (February 1984): 43-55.
    Uses data on 385 adolescent females (13-18) to test the hypothesis that an adolescent female's sexual and contraceptive behavior can be predicted from a linear combination of her attitude toward performing that behavior and her normative beliefs, weighted by her motivation to comply with those norms. The model employed explains only a limited amount of the total variance in the pregnancy risk taking behavior of female adolescents. Attitudes and parental norms, weighted by motivation to comply, were related to two measures of contraceptive use but not to frequency of intercourse. The norms of peers were not related to any of the pregnancy risk behaviors. Discusses why this study found only mixed support for the model and why the model is still useful.

126. Jorgensen, Valerie. "One Year Contraceptive Follow-up of Adolescent Patients." AMERICAN JOURNAL OF OBSTETRICS AND GYNECOLOGY 115 (February 1973): 483-486.
    Describes the one year contraceptive follow-up of 221 postpartum adolescent patients 11-17 years old. Sixty percent of the original sample was available at the time of the one year follow-up. The routine contraceptives prescribed were judged to be safe and effective. The discontinuation of methods was more strongly associated with family and boyfriends considering them to be unsafe than with actual rate of complication.

127. Kantner, John F., and Melvin Zelnik. "Contraception and Pregnancy: Experience of Young Unmarried Women in the United States." FAMILY PLANNING PERSPECTIVES 5 (Winter 1973): 21-35.
    Analyzes data from a national random sample of U. S. females 15-19 years of age in order to describe the contraceptive behavior of those who are sexually active. Discusses the frequency and correlates of contraceptive usage, the methods used and the sources. Among the many findings are that there is considerable occasional usage but less than half used a method at last intercourse. Race and social class are associated with use. More than 70 percent report that the pill, the condom or withdrawal

was the most recently used method. The primary distribution point is the drugstore.

128. Kastner, Laura S. "Ecological Factors Predicting Adolescent Contraceptive Use. Implications for Intervention." JOURNAL OF ADOLESCENT HEALTH CARE 5 (1984): 70-86.

Employs data on 230 female adolescents to investigate whether their contraceptive use can be predicted from a model composed of individual, family, peer, and community variables. Found that contraceptive use can be successfully predicted by a model of 12 scales assessing social permissiveness, costs and benefits of contraception, parent communication, boy friend support, perceived amount of learning and instruction in sexual education, objective contraceptive knowledge, attitudes about adolescent pregnancy, perceived access to contraceptive services and perceived attitudes of parents and peers about contraception.

129. Kirby, Douglas; Harvey, Philip D.; Classenius, David; and Marty Novar. "A Direct Mailing to Teenage Males About Condom Use: Its Impact on Knowledge Attitudes and Sexual Behavior." FAMILY PLANNING PERSPECTIVES 21 (January/February 1989): 12-18.

Describes an experimental study in which 985 members of an experimental group (who were mailed a letter, an informational pamphlet and a coupon for free mail order condoms) were compared to 1,033 members of a control group (who received no mailing). There were small but significant differences between the two groups in terms of knowledge about sexually transmitted diseases, pregnancy and contraception. There were no differences between the two groups in attitudes toward sexually transmitted diseases or birth control nor in sexual activity and contraceptive behavior. A sizeable proportion of the experimental group ordered the free condoms before their first intercourse experience.

130. Kisker, Ellen Eliason. "Teenagers Talk About Sex, Pregnancy and Contraception." FAMILY PLANNING PERSPECTIVES 17 (March/April 1985): 83-90.

Uses qualitative data from small group discussions with mostly white middle-class to lower-class adolescents to investigate some of the reasons for their poor level of contraceptive practices. Among the facts which emerged from these discussions were that adolescents, especially young females, do not plan for their sexual debut because to do so would require them to admit the fact that they are becoming sexually active. It also appears that many young people are quite sexually sophisticated even though much of their information is sketchy, ill digested or wrong. Many of their parents appear to be no better informed. Implications for action and future research are discussed.

131. Lowe, Candace S., and Susan M. Radius. "Young Adults Contraceptive Practices: An Investigation of Influences." ADOLESCENCE 22 (Summer 1987): 291-304.
Uses data on 283 unmarried college students between 18 and 22 to study the influences on their contraceptive behavior. Findings indicate that effective contraceptive behavior is associated with: (1) the respondents seeing few barriers to their use; (2) extensive interpersonal skills; and (3) the perception of peer norms as supporting effective contraceptive behavior. The findings also point out how uninformed young adults are about anatomy, physiology and contraceptives.

132. McCormick, Naomi; Izzo, Angela; and John Folcik. "Adolescents' Values, Sexuality and Contraception in a Rural New York County." ADOLESCENCE 20 (Summer 1985): 385-395.
Utilizes data from questionnaires filled out by 75 males and 88 females who were high school students in a rural county of New York. Found that measures of religiosity, premarital sexual standards, and sex role attitudes were not useful in explaining or predicting the sexual and contraceptive behavior in this group of adolescents. The most effective method of contraception used by the sexually active was the condom. The high level of risk taking in this group is clearly demonstrated by the fact that 21 percent of those who are sexually active rely on withdrawal, douching, and trusting in luck. The failure to contracept effectively is seen as related to the low frequency of intercourse (about twice a month).

133. Miller, Warren B. "Sexual and Contraceptive Behavior in Young Unmarried Women." PRIMARY CARE 3 (September 1976): 427-453.
Compares 26 sexually active never pregnant white women to an equal number of similar women who had recently discovered an unplanned pregnancy and were seeking a therapeutic abortion.

Concludes that the psychological determinants of the sexual and contraceptive behavior of young women are complex, variable and unique. Argues that these characteristics mean that the most effective therapy will be one-on-one face to face interactions between client and practitioner.

134. Morrison, Diane M. "Adolescent Contraceptive Behavior: A Review." PSYCHOLOGICAL BULLETIN 98 (1985): 538-568.
    Reviews the literature concerned with the contraceptive behavior of adolescents. Concludes that the research suggests that adolescents largely lack information about the physiology of reproduction and about many methods of contraception. They tend to hold negative attitudes about contraceptives in general and about contraceptive use. Argues that, given this low level of information about and negative attitude toward contraception, its nonuse by adolescents cannot be seen as irrational behavior. States that sufficient descriptive and comparative research which documents the simple relationships between predictor variables and contraceptive use has been done. Future research should be multivariate, integrative and theory based, representing cognitive, emotional and developmental perspectives.

135. Mosher, William D., and Marjorie C. Horn. "First Family Planning Visits by Young Women." FAMILY PLANNING PERSPECTIVES 20 (January/February 1988): 33-40.
    Uses data from the 1982 National Survey of Family Growth to describe the first visit that young women make to providers of family planning services. Finds that in the United States young women typically do not seek family planning services until after they have not only made their sexual debut but have been having intercourse regularly and frequently. Only 17 percent of those making first visits were not yet sexually active. Those making their first visit have, on the average, been sexually active for 23 months.

136. Mudd, Emily H.; Dickens, Helen O.; Garcia, Celso-Ramon; Rickels, Karl; Freeman, Ellen; Huggins, George and Jacqueline J. Logan. "Adolescent Health Services and Contraceptive Use." AMERICAN JOURNAL OF ORTHOPSYCHIATRY 48 (July 1978): 495-504.
    Describes a pilot study using data on 161 black females enrolled in a health services program for never pregnant adolescents which

was designed to measure contraceptive continuation. Also set out to explore the social and/or emotional differences between those girls who continued and those who discontinued a method. Found that in a program emphasizing education and support even the youngest adolescents can use contraception effectively. Adolescents who continued did not differ on any of the measured dimensions from those who did not continue. Those who became pregnant differed from the rest on the somatization dimension of the SLC-90, an out-patient psychiatric rating scale.

137. Namerow, Pearila Brickner; Lawton, Amelia I.; and Susan G. Philliber. "Teenagers' Perceived and Actual Probabilities of Pregnancy." ADOLESCENCE 22 (Summer 19897): 475-485.
     Utilizes data on 425 female adolescents attending a New York City multiservice center for youth to investigate the relationship between their perceived and actual risk of pregnancy at their last intercourse. Also examines the relationship between perceived and actual risk of pregnancy and contraceptive use. Found very little correlation between perceived and actual risk of pregnancy. Less than half of the sample correctly perceived their risk of pregnancy. Even among those who scored high on a test of knowledge about ovulation there was very little ability to apply this knowledge to their own fertility status. The behavior of adolescents in regard to contraception was more a function of how likely they thought they were to get pregnant rather than how likely they really were.

138. Namerow, Pearila B., and Judith E. Jones. "Ethnic Variation in Adolescent Use of a Contraceptive." JOURNAL OF ADOLESCENT HEALTH CARE 3 (1982): 165-172.
     Compares black, white and Hispanic youths in terms of their reason for attending a contraceptive facility; their visit patterns; clinic continuation rates; methods accepted; patterns of method utilization as well as pregnancy rates and pregnancy resolution decisions. Uses data on 11,665 visits made by 4,180 patients during the first three years of the operation of a clinic for young people in New York City.

139. Nathanson, Constance A., and Marshall H. Becker. "Family and Peer Influence on Obtaining a Contraceptive Method." JOURNAL OF MARRIAGE AND THE FAMILY 48 (August 1985): 513-525.

Uses data on 2,884 unmarried women under 20 who made a
first visit to a county health department family planning clinic in
Maryland between October 1980 and July 1981 to examine the
role of significant others in obtaining contraception. It was found
that the majority of these young women did not seek
contraception in isolation but rather with the active participation
of significant others. The involvement of parents or friends seem
to indicate alternative strategies; those girls who involve the
parents do not tend to involve their friends and vice versa. The
young black women were the most likely to report parental
involvement while white girls with relatively well educated
mothers were the least likely to report it. The findings are
interpreted in terms of structural and normative differences in
black and white families.

140. Peacock, Nancy. "Contraceptive Decision Making Among
     Adolescent Girls." JOURNAL OF SEX EDUCATION AND
     THERAPY 8 (1982): 31-34.
     Analyzes data on the contraceptive decision making process of
     132 sexually active female adolescents. Only one of the items
     studied, the respondent's assessment of the cost of contraceptive
     use, was predictive of actual contraceptive use. Concludes that
     the process adolescents use in deciding whether or not to
     contracept is complex and not yet well understood.

141. Polit-O'Hara, Denise, and Janet R. Kahn. "Communication and
     Contraceptive Practices in Adolescent Couples."
     ADOLESCENCE 20 (Spring 1985): 33-43.
     Describes the content, frequency and timing of communication
     about birth control in 83 sexually active couples where the female
     was between 15 and 18 years old. Most of the couples had
     discussed birth control at least once but only 45.8 percent had
     such discussions prior to their first intercourse. The couples with
     good communication were most likely to contracept effectively.
     Those at most risk of an unplanned pregnancy were the one-
     fourth of respondents who felt that contraception had not been
     adequately discussed.

142. Reichelt, Paul A. "Coital and Contraceptive Behavior of
     Female Adolescents." ARCHIVES OF SEXUAL
     BEHAVIOR 8 (March 1979): 159-172.
     Describes the coital and contraceptive behavior of 532 female
     adolescents using data collected from interviews with them before

they actually received contraceptive services at a Teen Center operated by Planned Parenthood. At the time they came to the Teen Center 92 percent of the young women had already experienced intercourse. The average delay between the initiation of sexual activity and coming to the clinic was one year. Almost all of the young women, 92 percent, were involved with only one sexual partner. Sixty percent of the young women had risked pregnancy by engaging in intercourse while using no form of contraception. This is seen as related to the sporadic nature of and the low frequency of their intercourse activity.

143. Schwartz, Dana Belmonte, and Katherine F. Darabi.
     "Motivations For Adolescents' First Visit to a Family Planning Clinic." ADOLESCENCE 21 (Fall 1986): 535-545.
     Describes what factors or events motivated 150 young women to make their first visit to a family planning clinic. The most important finding was how critical a pregnancy scare was as an catalyst for the first visit to the birth control clinic. Confirmed findings from earlier studies that Hispanics often delay clinic visits and were more likely to be pregnant before they made the first visit. Argues that the percentage of Hispanics reporting that their parents or partners knew of their clinic visit was surprisingly large.

144. Shah, Farida; Zelnik, Melvin; and John F. Kantner.
     "Unprotected Intercourse Among Unwed Teenagers."
     FAMILY PLANNING PERSPECTIVES 7
     (January/February 1975): 39-44.
     Addresses the question of why so many adolescents risk pregnancy by engaging in intercourse without contraception using data from a national survey of unmarried females 15-19 years old. The findings indicate that seventy percent of those who reported engaging in unprotected intercourse did not think they could become pregnant. Blacks tended to believe that their risk of pregnancy was low because of their age, that they had sex infrequently or because of a general belief that they could not become pregnant. Whites, on the other hand, thought that they were having sex during a safe part of the month. A little more than 15 percent of the respondents reported wanting to be pregnant or not caring, while 12.5 percent had medical or moral objections to contraception. Each of these choices is discussed in terms of race, the educational level of the women who raised the respondent and the respondent's level of completed education or educational aspirations.

145. Shah, Farida, and Melvin Zelnik. "Parent and Peer Influence on Sexual Behavior, Contraceptive Use, and Pregnancy Experience of Young Women." JOURNAL OF MARRIAGE AND THE FAMILY 43 (May 1981): 339-348.

Analyzes data on a national probability sample of 15-19 year old women, conducted in 1976, to determine the influence of parents and peers on the attitudes that young women have about premarital sexuality and their sexual and contraceptive behavior. White women with attitudes about premarital sex which are similar to those of their parents have low levels of sexual experience. When such women are sexually experienced, they tend not to be casual contraceptors but fall into either the never-contracept or always-contracept group. Those women who are most like their friends in attitudes have higher levels of sexual activity, contracept inconsistently and therefore have higher pregnancy rates. Among blacks there is a much lower level of congruency between attitudes and behaviors.

146. Sheehan, Mary Kroll; Ostwald, Sharon K.; and James Rothenberger. "Perceptions of Sexual Responsibility: Do Young Men and Women Agree?" PEDIATRIC NURSING 12 (January/February 1986): 17-21.

Uses data collected from a convenience sample of 248 undergraduates to explore questions about sexuality and contraceptive responsibility. Found that 63 percent of the sample had engaged in intercourse at least once and that 91 percent saw contraception as a shared responsibility. Neither age, intercourse experience nor gender were related to the perception of contraceptive responsibility. Slightly more than half of the sexually active students reported using effective methods of birth control at first intercourse, (52%), while the remainder used less effective methods, or no method at all (37.2%). At last intercourse only 5.6 percent used no method, 29 percent used condoms, and 46.7 percent used a prescription method. No relationship was found between the method used and perception of responsibility.

147. Strahle, W.M. "A Model of Premarital Coitus and Contraceptive Behavior among Female Adolescents." ARCHIVES SEXUAL BEHAVIOR 12 (February 1983): 67-94.

Abstracts a list of pertinent variables from the literature on female adolescent sexuality and contraceptive behavior and using exchange theory as a general framework constructs a two stage model from which 40 hypotheses are derived. The type of research design needed to test these hypotheses is discussed.

148. Strassberg, Donald L., and John M. Mahoney. "Correlates of the Contraceptive Behavior of Adolescents/Young Adults." JOURNAL OF SEX RESEARCH 25 (November 1988): 531-536.

149. Urberg, Kathryn. "A Theoretical Framework for Studying Contraceptive Practice." ADOLESCENCE 17 (Fall 1982): 527-540.
Attempts to elaborate a theoretical framework for studying the use of contraceptives by adolescents. The framework assumes that given the information they have, the pressures on them and their level of development, adolescents make rational decisions.

150. Westoff, Charles. "Contraceptive Paths Toward The Reduction of Unintended Pregnancy and Abortion." FAMILY PLANNING PERSPECTIVES 20 (January/February 1988): 4-13.
Uses data from the 1982 National Survey of Family Growth to estimate the potential impact of improved contraceptive practices on the rate of unintended pregnancies and abortions in the United States. Three hypothetical models of contraceptive improvement are applied to the data for both blacks and whites, the married and the unmarried, and for all age groups. The first model assumes increases in the utilization of existing methods of contraception. Model I implies a 32 percent reduction in the rate of unintended pregnancy among all women 15-44. Model II also assumes the introduction of new contraceptive methods and implies an overall reduction of 56 percent in unintended pregnancies. The third model assumes the complete elimination of contraceptive nonuse and implies a 57 percent reduction.

151. Winter, Laraine. "The Role of Self-Concept In the Use of Contraceptives." FAMILY PLANNING PERSPECTIVES 20 (May/June 1988): 123-127.
Describes a scale designed to measure the sexual self-concept and the results of administering it to a sample of high school and college students. The sexual self-concept construct did predict several aspects of contraceptive use, general consistency, use at most recent intercourse and method choice. The scores on the

scale did increase with age, but the design did not allow a determination of whether this was due to the developmental nature of the construct or to the cohort effect.

152. Zabin, Laurie Schwab. "Institutional Factors Affecting Teenagers' Choice and Reasons for Delay in Attending a Family Planning Clinic." FAMILY PLANNING PERSPECTIVES 15 (January/February 1983): 25-29.
Employs data on 1,243 never pregnant teenage family planning clinic patients to determine why they chose a particular clinic. The findings include the facts that adolescents choose a clinic on the basis of confidentiality, a caring staff and proximity. Among blacks it was often the mother who selected the clinic.

153. Zabin, Laurie Schwab. "The Impact of Early Use of Prescription Contraceptives on Reducing Premarital Teenage Pregnancies." FAMILY PLANNING PERSPECTIVES 13 (March/April 1981): 72-74.
Uses life table analysis to estimate the effect of all unmarried adolescent women using prescription contraceptives on the risk of teenage pregnancy. The model estimates that if all young women in the cohort made their sexual and contraceptive debut at the same time, the risk of pregnancy would be reduced by 79 percent at the end of 24 months. If they adopted prescription methods of contraception one month after first intercourse the risk would be reduced by 59 percent, while waiting six months would only bring a 30 percent reduction. The high level of risk which remains even if only a month elapses is due to the high risk of pregnancy in the first month and the problems that young women have with continuing a method and using it consistently as prescribed.

154. Zelnik, Melvin, and John F. Kantner. "Sexual Activity Contraceptive Use and Pregnancy Among Metropolitan Area Teenagers, 1971-1979." FAMILY PLANNING PERSPECTIVES 12 (September/ October 1980): 230-237.
Presents data from a 1979 national survey to describe the sexual activity, contraceptive use and pregnancy experience of 15-19 year old women living in metropolitan areas. Also provides data, for the first time, on the sexual activity of males 17-21. The 1979 data for women are compared to the data from the 1971 and 1976 surveys. Argues that while the level of sexual activity among young women is increasing, there is evidence that they are trying harder than ever to avoid pregnancy and childbirth outside of

marriage. Even so young women appear to not be very successful at avoiding unwanted pregnancies at least partially because the most effective methods of contraception have become less popular. The increased use of abortion by adolescents has, however, meant that proportionately fewer adolescent pregnancies end in live births.

155. Zelnik, Melvin, and John F. Kantner. "Contraceptive Patterns and Premarital Pregnancy among Women aged 15-19 in 1976." FAMILY PLANNING PERSPECTIVES 10 (May-June 1978): 135-142.

Uses data from a 1976 national survey of women aged 15-19 living in households in the United States to describe their contraceptive and pregnancy experience. Finds that 80 percent of those adolescents who experienced an unwanted pregnancy were not using any contraceptive method at the time the pregnancy occurred. The sexually active young woman who never uses a contraceptive method has a 58 percent chance of becoming pregnant. If, on the other hand, she contracepts regularly her chances of becoming pregnant are 11 percent. When she uses a medical method, the chance of becoming pregnant is only six percent.

156. Zelnik, Melvin, and John F. Kantner. "Sexual and Contraceptive Experience of Young Unmarried Women in the United States, 1976 and 1971." FAMILY PLANNING PERSPECTIVES 9 (March/April 1977): 55-71.

Analyzes data from national surveys carried out in 1971 and 1976 to describe changes in the sexual and contraceptive experiences of unmarried 15-19 year old females in the U.S. It was found that the prevalence of unmarried intercourse increased between 1971 and 1976 for both races and in each of the age categories. At the time of both surveys knowledge about what point in the menstrual cycle conception was most likely to occur was very poor. Contraceptive practices improved greatly in the time between the two surveys with increases in the proportions of young women who always used contraceptives and those who used a method at last intercourse. This growth was moderated by a smaller but simultaneous increase in the proportion who never contracept. Describes many other aspects of the sexual and contraceptive behavior of adolescents with the data broken down by age and race.

B. Chapters in Books

157. Ager, Joel W.; Shea, Fredericka P.; and Samuel J. Agronow.
"Method Discontinuance in Teenage Women: Implications for
Teen Contraceptive Programs." PREGNANCY IN
ADOLESCENCE: NEEDS, PROBLEMS, AND
MANAGEMENT. Edited by Irving R. Stuart and Carl F.
Wells. New York: Van Nostrand Reinhold Company, 1982,
pp. 236-263.
Uses data on 143 adolescents studied over 18 months in order
to assess the incidence of, the reasons for, and the consequences
of discontinuation of contraceptive methods.

158. Allegeier, Elizabeth Rice. "Informational Barriers to
Contraception." ADOLESCENTS, SEX AND
CONTRACEPTION. Edited by Donn Byrne and William A.
Fisher. Hillsdale, New Jersey: Lawrence Erlbaum Associates,
1983, pp. 143-170.

159. Allegeier, Elizabeth Rice. "Ideological Barriers to
Contraception." ADOLESCENTS, SEX AND
CONTRACEPTION. Edited by Donn Byrne and William A.
Fisher. Hillsdale, New Jersey: Lawrence Erlbaum Associates,
1983, pp. 171-205.

160. Byrne, Donn. "Sex Without Contraception." ADOLESCENTS,
SEX AND CONTRACEPTION. Edited by Donn Byrne and
William A. Fisher. Hillsdale, New Jersey: Lawrence Erlbaum
Associates, 1983, pp. 3-31.

161. DeLamater, John. "An Interpersonal and Interactional Model
of Contraceptive Behavior." ADOLESCENTS, SEX AND
CONTRACEPTION. Edited by Donn Byrne and William A.
Fisher. Hillsdale, New Jersey: Lawrence Erlbaum Associates,
1983, pp. 33-61.

162. Edmunds, Marilyn. "Providing Contraceptive Care on a College
Campus." ADOLESCENTS, SEX AND
CONTRACEPTION. Edited by Donn Byrne and William A.
Fisher. Hillsdale, New Jersey: Lawrence Erlbaum Associates,
1983, pp. 243-262.

163. Fisher, William A.; Byrne, Donn; and Leonard A. White. "Emotional Barriers to Contraception." ADOLESCENTS, SEX AND CONTRACEPTION. Edited by Donn Byrne and William A. Fisher. Hillsdale, New Jersey: Lawrence Erlbaum Associates, 1983, pp. 207-242.

164. Fisher, William A. "Adolescent Contraception: Summary and Recommendations." ADOLESCENTS, SEX AND CONTRACEPTION. Edited by Donn Byrne and William A. Fisher. Hillsdale, New Jersey: Lawrence Erlbaum Associates, 1983, pp. 273-300.

165. Furstenberg, Frank F., Jr.; Herceg-Baron, Roberta; Shea, Judy; and David Webb. "Family Communication and Contraceptive Use Among Sexually Active Adolescents." SCHOOL-AGE PREGNANCY: BIOSOCIAL DIMENSIONS. Edited by Jane B. Lancaster and Beatrix A. Hamburg. New York: Aldine De Gruyter, 1986, pp. 219-243.

166. Greydanus, Donald E. "Alternatives to Adolescent Pregnancy: Review of Contraceptive Literature." PREMATURE ADOLESCENT PREGNANCY AND PARENTHOOD. Edited by Elizabeth McAnarney. New York: Grune and Stratton, 1983, pp. 61-105.
Describes the available methods of contraception, their effectiveness, side effects and contraindications.

167. Gross, Alan E., and Martha Bellew-Smith. "A Social Psychological Approach to Reducing Pregnancy Risk in Adolescence." ADOLESCENTS, SEX AND CONTRACEPTION. Edited by Donn Byrne and William A. Fisher. Hillsdale, New Jersey: Lawrence Erlbaum Associates, 1983, pp. 263-272.

168. Mindick, Burton, and Stuart Oskamp. "Individual Differences Among Adolescent Contraceptors: Some Implications for Intervention." PREGNANCY IN ADOLESCENCE: NEEDS, PROBLEMS, AND MANAGEMENT. Edited by Irving R. Stuart and Carl F. Wells. New York: Van Nostrand Reinhold Company, 1982, pp. 140-176.
Discusses factors associated with effective contraception on the part of adolescents. The factors discussed include: (1) early relationships; (2) socialization processes; (3) development of

positive self-image; (4) the ability to reason cognitively; and (5) the ability to plan for future roles.

169. Olson, Lucy, and Joan Rollins. "Psychological Barriers to Contraceptive Use Among Adolescent Women." PREGNANCY IN ADOLESCENCE: NEEDS, PROBLEMS, AND MANAGEMENT. Edited by Irving R. Stuart and Carl F. Wells. New York: Van Nostrand Reinhold Company, 1982, pp. 177-193.
Describes how the perceptions that contraceptives are difficult to obtain and/or injurious to health act as psychological barriers to contraceptive utilization.

170. Rogel, Mary J., and Martha E. Zuehike. "Adolescent Contraceptive Behavior: Influences and Implications." PREGNANCY IN ADOLESCENCE: NEEDS, PROBLEMS, AND MANAGEMENT. Edited by Irving R. Stuart and Carl F. Wells. New York: Van Nostrand Reinhold Company, 1982, pp. 194-218.
Describes the set of factors seen as important in recruiting low income urban adolescents into the effective practice of contraception and retaining them. Discusses a program designed with this set of factors in mind.

171. Shopper, Moisy. "From (Re) Discovery to Ownership of the Vagina--A Contribution to the Explanation of Nonuse of Contraceptives in the Female Adolescent." ADOLESCENT PARENTHOOD. Edited by Max Sugar. New York: SP Medical and Scientific Books, 1984, pp. 35-54.
Describes a stage of psychological development in which the adolescent female comes to recognize her ownership of her own genitals. Argues that the nonuse of contraceptives by female adolescents can be partially explained by the fact that this stage of ownership must be reached before the adolescent can become an effective contraceptor but that the stage can only be reached by experiencing genital sexuality. When the form of genital sexuality experienced is intercourse, then a window is left for the occurrence of an unplanned adolescent pregnancy.

172. Tighe, Patti. "A Social Psychiatric View of Female Adolescent Contraception." THE TEENAGE PREGNANT GIRL. Edited by Jack Zackler and Wayne Brandstadt. Springfield, Illinois: Charles C. Thomas, 1975, pp. 203-230.

Points out how adolescent pregnancy is studied differently by race and class. Discusses the internal and external factors associated with the failure to contracept in adolescent females.

C. Books

173. Byrne, Donn, and William Fisher. ADOLESCENTS, SEX, AND CONTRACEPTION. Hillsdale, New Jersey: Lawrence Erlbaum Associates, 1983.
     Contains items 158-164, and 167.

V. SEX EDUCATION

A. Articles

174. Aldous, Joan. "Birth Control Socialization: How to Avoid Discussing the Subject." POPULATION AND ENVIRONMENT 6 (Spring 1983): 27-38.
    Analyzed transcripts of the discussions of 22 families (mother-father-adolescent triads) who were observed as they discussed a poster concerned with birth control. The content analysis, as well as the data derived from questionnaires, revealed the diverse strategies used by both parents and adolescents to avoid really communicating about the topic.

175. Alexander, Sharon J. and Stephen R. Jorgensen. "Sex Education for Early Adolescents: A Study of Parents and Students." JOURNAL OF EARLY ADOLESCENCE 3 (1983): 315-325.
    Utilizes data from 217 parents and 278 students to address questions concerned with how both groups view sex education. Both groups agreed that parents should be the primary providers of sex education who receive backup from the schools. The parents and the children did not agree, however, on which sex related topics had in fact been discussed in their home. Offers suggestions for further research and discusses the implications of findings for parents and educators, as well as, researchers.

176. Anchell, Melvin. "Psychoanalysis vs. Sex Education." NATIONAL REVIEW 38 (June 1986): 33-61.
    Argues that typical sex education courses are designed in such a way as to produce personality problems and even perversions in later life.

177. Arcus, Margaret. "Should Family Life Education Be Required for High School Students?: An Examination of the Issues." FAMILY RELATIONS 35 (July 1986): 347-356.
    Summarizes the literature concerned with whether or not high school students in the U.S. should be required to take a course in family life education. Points out that the research which has been carried out in this area shows a great deal of support for offering such courses, but often does not really address whether they should be required. Discusses the meaning of the concept of "family life education" and what are purported to be its benefits and its drawbacks. Also discusses the training of family life educators and the legal rights of parents and children.

178. Bennett, Susan M. and Winifred B. Dickinson. "Student Parent
     Rapport and Parent Involvement in Sex, Birth Control and
     Venereal Disease Education." JOURNAL OF SEX
     RESEARCH 16 (May 1980): 114-130.
     Explores how student parent rapport and the involvement of
     parents in sex education affect students' knowledge of sex, birth
     control and venereal diseases using data collected from 199
     students aged 18 and 19. Found that these young people did see
     parents as having the primary responsibility for providing sex
     education and that student parent rapport was associated with
     discussions of sex. However, there was no relationship between
     parent involvement or rapport and the students' practical
     knowledge in the three areas covered.

179. Benson, Michael D.; Perlman, Carole and John J. Sciarra. "Sex
     Education in the Inner City: Learning and Retention."
     JOURNAL OF THE AMERICAN MEDICAL
     ASSOCIATION 255 (January 1986): 43-47.
     Presents data on 1,333 students who participated in two separate
     one hour presentations on sex education (the Discovery Program).
     Overall, the students who participated in the program scored 32
     percent higher on the posttest than on the pretest. A third test,
     given ten weeks after the presentation, demonstrated a high
     degree of retention. The use of a control group which did not
     participate in the program but which was also tested three times
     demonstrated that the gains in knowledge were not the result of
     testing alone. Sex, age and socioeconomic status were related to
     the students' preinstruction knowledge but not to the degree of
     learning.

180. Bloch, Doris. "Attitudes of Mothers Toward Sex Education."
     AMERICAN JOURNAL OF PUBLIC HEALTH 69
     (September 1979): 911-915.
     Presents data from interviews with 124 mothers of seventh grade
     daughters in two California communities which assesses their
     attitudes toward the content and timing of sex education for their
     children and their attitudes toward sex education in the schools.
     Found that the mothers fell into four distinct groups. The first
     group of mothers was those who were seen as liberal in regard
     to their attitudes about the timing and content of sex education
     and favored sex education in the schools. The second group of
     mothers held liberal attitudes about the timing and content of sex
     education but was opposed to having it taught in schools. The

third group consisted of those who were conservative in regard to content and timing but also favored having sex education taught in school. The final group included those mothers who were conservative in regard to timing and content and who were opposed to having sex education taught in the school. This four-fold typology is seen as having implications for the planning of sex education programs.

181. Bloch, Doris. "Sex Education Practices of Mothers." JOURNAL OF SEX EDUCATION AND THERAPY 7 (1982): 7-12.
Presents data on the amount of sex education 124 California mothers have given their seventh grade daughters in three areas. Eighty percent of the mothers had told their daughters about menstruation, 50 percent had talked about the father's role, and thirty-two percent had talked about some aspect of birth control.

182. Brick, Peggy. "Sex and Society: Teaching the Connection." JOURNAL OF SCHOOL HEALTH (April 1981): 226-232.
Discusses the high level of need that American adolescents have for sex education that is integrated with the rest of the curriculum. Then describes the eight week section on human sexuality that the author includes in a full year behavioral science course.

183. Committee on Adolescence, American Academy of Pediatrics. "Counseling the Adolescent About Pregnancy Options." PEDIATRICS 83 (January 1989): 135-137.

184. Darling, Carol J. and Mary W. Hicks. "Parental Influence on Adolescent Sexuality: Implications for Parents as Educators." JOURNAL OF YOUTH AND ADOLESCENCE 11 (1982): 231-245.
Points out that whether consciously or not parents communicate both verbal and nonverbal messages about sex to their children. It was found that both negative and positive messages from parents, indirectly, have a significant and positive effect on the satisfaction that males report having with their sexual lives. For the females in the sample, however, while the negative messages had no impact the positive sexual messages were inversely related to sexual satisfaction. The authors explain this as being a case where more has been promised than delivered.

185. Davis, Sally M. and Mary B. Harris. "Sexual Knowledge, Sexual Interest and Sources of Sexual Information of Rural and Urban Adolescents from Three Cultures." ADOLESCENCE 17 (Summer 1982): 471-492.
     Reports on interviews with 288 students (39% Anglo, 36% Hispanic, and 24% Native American). The results indicate that sex, age or grade, ethnicity and urban-rural residence are all related to sexual knowledge, interests and sources of sexual information. For example, females, older students, urban students and Anglos scored higher on the test of knowledge. Females also showed more interest in a number of sexual terms and reported receiving more information from parents. Older students demonstrated greater interest in the concepts of pregnancy and birth control and reported receiving more information from their friends. The implications of these differences for designing courses in sex education are discussed.

186. Dawson, Deborah Anne. "The Effects of Sex Education on Adolescent Behavior." FAMILY PLANNING PERSPECTIVES 18 (July/August 1986): 162-170.

187. Dickinson, George E. "Adolescent Sex Information Sources: 1964-1974." ADOLESCENCE 13 (Winter 1978): 653-658.
     Examines the sources of sex information for high school students in a Northeast Texas community in 1964 and 1974. The major change over the decade was an increased degree of reliance on friends for sexual information. Argues that parents, who remained the preferred source of information, need encouragement to be more open. Also argues that since friends are such an important source of information every effort should be made to make sure that the information they share is reliable.

188. Flaherty, Carol and Peggy B. Smith. "Teacher Training for Sex Education." THE JOURNAL OF SCHOOL HEALTH (April 1981): 261-264.
     Describes a sex education teacher training program operated by the Baylor College of Medicine in Houston, Texas. Based upon the experience with this three year project, recommendations are given to help design and implement other sex education teacher training programs.

189. Fox, Greer L. and Judith K. Inazu. "Mother-Daughter Communication About Sex." FAMILY RELATIONS 29 (July 1980): 347-352.

Uses data from interviews with 449 Detroit mothers and their 14-16 year old daughters in order to examine what factors differentiate mothers who actively seek to provide their daughters with sexual socialization from those who do not. Also addresses what sexual topics are discussed by the involved mothers and compares their description of these discussions to those of their daughters. Almost all of the mothers and daughters report discussing menstruation, dating and boyfriends, sexual morality, how babies are made, sexual intercourse and birth control. The mothers' and daughters' tended to agree about the age of the daughter at the time these discussions took place. Also compares mothers and daughters in terms of which areas they initiate discussion in, which areas they feel most comfortable discussing and which area they would like to discuss further.

190. Fox, Greer L. "The Mother-Adolescent Daughter Relationship as A Sexual Socialization Structure: A Research Review." FAMILY RELATIONS 29 (January 1980): 21-28.
    Reviews the research literature concerned with how the mother-daughter relationship serves as a transmission structure for sexual socialization. Points out that the existing literature clearly reveals that there is little direct communication about sexual matters between mothers and their adolescent daughters. Where communication does exist, however, it appears to influence both the timing of the sexual debut and the use of contraception. Attempts to explain the low level of communication. Argues that mothers and daughters underutilize their relationship as a vehicle of socialization about sexual matters and that agencies seem to often overlook this important resource.

191. Fox, Greer L. "The Family's Influence on Adolescent Sexual Behavior." CHILDREN TODAY (May/June 1979): 21-36.
    Reviews what is known about the family's influence on adolescent sexual behavior. Overall, the studies reviewed indicate that there is little open communication about sex in the home. The small amount of sex education which does occur in the home is due largely to the efforts of mothers. Even minimal communication from the mother may serve to postpone the child's sexual involvement and/or promote more effective contraception. The mother-daughter bond is seen as critically important and the father-mother relationship is also seen as important. Points out that while more research needs to be carried out, programs concerned with all phases of adolescent

sexuality need to take the family into account and support rather than undermine its efforts.

192. Gordon, Sol. "The Case for a Moral Sex Education in the Schools." JOURNAL OF SCHOOL HEALTH (April 1981): 214-218.
Argues that sex education in U.S. schools should be moral rather than moralistic. Such programs could contribute to sexual health and could be important in preventing sexual problems later in life.

193. Hacker, Sylvia S. "It Isn't Sex Education Unless ..." JOURNAL OF SCHOOL HEALTH (April 1981): 207-218.
Presents an overview of what a sex education curriculum could and should be. That is it should go beyond a technical description of sexual "plumbing" and deal with the students' self-concept, the non-exploitation of others, the clarification of values, problem solving and decision making.

194. Herz, Elicia and Janet S. Reis. "Family Life Education for Young Inner City Teens: Identifying Needs." JOURNAL OF YOUTH AND ADOLESCENCE 16 (1987): 361-377.
Uses data collected from 251 black seventh and eighth graders, residing in economically disadvantaged sections of the Chicago, to assess their knowledge about sexuality, attitudes about premarital sexual behavior, and their perceived personal responsibility in regard to sexuality. Found that females and eighth graders scored higher on the test of knowledge. The young adolescents were aware of the existence of various contraceptive methods but did not have much practical knowledge about their effectiveness or how they could be obtained. Overall the students were not well informed about the risk of pregnancy. Both males and females saw the primary responsibility for contraception as belonging to females but the responsibility for an unplanned pregnancy as shared. Discusses the implications of these findings for designing family life education programs for this population of young adolescents.

195. Herz, Elicia; Goldberg, Wendy A. and Janet S. Reis. "Family Life Education for Young Adolescents: A Quasi-Experiment." JOURNAL OF YOUTH AND ADOLESCENCE 13 (1984): 309-327.

Uses data on 28 students who participated in a family life education intervention and 28 controls to test the effectiveness of the intervention. The students were all black, seventh and eighth graders living in one of Chicago's poorest neighborhoods. Compared to students in the control group, program participants showed: (1) an improved knowledge of reproductive physiology, contraception, and adolescent pregnancy outcomes; (2) an increase in awareness of specific methods of contraception; (3) a shift in attitudes about personal premarital sexuality, with seventh graders becoming more conservative and eighth graders more liberal; (4) a greater tendency toward recognizing shared responsibility for contraception. Sees the program as successful and suggests alterations which could increase its effectiveness as well as that of other family life education programs.

196. Imber, Michael. "Toward a Theory of Educational Origins: The Genesis of Sex Education." EDUCATIONAL THEORY 34 (SUMMER 1984): 275-286.
    Argues that the demand for new educational programs often results from new discoveries in such fields as science, medicine and psychology and from important changes in social conditions. Darwin's theory of evolution, breakthroughs in the fight against yellow fever and malaria, along with new ideas about the treatment of gonorrhea and syphilis all served to create an atmosphere in this country that was open to the development of sex education. The stock market crash and the Depression which followed it served, however, to slow down the push for sex education in the United States.

197. Kenney, Asta M. and Margaret Terry Orr. "Sex Education: An Overview of Current Programs, Policies and Research." PHI DELTA KAPPAN 65 (March 1984): 491-496.
    Reviews studies of sex education programs with an emphasis on those which appear to have the potential to reduce unwanted pregnancies. Points out that a national study has found that sex education does not appear to lead to increased sexual activity among adolescents but does appear to increase the likelihood that the sexually active will use contraception and thereby reduce their rate of pregnancy. Argues that while there is broad based support for sex education it remains a controversial issue. Programs need to reflect the standards of the community as well as its needs. Medical services need to be provided along with information.

198. Kirby, Douglas. "Sexuality Education: A More Realistic View of Its Effects." JOURNAL OF SCHOOL HEALTH 55 (December 1985): 421-424.
     Compares the effects of sexuality education programs to those of other education programs and discusses why sex education classes can increase knowledge without significantly affecting values, attitudes or behavior.

199. Leo, John. "Sex and Schools." TIME 128 (November 24, 1986): 54-63.
     Points out that there is a continuing debate in this country among factions regarding sex education. The questions involved include, what is sex education and how should it be taught. According to public opinion polls a majority of Americans, more than 80 percent, favor sex education but the opposition is highly vocal. Three issues appear to be very important: (1) homosexuality (normal or deviant); (2) abortion (moral or immoral); and (3) contraceptive information (pro-chastity or pro-pregnancy prevention). AIDS appears to have carried the day for those who favor sex education and it will appear in some form in most school districts.

200. Marsiglio, William and Frank L. Mott. "The Impact of Sex Education on Sexual Activity, Contraceptive Use and Premarital Pregnancy Among American Teenagers." FAMILY PLANNING PERSPECTIVES 18 (July/August 1986): 151-162.

201. Maslach, Germaine and Graham B. Kerr. "Tailoring Sex-Education Programs to Adolescents-A Strategy for the Primary Prevention of Unwanted Adolescent Pregnancies." ADOLESCENCE 18 (Summer 1983): 449-456.
     Reports on interviews with 88 adolescents, mostly white females, in which they were asked to make comments on and/or suggestions for sex education programs. The interviews were tape recorded and their content analyzed. Three facets of sex education classes were identified as being in need of revision, the curriculum, the format, and the lecturer. These students expressed a desire for small single gender classes taught by outside lecturers who want to teach the subject and do so comfortably. They want courses that go beyond instruction in biological plumbing and deal with related and sensitive topics.

The findings are interpreted to mean that students need and want, but do not have, sensitive sex education courses.

202. Orr, Margaret Terry. "Sex Education and Contraception Education in U.S. High Schools." FAMILY PLANNING PERSPECTIVES 13 (November/December 1982): 304-313.

Uses data from a survey of high school principals which shows that 36 percent of U.S. public high schools offer a sex education course, compared to 38 percent of Catholic high schools and 24 percent of other nonpublic schools. Sex education is offered more often than many other "nontraditional" courses and is offered more frequently than some academic subjects, such as Latin. Two characteristics of the schools, the number of types of nontraditional courses offered and the number of courses of different lengths, have independent effects on whether sex education classes are offered. However, these characteristics account for only six percent of the difference between schools that offer sex education and those that do not. It appears that there are no important differences between the schools that offer sex education courses and those that do not. Information from a follow up survey of sex educators from schools that offer sex education courses show that 78 percent of such courses include information about contraception and abortion. The topic most commonly covered, 97 percent of the courses, is venereal disease, closely followed by pregnancy and childbirth. At least 90 percent of the courses cover such subjects as changes at puberty; anatomy and physiology; drugs, alcohol and sex; dating; and teenage pregnancy. The topic least often discussed, and the only topic that a majority of sex education teachers said should not be covered is sexual techniques.

203. Penland, Lynn R. "Sex Education in 1900, 1940 and 1980: An Historical Sketch." JOURNAL OF SCHOOL HEALTH (April 1981): 305-309.

Describes in broad strokes what sex education was like in the United States in 1900 and 1940 and compares it to the 1980s. Argues that the evolution of sex education from the end of the 19th century to the present leads to the prediction that sex education will continue to exist in the future. It will, however, be constantly redesigned until its form is congruent with the current philosophies of student needs and the best way to meet those needs.

204. Poertner, John, and Jill Marks. "Role of the School Social Worker in Sex Education." SOCIAL WORK IN EDUCATION 11 (Fall 1988): 21-35.

Points out that the high level of current interest in sex education grows out of a dual concern with adolescent pregnancy and AIDS. Argues that school social workers can play a key role in the development of meaningful sex education programs. Provides information from a survey that school social workers can use in their advocacy efforts.

205. Polit, Denise F.; White, Cozette Morrow and Thomas D. Morton. "Sex Education and Family Planning Services for Adolescents in Foster Care." FAMILY PLANNING PERSPECTIVES 19 (January/February 1987): 18-23.

Reports the results of a survey of public child welfare agency representatives in 48 states designed to ascertain their policies in regard to sex education and family planning services for adolescents in foster care. Thirty nine of the states have no formal written policies on the issue. Southern states are most likely to be among the nine which have such policies and the western states least likely. Some states offer special training in adolescent sexuality to foster parents (29) and case workers (19). But such training is required for foster parents in only five states and for social workers in only four. In some states, the officials explain the absence of formal policy on the basis that a low key approach is the most effective way to deal with the problem while others admit that they simply have not given it much thought.

206. Reichelt, Paul A., and Harriet H. Werley. "Contraception, Abortion and Venereal Disease: Teenagers' Knowledge and the Effect of Education." FAMILY PLANNING PERSPECTIVES 7 (March /April 1975): 83-88.

Uses data on 1,190 adolescents attending the "rap session" at a Planned Parenthood clinic to describe their level of knowledge both before and after the session. The level of knowledge was much higher after the intervention.

207. Reichelt, Paul A., and Harriet H. Werley. "A Sex Information Program for Sexually Active Teenagers." JOURNAL OF SCHOOL HEALTH 45 (February 1975): 100-107.

Measures the effects of a sex education intervention by comparing the extent of sex knowledge in a sample of 367 adolescent females before and after they had attended a "rap session." The results indicated that the intervention was needed and valuable.

208. Rothenberg, Perila B. "Communication about Sex and Birth Control between Mothers and Their Adolescent Children." POPULATION AND ENVIRONMENT 3 (Spring 1980): 35-50.
Examines issues surrounding mother-child communications about sex and contraception using data from interviews with a stratified random sample consisting of 163 Cincinnati mothers and two of their children between 10 and 18. The findings indicate that only one-third of these mothers had provided their children with reading material about sex, while 45 percent had explained intercourse and a little more than half had discussed contraception with them. The mother's eduction, race and income were not related to whether she explained intercourse. There was also no relationship between these variables and whether she discussed birth control. The mother's attitudes, her sexual and contraceptive behavior were related to the likelihood that she would discuss these areas with her children. The reports of mothers and children are compared and the children's contraceptive knowledge examined.

209. Scales, Peter, and Douglas Kirby. "A Review of Exemplary Sex Education Programs for Teenagers by Nonschool Organizations." FAMILY RELATIONS 30 (April 1981): 238-245.
Reviews sex education in twenty-seven exemplary programs across the country; Planned Parenthood programs, church sponsored activities, and state and local government department efforts. Programs are rated on several features describing structure, activities, and content, and on methods of evaluation. Similarities and differences among nonschool sex education programs are described and differences between nonschool and school sex education programs are presented. Several of the programs are described in detail. In general it is concluded that nonschool programs provide more detailed coverage of such topics as contraception, values and decision making; are more extensively "linked" with other community groups; have less organized opposition; make greater use of mass media approaches, counseling, and experimental activities; and make more frequent use of teenagers themselves as program planners and leaders. Finally it is suggested that procedures for evaluating program impact need substantial development and improvement.

210. Silverman-Watkins, L. Theresa. "Adolescents'
      Comprehension of Televised Sexual Innuendos."
      JOURNAL OF APPLIED DEVELOPMENTAL
      PSYCHOLOGY 4 (October/December 1983): 359-369.
      Describes a study in which 108 adolescents, 18 males and 18
      females at each of three ages (12, 14, and 16) were shown 24
      television excerpts which presented either a sexual joke or a
      nonsexual filler and were asked to interpret it. The age of the
      adolescent and the content of the excerpt were both related to the
      adolescent's comprehension. The adolescents were able to most
      adequately explain innuendos referring to discouraged sexual
      practices and were least able to explain those referring to
      intercourse.

211. Stout, James W., and Frederick P. Rivara. "Schools and Sex
      Education: Does It Work?" PEDIATRICS 83 (March 1989):
      375-379.

212. Strouse, Jeremiah, and Richard A. Fabes. "Formal Versus
      Informal Sources of Sex Education: Competing Forces in the
      Sexual Social of Adolescents." ADOLESCENCE 20
      (Summer 1985):251-263.
      Points out that much of the research evaluating formal sex
      education programs suggests that these programs have not been
      successful in getting adolescents to behave in a sexually
      responsible way. Examines several logical explanations for the
      failure of these programs to achieve their goal. Reviews the
      literature which highlights the importance of informal sources of
      education about sexually related issues and discusses the
      implications of this importance for parents and educators.

213. Sonenstein, Freya, and Karen Pittman. "The Availability of Sex
      Education in Large City School Districts." FAMILY
      PLANNING PERSPECTIVES 16 (January/February 1984):
      19-25.
      Reports the results of a survey to determine the extent of sex
      education in U.S. school districts in cities with populations of
      100,000 or more. Found that some form of sex education is
      offered in 80 percent of such districts. Describes differences in
      availability, program goal and content and grade and participation
      level.

214. Walters, James; McKenry, Patrick C. and Lynda H. Walters.
     "Adolescent's Knowledge of Childbearing." THE FAMILY
     COORDINATOR 28 (April 1979): 163-171.
     Reports on a study in which 1200 high school students were
     asked 30 questions about the consequences of adolescent
     childbearing. The answers given by pregnant adolescents were
     compared to those given by nonpregnant adolescents. Concludes
     that most adolescents have inadequate knowledge of the
     consequence of teenage childbearing, that it may be counter
     productive to try and identify a high risk group. Instead all
     adolescents should be the beneficiaries of service and educational
     efforts.

215. Zelnik, Melvin, and Young J. Kim. "Sex Education and Its
     Association with Teenage Sexual Activity, Pregnancy and
     Contraceptive Use." FAMILY PLANNING
     PERSPECTIVES 14 (May/June): 117-139.
     Uses data from surveys of national representative samples of 15-
     19 year old women carried out in 1976 and 1979 (the latter survey
     also gathered data on young men) to examine the association
     between sex education and the sexual, contraceptive and
     pregnancy experience of adolescents in the United States. Finds
     that approximately three fourths of this age group living in
     metropolitan areas of the United States have taken courses
     concerned with sex education in schools. In nearly three fourths
     of the cases the respondents reported that the courses included
     information on contraception, including where they can be
     obtained or their possible side effects. Those who had taken a
     sex education class were no more likely to be sexually active than
     those who had not. The data also indicate that those who have
     taken a sex education class are more likely to use birth control at
     first intercourse and are less likely to get pregnant.

B. Chapters in Books

216. Fox, Greer Litton. "The Family Context of Adolescent Sexuality and Sex Roles." ADOLESCENTS IN FAMILIES. Edited by Geoffrey K. Leigh and Gary W. Peterson. Cincinnati: South-Western Publishing.

217. Fox, Greer Litton. "The Family's Role in Adolescent Sexual Behavior." TEENAGE PREGNANCY IN A FAMILY CONTEXT. Edited by Theodora Ooms. Philadelphia: Temple University Press, 1981, pp. 73-130.
Discusses what is known about the family's direct and indirect sexual socialization of adolescents and recommends that policies need to include provisions of family involvement.

218. Inman, Marilee. "What Teen-Agers Want in Sex Education." NURSING OF CHILDREN AND ADOLESCENTS. Compiled by Andrea B. O'Connor. New York: The American Journal of Nursing Co., 1975, pp. 217-219.

219. Kolenda, Konstantin. "Ethical Issues of Adolescent Pregnancy." ADOLESCENT PREGNANCY: PERSPECTIVES FOR THE HEALTH CARE PROFESSIONAL. Edited by Peggy B. Smith and David M. Mumford. Boston: G.K. Hall, 1980, pp. 198-214.
Argues that there is a need to really broaden the definition of sex education so that it deals with the important role of sexuality in human life rather than simply the facts of reproduction.

220. Scales, Peter. "Adolescent Sexuality and Education: Principles, Approaches, and Resources." ADOLESCENT SEXUALITY IN A CHANGING AMERICAN SOCIETY. by Catherine S. Chilman. New York: John Wiley and Sons, 1983, pp. 207-229.

221. Scales, Peter. "Sex Education and the Prevention of Teenage Pregnancy: An Overview of Policies and Programs in the United States." TEENAGE PREGNANCY IN A FAMILY CONTEXT. Edited by Theodora Ooms. Philadelphia: Temple University Press, 1981, pp. 213-253.
Describes the variety of sex and family life education being offered in the U.S. in terms of goals, definitions, values, and

program evaluations as well as in terms of content, extent, and sponsorship.

222. Schiller, Patricia. "Sexual Counseling for Adolescents." ADOLESCENT PREGNANCY: PERSPECTIVES FOR THE HEALTH CARE PROFESSIONAL. Edited by Peggy B. Smith and David M. Mumford. Boston: G.K. Hall, 1980, pp. 240-249.
Argues that sex counseling should deal with the broad area of human sexuality rather than simply focus on its reproductive function.

223. Smith, Peggy B. "Sex Education." ADOLESCENT PREGNANCY: PERSPECTIVES FOR THE HEALTH CARE PROFESSIONAL. Edited by Peggy B. Smith and David M. Mumford. Boston: G.K. Hall, 1980, pp. 215-239.
Deals with the history of sex education, its diverse sources and implementations as well as the conflicts surrounding these.

224. Smith, Peggy B. "Parenting Education." ADOLESCENT PREGNANCY: PERSPECTIVES FOR THE HEALTH CARE PROFESSIONAL. Edited by Peggy B. Smith and David M. Mumford. Boston: G.K. Hall, 1980, pp. 155-172.
Discusses the overall idea that parenting is a learned rather than an instinctive behavior. Also discusses the problems which have made it difficult to establish universal parenting education in this society including the fact that parenting education is often confused with sex education.

C. Books

225. Kelly, Gary F. SEX COUNSELING FOR ADOLESCENTS AND YOUTH. Washington, D.C.: American Association of Sex Educators, Counselors and Therapists, 1977.
Defines sex counseling and discusses sex counseling with young people, the sexual concerns of adolescents and youth, sex counseling in schools and colleges, and the evaluation of sex counseling services.

VI. RISK FACTORS

A. Articles

226. Abernathy, Virginia. "Illegitimate Conception Among Teenagers." AMERICAN JOURNAL OF PUBLIC HEALTH 64 (July 1974): 662-665.
    Suggests that it is possible to identify adolescents at high risk of unwanted pregnancy without knowledge of their sexual or contraceptive behavior. Argues that there are identifiable psychological factors which underlie a predisposition to risk pregnancy. The primary dimensions of the high risk profile presented are family history and attitudes toward self and others. The three aspects of family history considered to be important include: (1) not liking the mother and/or finding that she is not an adequate role model; (2) liking the father better than the mother; (3) hostility in the parents' marriage. The two self and other attitudes seen as important are low self esteem and anxiety over the nature of the relationship with the father.

227. Abrahamse, Allan F.; Morrison, Peter A.; and Linda J. Waite. "Teenagers Willing to Consider Single Parenthood: Who Is at Greatest Risk?" FAMILY PLANNING PERSPECTIVES 20 (January/February 1988): 13-19.
    Analyzes data from a subsample of the High School and Beyond panel study (the 13,061 young women in the 1980 sophomore cohort who responded in 1981 and 1982) in order to determine if the respondents who communicated a willingness to consider nonmarital childbearing were actually more likely to become adolescent mothers. In fact, over the two year period willing respondents generally had much higher rates of childbearing at each level of risk. Those who totally refused to consider unmarried parenthood appeared better able to evade it. It is argued that the willingness to consider unmarried parenthood can be traced to patterns of nonconforming behavior, to the educational opportunity costs of unmarried motherhood, and at least for the whites and the Hispanics in the sample self reported depression.

228. Babikian, Hrair M., and Adila Goldman. "Study of Teenage Pregnancy." AMERICAN JOURNAL OF PSYCHIATRY 128 (December 1971): 760-765.

Reports on a study of 30 psychiatric patients under the age of 17 who were approximately 20 weeks pregnant in order to understand their social contexts, family relationships and the motivations behind their pregnancies. Most conspicuous in the life histories of these girls were chaotic family lives during their formative years which had contributed to poor structuralization of the ego. The study also indicated a severe lack of superego derivatives. It should also be noted that while eight of the girls were diagnosed as having transient problems associated with the adjustment to their pregnancy, the remainder were given more severe diagnoses, including nine diagnoses of psychosis.

229. Brundtland, G. H., and L. Walloe. "Menarcheal Age In Norway: Halt in the Trend Towards Earlier Maturation." NATURE 241 (February 1973): 478-479.

Utilized data on physical measurements and age at menarche from 7,155 girls in Oslo Norway to determine whether the trend toward earlier age at onset of menses continues. The data indicate that while the mean menarcheal age decreased from 1928 to 1952, it did not change at all between 1952 and 1970. These data are interpreted to be the first indication from any country that there is a halt in the trend toward earlier age at menarche.

230. Bullough, Vern L. "Age at Menarche: A Misunderstanding." SCIENCE 213 (July 1981): 365-366.

Argues that through a misinterpretation of historical data, the average age of menarche in the 19th century is believed by many to have been 17 years. What appears to in fact be the case is that the age of 17 is derived from one isolated report on a small sample. This mistake has resulted in erroneous beliefs about change in female sexual maturation in the United States. Change has occurred, but it has been much smaller than that suggested by the misinterpretation.

231. Coddington, R. Dean. "Life Events Associated with Adolescent Pregnancies." JOURNAL OF CLINICAL PSYCHIATRY 40 (April 1979): 180-185.

Studies 121 women who were adolescent mothers and 261 nonpregnant controls to explore the social and cultural factors leading to adolescent pregnancy. The study and control groups were very different in terms of race and class. The difference between the two groups which was seen as most important is the greater loss of family members experienced by the study group.

232. Cohen, Stuart Joseph. "Intentional Teenage Pregnancies."
     JOURNAL OF SCHOOL HEALTH (March 1983): 210-211.
     Briefly reviews the literature and argues that many adolescent
     pregnancies are intentional because adolescents have access to
     contraceptives yet continue to engage in unprotected intercourse.
     Then offers eight suggestions for how the problem can be
     addressed.

233. Cutright, Phillips. "The Teenage Sexual Revolution and the
     Myth of an Abstinent Past." FAMILY PLANNING
     PERSPECTIVE 4 (January 1972): 24-31.
     Points out that we do not in fact know a very great deal about
     adolescent sexuality in the past but still take the position that
     abstinence among adolescents was much more widespread than
     it is today. Argues that in the past, relatively poor health
     conditions may have restrained the consequences of nonmarital
     adolescent sexuality and that when considering the current levels
     of adolescent fertility two factors need to be considered. First,
     improved health conditions probably have increased the chances
     that an out of wedlock conception will be carried to term (hence,
     become visible, and a problem). Secondly, these improved health
     conditions have probably also increased the capacity of sexually
     active young girls to conceive.

234. Damon, Albert. "Larger Body Size and Earlier Menarche: The
     End May Be in Sight." SOCIAL BIOLOGY 21 (1974): 8-11.
     Addresses the question of whether larger body size and age of
     menarche has stabilized for the wealthy classes in the United
     States. Data were collected on the body size and age at
     menarche for 500 mothers and 522 daughters. These women who
     attended Mt. Holyoke and Wellesley between 1930 and 1970 were
     white and of Northern and Western European descent. This
     comparison of trends for successive generations within families
     attending private colleges is an approach which reduces genetic
     and environmental variance. The sample has basically
     experienced a uniform, optimal environment in regard to nutrition
     and health. The study found that while the rate of increase in
     height had slowed there was an increase in weight and the age of
     menarche has stabilized at an age of 13.1. Daughters were very
     slightly taller and leaner but the age at menarche was identical.
     For the well to do then menarche has stabilized.

235. Elster, Arthur B.; Panzarine, Susan; and Elizabeth R.
     McAnarney. "Causes of Adolescent Pregnancy." MEDICAL
     ASPECTS OF HUMAN SEXUALITY 14 (July 1980): 83-87.
     Describes the causes of both unintentional and intentional
     adolescent pregnancies. Presents the causes of unintentional teen
     pregnancies as psychosocial and cognitive immaturity, lack of
     knowledge regarding reproduction, and contraceptive failure.
     Intentional pregnancies are seen as resulting from depression,
     rebellious acting out behavior, fear of abandonment and reduced
     sanctions against premarital pregnancies. Argues that the
     availability of family planning services may eliminate some, but
     certainly not all adolescent pregnancies.

236. Evans, Therman E. "Societal Hypocrisy Helps to Promote
     Teenage Pregnancy." JOURNAL OF THE NATIONAL
     MEDICAL ASSOCIATION (May 1986): 361-364.
     States that the broadcast media (television and radio) which
     teens watch (30 hours of television per week) and listen to (20
     hours of radio) are rife with sexual comment, innuendo and
     behavior. Yet the media do not broadcast birth control
     information. Claims that broadcast media rank either just ahead
     or just behind parents and peers as the greatest force in
     influencing the values and behaviors of teenagers.

237. Frisch, Rose E. "Body Fat, Puberty and Fertility."
     BIOLOGICAL REVIEW 59 (1984): 161-188.
     Discusses the relationship between nutrition and fertility.
     Argues that not only is there a minimum weight required but also
     a certain proportion of body fat.

238. Goldfarb, Joyce L.; Mumford, David M.; Schum, David A.;
     Smith, Peggy B.; Flowers, Charles and Carolyn Schum. "An
     Attempt to Detect 'Pregnancy Susceptibility' in Indigent
     Adolescent Girls." JOURNAL OF YOUTH AND
     ADOLESCENCE 6 (1977): 127-144.
     Uses concepts from Bayesian inference theory and signal
     detection theory to arrive at an indirect index of pregnancy
     susceptibility which can be expressed in probabilistic terms.

239. Hanson, Sandra L.; Myers, David E. and Alan L. Ginsburg.
     "The Role of Responsibility and Knowledge in Reducing
     Teenage Out-of-Wedlock Childbearing." JOURNAL OF
     MARRIAGE AND THE FAMILY 49 (May 1987): 241-253.

Examines the impact of knowledge and attitudes on adolescent childbearing in the United States using data on more than 10,000 never married female adolescents taken from the nationally representative High School and Beyond Survey. Finds that the chances of an unmarried adolescent birth are not reduced by sex education and birth control knowledge. On the other hand, the attitudes of adolescents and their parents are seen as having an influence in that those adolescents who have high educational aspirations and parents who supervise their activities are less likely to give birth as adolescents. Behavior in school and going steady are also factors which influence the likelihood of pregnancy. For whites, locus of control and the educational aspirations that parents have for their daughter also exert an important influence. For blacks an important variable is the young woman's willingness to even consider an unwed pregnancy.

240. Hart, Beth, and Irma Hilton. "Dimensions of Personality Organization as Predictors of Teenage Pregnancy Risk." JOURNAL OF PERSONALITY ASSESSMENT 52 (1988): 116-132.

Describes the results of a study which involved administering projective tests to and interviewing 161 college students between 17 and 19. The subjects were divided into four groups. Group one consisted of 60 women who had never engaged in intercourse. Group two consisted of 35 sexually active women who always used a reliable method of birth control. Group three consisted of 34 sexually active women who never used birth control or did not use it reliably. Group four consisted of 32 young women who were pregnant and planning to carry to term. The tests of personality development given (Loevinger's Washington University Sentence Completion Test, The Friedman Developmental Level Scoring System for the Rorschach, The Urist Mutuality of Autonomy Scale and the Thematic Apperception Test) successfully discriminated between those at high and low risk for pregnancy.

241. Hogan, Dennis P., and Evelyn M. Kitagawa. "The Impact of Social Status, Family Structure, and Neighborhood on the Fertility of Black Adolescents." AMERICAN JOURNAL OF SOCIOLOGY 90 (January 1985): 825-855.

Uses data collected through interviews with 1,078 randomly selected black female adolescents residing in Chicago to test hypotheses concerning black adolescent fertility which have been generated by ethnographic research and by demographic research. These data confirm the demographic view that a relatively large proportion of black adolescents from all types of family and economic backgrounds become pregnant before 20. As suggested by the ethnographic research, however, family factors, socioeconomic status, neighborhood characteristics and career aspirations also have a considerable effect on the rate of pregnancy. By age 19 a larger proportion of girls with unfavorable characteristics in these areas have become pregnant.

242. Horn, Mary Elaine, and Linda B. Rudolph. "An Investigation of Verbal Interaction, Knowledge of Sexual Behavior and Self Concept in Adolescent Mothers." ADOLESCENCE 22 (Fall 1987): 591-507.

Utilizes data on 23 unmarried first time adolescent mothers to investigate the pattern of communication between adolescent females and their parents and to determine if the self-concept of adolescent mothers differs significantly from that of the general population. The adolescents indicated that their relationship with their mothers was "good." These adolescents present their mothers as understanding of their problems, as giving them freedom, not invading their privacy, and as being someone they enjoy talking things over with. They did not indicate having close relationships with their fathers. The mothers in this sample scored lower than the norm group on the Tennessee Self-Concept Scale. In the interviews, however, they reported having positive feelings about themselves.

243. Ireson, Carol J. "Adolescent Pregnancy and Sex Roles." SEX ROLES 11 (1984): 189-201.

Analyzes data on 161 adolescents (13-18) who sought services at health related agencies to examine the relationship between sex roles and adolescent pregnancy. When the adolescents who were already pregnant were compared to those seeking contraceptive services, it was found that the pregnant teens saw themselves as competent in more highly sex typed activities and as having less control over their lives. The pregnant teens also had lower grades in school and lower educational aspirations. The most significant difference between the two groups was socioeconomic status, with the pregnant teens having lower SES. The two groups did not differ in regard to sex role values, and it was the pregnant teens who were the least likely to aspire to the traditionally female occupational specialties.

244. Jorgensen, Stephen R.; King, Susan L.; and Barbara A. Torrey.
"Dyadic and Social Network Influences on Adolescent
Exposure to Pregnancy Risk." JOURNAL OF MARRIAGE
AND THE FAMILY 42 (February 1980): 141-155.
Uses data on 127 females aged 12-18 years old attending county
health and family planning clinics in both urban and rural Arizona
to test hypotheses concerned with the association between dyadic
relationship, and family and peer context on the risk of exposure
to pregnancy. The multivariate analysis yielded three major
findings: (1) qualities of the interpersonal relationship of the
adolescent dyad, such as power and satisfaction, have a stronger
and more consistent bearing on exposure to risk of pregnancy
than either peer or family relationships; (2) certain variables
which are often thought to have a simple one way relationship to
exposure to pregnancy risk actually have counter balancing
influences; and (3) dyadic relationship, family, and peer variables
actually explain only a small portion of the variance in exposure
to pregnancy risk.

245. Jurs, Jan. "Correlation of Moral Development with Use of
Birth Control and Pregnancy Among Teenage Girls."
PSYCHOLOGICAL REPORTS 55 (1984): 1009-1010.
Compares the moral development of pregnant and never
pregnant adolescent females, responsible and nonresponsible birth
control users and those who elect to abort and those who choose
to carry to term (N = 75). Found no significant differences
between these groups in moral development. Higher moral
development scores were associated with having taken a sex
education course.

246. Kane, Francis J.; Moan, Charles A.; and Barbara Bolling.
"Motivational Factors in Pregnant Adolescents." DISEASES
OF THE NERVOUS SYSTEM 35 (March 1974): 131-134.
Uses data on 52 pregnant adolescents who were living in
maternity homes in New Orleans. Found that information about
birth control was widespread and accurate. Argues that
motivational factors and reactions to psychological loss played a
more important role in these pregnancies. Also argues that the
MMPI can separate out pregnant adolescents who are "normal"
from those who are "abnormal."

247. Keeve, J. Phillip. "Selected Social Educational and Medical
     Characteristics of Primiparous 12-16 Year Old Girls."
     PEDIATRICS 36 (September 1965): 394-401.
     Estimates the adolescent fertility rate of the school age
     population of a moderate sized New York community through the
     use of hospital records. The rate between 1959-63 remained
     stable at about 10 percent. The study was not able to produce a
     predictive profile but did find that the pregnant adolescent tended
     not to participate in organized extracurricular activities. Such
     programs then do not provide an appropriate vehicle for
     preventive strategies.

248. Koenig, M.A., and Melvin Zelnik. "The Risk of First Pregnancy
     Among Metropolitan Area Teenagers: 1976 and 1979."
     FAMILY PLANNING PERSPECTIVES 14
     (September/October 1982): 239-247.
     Employs data from two national studies to compare the risk of
     first premarital pregnancy between 1976 and 1979. The risk of
     pregnancy increased from 32 to 36 percent between the two study
     dates. The increased risk was relatively greater for whites than
     for blacks. The most pronounced increase was among whites who
     begin intercourse before age 15. This increase is attributed to
     decreased reliance on the most effective methods of contraception
     at the time of first intercourse and a distinct increase in the
     frequency of sexual activity.

249. Larsen, John J., and Anne McCreary Juhasz. "The Effects of
     Knowledge of Child Development and Social-Emotional
     Maturity on Adolescent Attitudes Toward Parenting."
     ADOLESCENCE 20 (Winter 1985): 823-839.
     Employs data on 430 high school, junior college and university
     students to investigate the relationship between the combined
     effect of knowledge about child development and socio-emotional
     maturity and the degree to which this relationship affects attitudes
     toward parenting. Together knowledge of child development and
     socio-emotional maturity account for 51 percent of the variation
     among the variables. In general, the data indicated that negative
     attitudes toward parenting were related to lack of knowledge
     about child development and low levels of socio-emotional
     maturity.

250. Miller, Warren B. "Psychological Vulnerability to Unwanted Pregnancy." FAMILY PLANNING PERSPECTIVES 5 (Fall 1973): 199-201.
     Sets out to address the question of why do women have unwanted pregnancies? Why do such unwanted pregnancies seem to occur at certain specific times during the life cycle of females. Based on observations over a four year period at Stanford University Medical Center, it is concluded that there are stages in a woman's reproductive career when she is especially vulnerable psychologically to unwanted pregnancy. The author identifies eight stages of the life cycle when such vulnerability tends to occur.

251. Moore, Kristin A., and Steven B. Caldwell. "The Effect of Government Policies on Out-of-Wedlock Sex and Pregnancy." FAMILY PLANNING PERSPECTIVES 9 (July/August 1977): 164-225.
     Uses data from a national probability survey conducted in 1971 (Zelnik and Kantner 1971) to determine: (1) if those states with generous and easily available Aid to Families With Dependent Children (AFDC) benefits encourage childbearing among unmarried women; (2) if the absence of AFDC benefits where there is a father in the house discourages marriage; (3) does the availability of abortion services reduce the likelihood of premarital births; (4) does the availability of abortion encourage contraceptive irresponsibility; (5) does the availability of family planning services decrease the probability of conception or does it lead to increased sexual activity without reducing the rate of conception. The findings indicate that neither the level of AFDC benefits nor the AFDC acceptance rates serve as incentives for unmarried child bearing among either blacks or whites. The availability of contraceptive and abortion services do not encourage the initiation of sexual activity. The availability of subsidized family planning services does lower pregnancy rates especially among black teens, while the availability of abortion reduces the rate of premarital births, especially for whites.

252. Norbert, Ralph; Lochman, John; and Truman Thomas. "Psychosocial Characteristics of Pregnant and Nulliparous Adolescents." ADOLESCENCE 19 (Summer 1984): 283-294.
     Utilizes data on a sample of low income black adolescents in order to ascertain if there are characteristics which distinguish the pregnant from the nulliparous and if the pregnant adolescents

have lower levels of personal and family adjustment. Found that the pregnant group was characterized by mothers with lower levels of education, later sex education, more brothers and better family adjustment. The pregnant group was also characterized by less vocational - educational adjustment. The pregnant group was not found to be characterized by significant psychological or family disturbances.

253. Olson, Colleen F., and John Worobey. "Perceived Mother-Daughter Relations in a Pregnant and Nonpregnant Adolescent Sample." ADOLESCENCE 19 (Winter 1984): 781-794.
    Investigates the differences in the mother-daughter relationship of 20 pregnant and 40 non-pregnant adolescents. The pregnant adolescents perceived significantly lower levels of love, attention and interdependence.

254. Presser, Harriet B. "Guessing and Misinformation About Pregnancy Risks Among Urban Mothers." FAMILY PLANNING PERSPECTIVES 9 (May/June 1977): 234-236.
    Uses data from interviews with 358 randomly selected women who had recently experienced their first birth to assess knowledge about when in the menstrual cycle a woman is most likely to get pregnant. The women were asked the pertinent question twice a year apart. In the first interview 45 percent answered correctly, while at time two 48 percent did. Only one third answered correctly both times.

255. Presser, Harriet B. "Age at Menarche, Socio-Sexual Behavior and Fertility." SOCIAL BIOLOGY 2 (1978): 94-101.
    Uses data from a sample of 408 black and white New York mothers aged 15-29 who had recently given birth to their first child to examine the nature of the relationship between age at menarche and age at first birth. In this sample, a slightly younger age at menarche was reported for whites than blacks and there was only a very slight relationship between mother's education and age at menarche. Age at menarche and age at first birth were very weakly related to each other in the entire sample but more strongly related among blacks. There was no statistically significant relationship between age at menarche and age at first birth when age at first intercourse was controlled. There is some evidence however that in the absence of contraceptive use age at menarche is somewhat related to age at first birth. For blacks,

age at menarche, viewed as an indicator of the timing of sexual maturation does, seem to have some influence on the timing of dating. Age at first date is related to age at first sexual intercourse for both races.

256. Protinsky, Howard; Sporakowski, Michael; and Patti Adams. "Identity Formation: Pregnant and Non-Pregnant Adolescents." ADOLESCENCE 17 (Summer 1982): 73-80.
Compares 30 pregnant adolescents to 30 non-pregnant adolescents in terms of ego identity, or the extent to which they have resolved the first five of the developmental tasks in Erikson's model of psychosocial development. Using the Rasmussen Ego Identity Scale there were significant differences between the two groups in their total scores, Trust vs. Mistrust, Initiative vs. Guilt, and Industry vs. Inferiority. Concludes that the pregnant adolescent is not as healthy in total identity formation as the non-pregnant. Recognizes that racial differences and differences in urban/rural residence between the two groups mean that they are not strictly comparable.

257. Rogeness, Graham A.; Ritchey, Susen; Alex, Patricia L.; Zuelzer, Margot; and R. Morris. "Family Patterns and Parenting Attitudes in Teenage Parents." JOURNAL OF COMMUNITY PSYCHOLOGY 9 (July 1981): 239-245.
Compares three groups of, largely Mexican American, adolescents in an attempt to determine if the group of adolescent parents was significantly different from a group of never pregnant teens from a local high school and/or from a group of teens in therapy at a community guidance center. The group of adolescent parents and the therapy group were both more likely than the high school group to come from single- parent families and to have more problems in their relationships with parents. The adolescent parents were also more likely to be isolated and were less interested in school or work.

258. Ryan, George M., and Patrick J. Sweeney. "Attitudes of Adolescents Toward Pregnancy and Contraception." AMERICAN JOURNAL OF OBSTETRICS AND GYNECOLOGY 137 (1980): 358-366.
Uses data on 87 pregnant adolescents living in inner-city Memphis. Found that 94 percent of these adolescents did have birth control knowledge and that 63 percent were pleased with their pregnancies.

259. Scott, Joseph. W. "The Sentiments of Love and Aspirations for Marriage and Their Associations with Teenage Sexual Activity and Pregnancy." ADOLESCENCE 18 (Winter 1983): 889-897.

Discusses the motivation for initiating sexual intercourse and becoming pregnant in a sample of 123 school-age mothers. Questions the now conventional view that pregnancy in adolescence is generally the unanticipated outcome of sexual activity. Found that 40 percent of the white and 35 percent of the black school-age mothers in this sample initiated sexual intercourse out of sentiments of love. The other reasons given for initial sexual activity were peer pressure and curiosity. Love appeared to be more related to pregnancy than to beginning intercourse. Being in love when pregnancy occurred was also related to the hope of some day marrying the loved one.

260. Shtarkshall, Ronny A. "Motherhood as a Dominant Feature in the Self Image of Female Adolescents of Low Socioeconomic Status." ADOLESCENCE 22 (Fall 1987): 565-570.

Reports that when groups of socioeconomically and educationally disadvantaged females in late adolescence project themselves into future roles, they most often see themselves as mothers. In their projections there is a direct transition from the daughter role to the mother role which excludes such roles as spouse or career woman.

261. Smith, Peggy B.; Nenney, Susan W.; Weinman, Maxine L.; and David Mumford. "Factors Affecting Perception of Pregnancy Risk in the Adolescent." JOURNAL OF YOUTH AND ADOLESCENCE 11 (1982): 207-215.

Uses data on 104 primiparous urban adolescents 13-18 years of age in their second or third trimester of pregnancy to describe their perception of pregnancy risk, fertility knowledge, and probability based examples. Concludes that the adolescent's biological knowledge, independent of demographic characteristics, may be the most important variable in preceding pregnancy.

262. Stiffman, Arlene Rubin; Earls, Felton; Robins, Lee N.; Jung, Kenneth G.; and Pamela Kulbok. "Adolescent Sexual Activity and Pregnancy: Socioenvironmental Problems, Physical Health and Mental Health." JOURNAL OF YOUTH AND ADOLESCENCE 16 (1987): 497-509.

Employs data on 1,590 adolescents, mostly black and from low socioeconomic status single parent homes, to examine the relationships between socioenvironmental, physical and mental health and their sexual activity and pregnancy status. When those who were not sexually active were compared to those who were sexually active but never pregnant and those who were pregnant, it was found that those who were pregnant had backgrounds which could be described as more psychosocially disadvantaged. Those who were not sexually active had the least disadvantaged backgrounds and those who were sexually active but never pregnant were intermediate in terms of background. There were no significant differences between the three groups in physical health. While the sexually inactive had the lower rates of mental health problems, those who had been pregnant had lower rates of anxiety and fewer conduct disorder symptoms than the sexually active never pregnant.

263. Streetman, Lee G. "Contrasts in the Self Esteem of Unwed Teenage Mothers." ADOLESCENCE 22 (Summer 1987): 459-464.
     Measures the self-esteem of 93 adolescent females 70 of whom were mothers. Found no significant difference in the self-esteem of childless adolescents and those who were parents.

264. Wilson, Fiona. "Antecedents of Adolescent Pregnancy." JOURNAL OF BIOSOCIAL SCIENCE 12 (April 1980): 141-152.
     Uses data from three studies carried out in Aberdeen to compare pregnant and nonpregnant adolescents. Found that those who became pregnant were more likely to have been academic underachievers at age 11, to have made an appearance in a juvenile court and to have been referred to a child guidance or psychiatric clinic at an early age.

265. Yamaguchi, Kazuo, and Denise Kandel. "Drug Use and Other Determinants of Premarital Pregnancy and Its Outcome: A Dynamic Analysis of Competing Life Events." JOURNAL OF MARRIAGE AND THE FAMILY 49 (May 1987): 257-270.
     Analyzes data on 706 young women to examine the extent to which drug use predicts premarital pregnancy and its resolution. Finds that three time-varying variables, current and former use of illicit drugs, other than marijuana and current cohabitation

strongly predict a high rate of premarital pregnancy. After a pregnancy has occurred, race has the strongest effect on its resolution. Premarital births are over-represented among blacks, while abortions are over-represented among users of illicit drugs other than marijuana.

266. Zabin, Laurie Schwab; Kantner, John F.; and Melvin Zelnik. "The Risk of Adolescent Pregnancy in the First Months of Intercourse." FAMILY PLANNING PERSPECTIVES 11 (July/August 1979): 215-222.
    Carries out a life-table analysis of data on 544 sexually active women aged 18-19. Finds that of the initial pregnancies in adolescents half occur within the first six months of sexual activity and more than 20 percent occur within the first month. The key explanatory factor is early age at initiation of intercourse which is associated with not using contraception.

267. Zacharias, L.; Wurtman, R.J.; and M. Schatzoff. "Sexual Maturation in Contemporary American Girls." AMERICAN JOURNAL OF OBSTETRICS AND GYNECOLOGY 108 (November 1970): 833-846.
    Reports that the mean age at menarche among 6,217 American born student nurses in 1964-65 was 151.8 months. This age is lower than that reported in most previous studies and is 4.5 months lower than that of the mothers of these subjects. These data tend to support the hypothesis that menarche is taking place earlier than before.

268. Zongker, Calvin. "The Self Concept of Pregnant Adolescent Girls." ADOLESCENCE 12 (Winter 1977): 477-488.
    Compares the self concept of 88 pregnant adolescents and 108 non-pregnant controls. Found that there were significant differences between the two groups on 13 out of 27 measures. The pregnant adolescents exhibited poor self-esteem, feelings of inadequacy and unworthiness and were more dissatisfied with their family relationships and bodies. The pregnant adolescents were also characterized by more conflict, unrealistic overcompensation, instability and defensiveness. There were also indications of personality disorders and maladjustments.

B. Chapters in Books

269. Butts, June Dobbs. "Adolescent Sexuality and Teenage
Pregnancy from a Black Perspective." TEENAGE
PREGNANCY IN A FAMILY CONTEXT. Edited by
Theodora Ooms. Philadelphia: Temple University Press,
1981, pp. 307-325.
Argues that the problem of adolescent pregnancy in the United
States is a symptom of the diseases of racism and sexism.
Describes three valued principles in the black community which
must be taken into account when policies and programs are
designed and implemented. These principles are a sex-positive
view of life, the extended family, and the historical value of
fecundity.

270. Curtis, Frances L.S. "Observations of Unwed Pregnant
Adolescents." NURSING OF CHILDREN AND
ADOLESCENTS. Compiled by Andrea B. O'Connor. New
York: The American Journal of Nursing Co., 1975, pp. 229-
233.

271. Cutright, Phillips. "The Rise in Teenage Illegitimacy in the
United States: 1940-1971." THE TEENAGE PREGNANT
GIRL. Edited by Jack Zackler and Wayne Brandstadt.
Springfield, Illinois: Charles C. Thomas, 1975, pp. 3-46.
Documents an increase in illegitimacy among teenagers in the
United States between 1940 and 1970. Explains this increase
primarily in terms of a difference by race in the culture of fertility
which has developed out the subordination of nonwhites by
whites.

272. Cvetkovich, George, and Barbara Grote. "Psychological
Development and the Social Problems of Teenage
Illegitimacy." ADOLESCENT PREGNANCY AND
CHILDBEARING: FINDINGS FROM RESEARCH.
Edited by Catherine S. Chilman. U. S. Department of Health
and Human Services, 1980, pp. 15-42.
Reports the first year results of a longitudinal study designed
to identify those psychosocial factors which identify adolescents
most likely to be at contraceptive risk early in their sexual lives.

273. Eveleth, Phyllis B. "Timing of Menarche: Secular Trend and Population Differences." SCHOOL-AGE PREGNANCY: BIOSOCIAL DIMENSIONS. Edited by Jane B. Lancaster and Beatrix A. Hamburg. New York: Aldine De Gruyter, 1986, pp. 39-52.

274. Field, Barry. "A Socioeconomic Analysis of Out-of-Wedlock Births Among Teenagers." TEENAGE PARENTS AND THEIR OFFSPRING. Edited by Keith G. Scott, Tiffany Field, and Euan G. Robertson. New York: Grune and Stratton, 1981, pp. 15-34.
Presents and tests a model for examining a variety of causal relationships between a number of socioeconomic variables and out-of-wedlock births among adolescents using data from standard metropolitan statistical areas. Concludes that black ethnicity, higher incomes, and increased age at first marriage are factors contributing to increasing rates of births to unmarried teen mothers. Liberalized abortion laws, more family planning services, higher labor market participation are factors which contribute to lower rates.

275. Konner, Melvin, and Marjorie Shostak. "Adolescent Pregnancy and Childbearing: An Anthropological Perspective." SCHOOL-AGE PREGNANCY: BIOSOCIAL DIMENSIONS. Edited by Jane B. Lancaster and Beatrix A. Hamburg. New York: Aldine De Gruyter, 1986, pp. 325-345.

276. Quay, Herbert C. "Psychological Factors in Teenage Pregnancy." TEENAGE PARENTS AND THEIR OFFSPRING. Edited by Keith G. Scott, Tiffany Field, and Euan G. Robertson. New York: Grune and Stratton, 1981, pp. 73-90.
Reviews in terms of methodology and conclusions those studies which attempt to assess the psychological risk factors associated with adolescent pregnancy. Concludes that few, if any differences can be found in intelligence, personality or psychopathology when unwed pregnant adolescents are compared to their nonpregnant peers using appropriate methodologies. It is further inferred that pregnant adolescents do not represent a psychologically homogeneous group. Suggests, however, that the population may include several identifiable subgroups.

277. Reiter, Edward O. "The Neuroendocrine Regulation of
Pubertal Onset." SCHOOL-AGE PREGNANCY:
BIOSOCIAL DIMENSIONS. Edited by Jane B. Lancaster
and Beatrix A. Hamburg. New York: Aldine De Gruyter,
1986, pp. 53-76.

278. Salguero, Carlos. "The Role of Ethnic Factors in Adolescent
Motherhood." ADOLESCENT PARENTHOOD. Edited by
Max Sugar. New York: SP Medical and Scientific Books,
1984, pp. 75-100.
Compares a sample of black and Hispanic adolescent mothers
in terms of seven sets of variables: economic, family, marital
status, education, contraception, parity, and prenatal, birth and
delivery data. Concludes that while black adolescent mothers are
gradually being assimilated into the mainstream of American life,
Hispanics are becoming more isolated and alienated. Makes
recommendations for dealing with Hispanic adolescent mothers
in such a way as to respect their values and cultural background
yet alter this drift toward increasing alienation.

VII. PREGNANCY RESOLUTION

A. Articles

279. Bracken, Michael B.; Klerman, Lorraine V.; and Maryann Bracken. "Abortion, Adoption or Motherhood: An Empirical Study of Decision Making During Pregnancy." AMERICAN JOURNAL OF OBSTETRICS AND GYNECOLOGY 130 (February 1978): 251-262.
Compares a sample of 249 never married women who were carrying a pregnancy to term to a matched sample of the same number who sought an abortion. Found that the decision to abort or to carry to term is more related to the circumstances of the pregnancy than to the characteristics of the women themselves. In this sample of young underprivileged women the pregnancy resolution decision was associated with the length and type of relationship with the partner, attitudes toward abortion and the existence of role models for the decision option.

280. Brazzell, Jan F., and Alan C. Acock. "Influence of Attitudes, Significant Others, and Aspirations on How Adolescents Intend to Resolve a Premarital Pregnancy." JOURNAL OF MARRIAGE AND THE FAMILY 50 (May 1988): 413-425.
Employs data on 129 white females under the age of 20 who were sexually active and never married to assess how their attitudes, significant others and aspirations would affect their resolution decision in case of an hypothetical pregnancy. It was found that those who feel closer to their boyfriends, hold less favorable attitudes toward abortion and aspire to more domestic pursuits tend more toward continuing the imaginary pregnancy. The attitudes of others had indirect effects through their relationship with the respondents' attitudes. The perceived attitudes of friends had more influence than the attitudes of parents.

281. Eisen, Marvin, and Gail L. Zellman. "Factors Predicting Pregnancy Resolution Decision Satisfaction of Unmarried Adolescents." JOURNAL OF GENETIC PSYCHOLOGY 145 (1985): 231-239.
Utilizes data collected in six month follow-up interviews with 238 white and 61 Mexican American adolescents who received services through the Public Health Department of Ventura County, California. At least 80 percent making each decision

reported that they would make the same decision again. Level of satisfaction at the time of the follow-up was not related to decision alternative, ethnicity/religion or age. Among those who chose to abort, four factors-- positive preprocedure abortion opinion, more liberal attitudes towards abortion for others, consistent contraceptive use following abortion, and their mothers' higher educational attainment--accounted for about 20 percent of the variance in satisfaction. Among single mothers positive preprocedure attitude towards single motherhood and lack of attempts to attend school in the six months after delivery were associated in bivariate analyses with decision satisfaction. Implications of these findings for adolescent pregnancy counseling are discussed.

282. Eisen, Marvin; Zellman, Gail; Leibowitz, Arleen; Chow, Winston K.; and Jerome R. Evans. "Factors Discriminating Pregnancy Resolution Decisions of Unmarried Adolescents. GENETIC PSYCHOLOGY MONOGRAPHS 108 (1983): 69-95.

Presents data collected in interviews with 238 white and 61 Mexican-American adolescents (13-19) who received services through the Public Health Department of Ventura County, California. Uses a utility decision model which includes psychological background and economic variables. Discriminant function analysis of the decision to have an abortion or to deliver the child indicated that psychological, background and economic variables each made significant contributions to the successful classification of teenagers (approximately 87.5 percent of the women were classified correctly). For adolescents who chose to deliver, a second discriminant function indicated that only one economic factor-- receipt of state financial aid-- successfully discriminated those who married from those who became single mothers (approximately 72 percent of the women were classified correctly). Findings are examined in terms of possible decision strategies and progressions used by adolescents and the value of using a decision framework that incorporates psychological, background and economic factors.

283. Fischman, Susan H. "Delivery or Abortion in Inner City Adolescents." AMERICAN JOURNAL OF ORTHOPSYCHIATRY 47 (January 1977): 127-133.

Employs data on 229 unmarried black adolescents, 151 of whom delivered and 78 of whom had abortions to address the question of what social and personal characteristics distinguish who chooses the divergent options. Reports on parental, boyfriend and individual factors. The deliverers tended to have a higher degree of social support than the aborters and longer, more lasting relationships with their boyfriends. The aborters came from families of higher socioeconomic status. The decisions that the adolescents made were moderately congruent with their attitudes toward abortion.

284. Geber, Gayle, and Michael D. Resnick. "Family Functioning of Adolescents Who Parent and Place for Adoptions." ADOLESCENCE 23 (Summer 1988): 417-428.

Employs data on 84 adolescent mothers in order to assess differences in the family environment of those who chose to place their children for adoption and those who chose to keep them. There were no differences between the two groups in terms of: (1) how they described their current perceptions of their families; (2) what their families should be like ideally; or (3) how satisfied they were with their families. Both the placers and the keepers are seen as functioning at a level that is less optimal than the norm.

285. Gispert, Maria, and Ruth Falk. "Sexual Experimentation and Pregnancy in Young Black Adolescents." AMERICAN JOURNAL OF OBSTETRICS AND GYNECOLOGY 126 (October 1976): 459-466.

Uses data from 214 black adolescents, 80 who chose abortion, 64 to deliver, and 70 never-pregnant controls. In the two pregnant groups the reaction of the adolescent and her parents to the pregnancy was assessed along with their attitudes toward the resolution decision. Those in all groups were measured in terms of their school performance and educational aspirations, their sexual behavior and their contraceptive use. Psychological tests were also administered. The controls had the highest educational ambitions and school performance and the fewest problems in school. The girls who had decided to deliver their babies had more problems in school, performed less well and had lower educational aspirations. The abortion group was intermediate on all of the these measures. Contraception was not used by the majority of those who were sexually active, but members of the control group were more consistent contraceptors. Neither of the groups showed a significant degree of psychopathology.

286. Jekel, James F.; Tyler, Natalie C.; and Lorraine V. Klerman. "Induced Abortion and Sterilization Among Women Who Became Mothers as Adolescents." AMERICAN JOURNAL OF PUBLIC HEALTH 67 (July 1977): 621-625.

Uses data on four groups of adolescent women who delivered a child at the Yale New Haven Hospital in order to determine their subsequent use of induced abortion and sterilization to control fertility. About 40 percent of all four groups used either abortion or sterilization to limit their subsequent fertility.

287. McLaughlin, Steven; Manninen, Diane L.; and Linda D. Winges. "Do Adolescents Who Relinquish Their Children Fare Better or Worse than Those Who Raise Them." FAMILY PLANNING PERSPECTIVES 20 (January/February 1988): 25-32.

Analyzes data on 269 first time mothers under the age of 20 who had been clients of a pregnancy counseling agency affiliated with a large adoption agency practicing open adoption. The sample included 146 women who had yielded their children up for adoption and 123 who had kept and were rearing the child. The two groups of mothers were compared in terms of their educational attainment, marriage and subsequent fertility, employment and household income, as well as in terms of social psychological consequences. Those mothers who kept their children are less likely to complete vocational training and to have aspirations for higher education. Those who elect to keep their children are more likely to marry, to be unemployed and to have lower household incomes. They are also more likely to become pregnant again sooner and to abort. Mothers in both groups indicate high levels of satisfaction with their pregnancy resolution decision, although those who decided to keep their children are slightly more satisfied with their decision than the relinquishers.

288. Mech, Edmund V. "Pregnant Adolescents: Communicating the Adoption Option." CHILD WELFARE 65 (November/December 1986): 555-567.

Investigates the extent to which 320 pregnant adolescents expressed interest in various aspects of adoption. These adolescents were seen as having four interest levels. None, (24%), slight, (42%), moderate (17%) and high (17%). The data indicate that white adolescents are more interested in adoption than non-whites. However, there was a consistent interest on the part of non-white adolescents which was higher than expected. Implications for counselors are discussed.

289. Nettleton, Carol A., and David W. Cline. "Dating Patterns, Sexual Relationships and Use of Contraceptives of 700 Unwed Mothers During a Two Year Period Following Delivery." ADOLESCENCE 10 (Spring 1975): 45-57.

Attempts to understand the adjustment following pregnancy resolution decisions by describing the dating patterns, sexual relationships and contraceptive usage of 550 unwed mothers (294 were between 14 and 20). Compares the behavior in each of these areas of those who kept and those who relinquished their children. There were differences in these areas which were associated with the divergent decisions.

290. Olson, Lucy. "Social and Psychological Correlates of Pregnancy Resolution Among Young Adolescent Women: A Review." AMERICAN JOURNAL OF ORTHOPSYCHIATRY 50 (July 1980): 432-445.

Presents a review of the literature on pregnancy resolution with an emphasis on adolescents. Looks first at sociodemographic and then the psychological variables that have been studied. Argues that there are some differences between those who select the divergent resolution options. Those who chose abortion, for example, are slightly older, better educated and more financially independent. Suggests, however, that those who seek and go through with an abortion do not comprise a "special" population but are similar to their age mates in many of their social and psychological characteristics.

291. Ortiz, Carmen G., and Ena Vasquez Nuttall. "Adolescent Pregnancy: Effects of Family Support, Education, and Religion on the Decision to Carry or Terminate Among Puerto Rican Teenagers." ADOLESCENCE 88 (Winter 1987): 897-917.

Utilizes data collected through interviews with a non-random sample of 43 pregnant Puerto Rican adolescents to examine how family relationships, religiosity and educational aspirations influence their decision to carry to term or to abort. Found that the teenagers divided into aborters and carriers received different levels of support from family members and friends both before and after their decisions. Those who chose to carry are not more

religious than those who decide to abort. The aborters have
higher educational aspirations.

292. Rosen, Raye Hudson. "Adolescent Pregnancy Decision Making:
Are Parents Important?" ADOLESCENCE 15 (Spring 1980):
43-54.

Examines data on 432 adolescent females who were less than 18
years old and unmarried at the time they experienced a first
pregnancy in order to determine the extent to which they involved
their parents in their pregnancy resolution decisions. The data
were obtained from 250 white and 182 black women through
anonymous self administered questionnaires. Most of the
teenagers did not involve their parents when they first assumed
they were pregnant. Parental assistance was sought to find a
place to verify the pregnancy in 23 percent of the cases. More
than half of the sample did involve their parents in their
resolution decisions. Mothers played a significant role in all
groups except whites who decided to keep their infant. In this
group the father of the child was the most significant other.

293. Rosen, Raye Hudson; Benson, Twylah; and Jack M. Stack.
"Help or Hindrance: Parental Impact on Teenagers'
Resolution Decisions." FAMILY RELATIONS 31 (April
1982): 271-280.

Analyzes data on the impact of parents on the pregnancy
resolution decisions of 100 rural, largely middle class, white (98%)
adolescents receiving care from a private physician. Two thirds
chose to abort, 12 percent to carry the infant to term, and 17 to
get married and keep the child. Parental impact was categorized
as involving direct pressure, indirect pressure, direct influence and
indirect influence. Very few respondents reported feeling direct
pressure from their parents. Indirect pressure was found to
operate entirely among aborters and was especially commonplace
among Catholics. Direct influence seemed to be the most
common form of parental impact among those who elected to
remain single and keep the child. Indirect influence was the
major form of impact on those who decided to marry and keep
the child.

294. Voss, Richard. "A Sociological Analysis and Theological
Reflection on Adoption Services in Catholic Charities
Agencies." SOCIAL THOUGHT 11 (Winter 1985): 32-43.

Reviews the trends in adolescent pregnancy resolution decision making over the past twenty years including the gradual but dramatic decline in adoption. Argues that adoption services fail to meet three threshold conditions for serving their clients. The adoption services are often not known to teenagers, they don't guarantee confidentiality or anonymity and they don't understand the needs and perceptions of teenagers in regard to affordability. Approaches used by adoption agencies often demonstrate small regard for the young unwed mother's feelings. She is often badgered, forced to sign forms that use terms like "illegitimate child" and "termination of parental rights" and treated like a criminal. Argues that adoption services must be made more accessible, affordable and sensitive to the dignity and privacy of their clients by adopting a theological rather than a bureaucratic approach to dealing with potential clients.

295. Zelnick, Melvin, and John F. Kantner. "The Resolution of Teenage First Pregnancies." FAMILY PLANNING PERSPECTIVES 6 (Spring 1974): 74-90.
    Uses data on a national probability sample of U.S. females 15-19 years of age to describe the outcomes of first pregnancies in this age group as well as the young woman's marital status at the time of that outcome. Approximately 30 percent of the women in this age group had experienced premarital intercourse, and of these about 30 percent experience a pregnancy before they marry. About 35 percent of those who become pregnant marry before the outcome. Whites are much more likely to marry than blacks. Illegitimate births are the outcome of two thirds of all premarital first pregnancies in blacks and one fifth in whites. Whites who do not marry terminate the pregnancy through abortion seven times more frequently than blacks. Two percent of the children born to unmarried black adolescents are given up for adoption, while 18 percent of those born to white teens are put up for adoption.

    B. Chapters in Books

296. Greer, Joanne G. "Adoptive Placement: Developmental and Psychotherapeutic Issues." PREGNANCY IN ADOLESCENCE: NEEDS, PROBLEMS, AND MANAGEMENT. Edited by Irving R. Stuart and Carl F.

Wells. New York: Van Nostrand Reinhold Company, 1982, pp. 386-406.
Describes the decrease in the extent to which adolescent pregnancies are resolved using the option of adoption. Argues that adoption should more frequently be seen as a feasible option when the young mother chooses not to abort but is unwilling or unable to parent.

297. Greydanus, Donald E. "Abortion in Adolescence." PREMATURE ADOLESCENT PREGNANCY AND PARENTHOOD. Edited by Elizabeth McAnarney. New York: Grune and Stratton, 1983, pp. 351-371.
Describes current techniques of abortion, laws in regard to adolescents and abortion. Gives advice to the clinician who is confronted with an adolescent who has chosen to resolve a pregnancy through abortion.

298. Klerman, Lorraine V.; Bracken, Michael B.; Jekel, James F.; and Maryann Bracken. "The Delivery-Abortion Decision Among Adolescents." PREGNANCY IN ADOLESCENCE: NEEDS, PROBLEMS, AND MANAGEMENT. Edited by Irving R. Stuart and Carl F. Wells. New York: Van Nostrand Reinhold Company, 1982, pp. 219-235.
Compares a sample of deliverers to a matched sample choosing the abortion option. Finds, for example, that teens do not make the decision to abort without experiencing a great deal of conflict, even though the aborters tend to be much more independent in decision making than those who elect to carry to term.

299. Poindexter, Alfred N., and Raymond H. Kaufman. "Issues Surrounding Adolescent Pregnancy Terminations." ADOLESCENT PREGNANCY: PERSPECTIVES FOR THE HEALTH CARE PROFESSIONAL. Edited by Peggy B. Smith and David M. Mumford. Boston: G.K. Hall, 1980, pp. 142-154.
Describes the pregnant adolescent who chooses to have an abortion and her knowledge of the procedure. Addresses how she became pregnant and what can be done to prevent a subsequent pregnancy.

VIII. SOCIAL CONSEQUENCES

A. Articles

1. *Conceptual Approaches*

300. Burr, Wesley R. "Role Transitions: A Reformulation of Theory." JOURNAL OF MARRIAGE AND THE FAMILY 34 (August 1972): 407-416.

Integrates several theoretical ideas in role theory with the empirical literature that has examined the ease of making such role transitions as adjusting to the coming of the first child, retirement and bereavement. Attempts to construct theory by identifying and reworking propositions that are sufficiently general and so precisely stated that they can be used as a basis for deductively explaining why the ease of making various role transitions varies.

301. Franklin, Donna L. "Race, Class and Adolescent Pregnancy: An Ecological Analysis." AMERICAN JOURNAL OF ORTHOPSYCHIATRY 58 (July 1988): 339-354.

Argues that an understanding of pregnancy among low income black adolescents requires a four part theoretical approach which is based on an ecological developmental model. The model involves variables at four levels of analysis: the individual, the family, the sociocultural and the social structural. Discusses the limitations of the approach as well as its utility for research and intervention.

302. Howe, Carol L. "Developmental Theory and Adolescent Sexual Behavior." NURSE PRACTITIONER February 11 (February 1986): 67-71.

Speculates on how the sexual behavior of adolescents may be related to the accomplishment of the central developmental task of each of Erickson's eight stages of psychosocial development. Argues, for example, that when adolescents, who have yet to acquire a sense of identity, move ahead in establishing a sense of intimacy, through early involvement in sexual activity, and a sense of generativity, through early parenthood, they may encounter obstacles to resolving the other developmental tasks.

303. Murcott, Anne. "The Social Construction of Teenage
     Pregnancy: A Problem in the Ideologies of Childhood and
     Reproduction." SOCIOLOGY OF HEALTH AND
     ILLNESS 2 (March 1980): 1-23.
     States that there is a common sense supposition that
     adolescent pregnancy is a social problem. But argues that this
     socially constructed problem cannot be fully understood by
     looking only at the ideologies of reproduction. The fact that
     adolescent pregnancies tend to be premarital is not their only
     problematic aspect. At least a part of the way the problem is
     constructed derives from the central fact that the underage
     pregnant are children. The presentation of adolescent
     pregnancy as a social problem then can be apprehended as a
     matter of contamination and can be seen as situated where the
     ideologies of reproduction and the ideologies of childhood
     cross.

304. Philliber, Susan G. "Socialization for Childbearing."
     JOURNAL OF SOCIAL ISSUES 36 (Winter 1980): 30-44.
     Outlines a conceptual approach for viewing fertility socialization
     which suggests at least six broad content areas: sexuality,
     contraception use, family formation, family composition and
     family function. Specific variables within each of these areas are
     suggested including the various agents of socialization and the
     timing of socialization. The framework generates a number of
     research questions, one of which is explored empirically. The
     analysis of data from a sample composed of both mothers and
     their children explicates several aspects of the fertility socialization
     process. Young women have beliefs about the value of children,
     correct family size, and predilections about sex of offspring even
     before they are at risk of pregnancy. The mother's own
     contraceptive behavior is generally not known, even though there
     is some communication about birth control. Children have a
     more accurate knowledge of their mother's preferred family size.

305. Presser, Harriet B. "The Timing of the First Birth, Female
     Roles and Black Fertility." MILBANK MEMORIAL FUND
     QUARTERLY 3 (1971): 329-361.
     Sets out to provide an explanatory framework for the racial
     differences in fertility which characterize the United States.
     Attempts to explain why black women have higher levels of
     fertility than white women even though they report wanting fewer
     children. The basic proposition explored here is that the timing

of the first birth is crucial in generating ensuing fertility. The initial hypothesis is that the earlier the first birth, the higher the completed fertility.

306. Russell, Candyce S. "Unscheduled Parenthood: Transition to 'Parent' for the Teenager." THE JOURNAL OF SOCIAL ISSUES 36 (Winter 1980): 45-63.
Points out that there are three conceptual approaches utilized in family sociology which are clearly applicable to the analysis of adolescent parenthood. The first approach discussed is the developmental or life cycle approach which deals with the transition to first time parenthood. The second perspective is that of "accelerated role transition" which, unlike the first perspective, does not concentrate on an unvaried sequence of stages in which marriage comes before parenthood. The third perspective which is considered is that of "family accession" which is concerned with crises brought on by the entry of new members into the family. The literature from these three areas is reviewed to yield two major conclusions. First, the variables associated with easing the transition to parenthood are not really clear. Second, recent longitudinal research indicates that adolescent mothers are not invariably doomed to a life of destitution and dependency.

2. Lost Opportunities

307. Atkyns, Glenn. "Trends in the Retention of Married and Pregnant Students in American Public Schools." SOCIOLOGY OF EDUCATION 41 (Winter 1968): 57-65.
Reports on a study designed to ascertain if there has been a distinguishable trend in school policy on the retention of students who are married, pregnant or who have already become mothers. Uses data on 127 of the 153 school districts in the continental United States with a student population of a 100,000 or more and 100 of the 120 districts in the state of Connecticut. In the large school districts a visible trend toward less restrictive policy is apparent since 1940.

308. Bacon, L. "Early Motherhood, Accelerated Role Transition, and Social Pathologies." SOCIAL FORCES 52 (March 1974): 331-341.

Uses data on ever married mothers from the 1967 Survey of Economic Opportunity to test the hypothesis that the younger women become mothers, the more likely they will be to experience marital instability, poverty and low levels of education. That the data appear to support the hypothesis is explained in terms of stress and pathologies produced by too early a transition to the role of mother.

309. Card, Josefina J., and Lauress L. Wise. "Teenage Mothers and Teenage Fathers: The Impact of Early Childbearing on the Parents' Personal and Professional Lives." FAMILY PLANNING PERSPECTIVES 10 (July/August 1978): 199-155.
    Utilizes data on a nationwide random sample of 375,000 students interviewed first in 1960 and then one, five, and 11 years after their expected high school completion date to examine the consequences of adolescent childbearing. Found that bearing a child has negative consequences for educational attainment, occupational achievement, marital stability and the ability to control subsequent fertility. The effects are negative for both those who become mothers and those who become fathers as teenagers, however, the negative consequences are more far reaching for young mothers.

310. Card, Josefina. "Long-term Consequences for Children of Teenage Parents." DEMOGRAPHY 18 (May 1981): 137-156.
    Analyzes the data on the 375,000 individuals included in Project TALENT to examine the long term consequences of being born to adolescent parents. The project participants who were born when their mother and/or father was an adolescent were compared to their classmates born to older parents. The children of adolescent parents, even when other variables were controlled, had lower academic achievement, were more likely to live in single or stepparent families, and were a little more likely to duplicate the early fertility, early marriage pattern of their parents.

311. Dillard, K. Denise, and Louis G. Pol. "The Individual Economic Costs of Teenage Childbearing." FAMILY RELATIONS 31 (April 1982): 249-259.
    First reviews prior research which has found that early motherhood is associated with lower levels of education, higher levels of completed fertility and less rewarding labor force

participation. Then reviews the prior research which has attempted to estimate the costs involved in rearing children. Next uses data from a number of sources to estimate the costs of rearing a child in terms of both direct maintenance costs and lost opportunity. Finally, explores the "hidden costs" which make children born to adolescent mothers more expensive than other children.

312. Furstenberg, Frank F., Jr. "The Social Consequences of Teenage Parenthood." FAMILY PLANNING PERSPECTIVES 8 (July/August 1976): 148-164.
Describes findings from a longitudinal study of 400 teenage mothers at a time approximately six years after the birth of their first child. Examines how experiencing motherhood before the age of 18 threatens the life chances of the young mother and her offspring. Compares the young mothers to a control group composed of their classmates. The adolescent mothers constantly faced greater adversity in realizing their life plans. Among the problems associated with early unplanned parenthood were marital instability, school disruption, economic problems, and difficulty in family size regulation and child rearing.

313. Furstenberg, Frank F., Jr.; Brooks-Gunn, J.; and S. Philip Morgan. "Adolescent Mothers and Their Children Later in Life." FAMILY PLANNING PERSPECTIVES 19 (July/August 1987): 142-151.
Presents some of the results from a longitudinal study of teenage mothers. This follow up takes place 17 years after the birth of the first child. At this time the major findings appear to be that the life course of adolescent mothers is much more varied than is generally recognized. The popular belief that adolescent motherhood invariably results in truncated education is called into question by the fact that a substantial number of these 300 urban black women who became mothers as adolescents returned to school. In many cases this only occurred after their younger child had started school. The general beliefs about the social consequences of adolescent parenthood also include the idea that it leads to increased levels of completed fertility. The women in this study, however, often did not have large families. In many more cases than was predicted these women also managed to avoid lifelong welfare dependency. The authors discuss several factors which play a role in allowing these women to overcome the obstacles imposed by early childbearing. These factors

include: (1) the economic security and level of education of the young mother's parents; (2) the educational ability and aspirations of the young mother; and (3) the extent to which they are able to rapidly control subsequent fertility.

314. Haggstrom, Gus W.; Kanouse, David E.; and Peter A. Morrison. "Accounting for Educational Shortfalls of Mothers." JOURNAL OF MARRIAGE AND THE FAMILY 48 (February 1986): 175-186.

Employs data from the National Longitudinal Study of the High School Class of 1972 in order to examine the role played by pre-existing differences in the relationship between early family formation and the educational attainment process. The findings suggest important self selection into early marriage and early parenthood. The first main finding indicates that the effects of late teenage parenthood on the current educational attainment and educational aspirations of young married women are less severe than might be inferred from a simple comparison of parents and non-parents. Even in the absence of parenthood, pre-existing differences would have led to different outcomes. The second main finding is that marriage and parenthood have effects that are separately identifiable with early marriage having the stronger effect.

315. Henderson, Gail H. "Consequences of School-Age Pregnancy and Motherhood." FAMILY RELATIONS 29 (April 1980): 185-190.

Compares the perceptions of the consequences of adolescent parenthood held by 30 school age mothers, their parents, and 14 school representatives. Found that the school representatives saw adolescent motherhood as having far reaching, long term consequences. The young mothers and their parents, on the other hand, saw the consequences as limited in quantity, degree and span.

316. Hoeft, Douglas L. "A Study of the Unwed Mother in the Public School." JOURNAL OF EDUCATION RESEARCH 61 (January 1968): 226-229.

Compares 37 unwed mothers attending a "culturally deprived" high school in a midwestern city to 37 of their randomly selected school mates in terms of grades, attendance and emotional behavior. The young mothers were significantly different from (did less well than) the control group in each area. In addition, the mothers were more likely than members of the control group to drop out of school. Argues that the young mother returning to school needs special treatment and guidance to remain in school.

317. Hofferth, Sandra L., and Kristin A. Moore. "Early Childbearing and Later Economic Well-Being." AMERICAN SOCIOLOGICAL REVIEW 44 (October 1979): 784-815.
Applies path analysis to a subsample, those who have borne a child by age 27 from the National Longitudinal Survey of Young Women. Addresses the question of how do those who become mothers as adolescents compare economically at age 27 to those women who delayed childbearing until they were in their twenties. Also seeks to evaluate the divergent explanations for why early child bearers do less well economically. The first argument sees early childbearing as causally related to lower economic attainment. The second suggests that the apparent relationship between these two variables is spurious, that is appears to exist only because they are both related to other variables such as low aspirations or social origins. The findings indicate that there is a complex set of relationships among the variables involved here. Analyzes the data for adolescent mothers and blacks and whites separately. Finds that having an early first birth is less injurious to blacks than whites.

318. Howell, Frank M., and Wolfgang Frese. "Adult Role Transitions, Parental Influence, and Status Early in the Life Course." JOURNAL OF MARRIAGE AND THE FAMILY 44 (February 1982): 35-49.
Employs data collected in a two wave panel design. The first set of interviews took place in 1969 when a sample of fifth and sixth graders and their parents were interviewed in six Southern states. The follow up interviews took place in 1975. Examined the relationship between social origins, academic ability or performance and adolescent marriage, parenthood and dropping out of school. The first three variables have a greater influence on leaving school than they do on the other two role transitions, even though none of the relationships were very strong. The associations among the three role transitions vary by race and sex. The authors see as their most important finding the substantial extent to which early role transitions led to reduced parental expectations, which, in turn, influence the aspirations of the young people going through the role transitions.

319. Ladner, Joyce. "Black Teenage Pregnancy: Challenge for
      Educators." JOURNAL OF NEGRO EDUCATION 56
      (1987): 53-63.
      Analyzes the effect of adolescent pregnancy on the education of
      black adolescents. Examines the scope and the context of the
      adolescent pregnancy problem, as well as its consequences.
      Discusses several successful approaches to dealing with the
      problem including sex/family life education, school based health
      clinics, life skills, school retention and self-esteem enhancement.

320. Marini, Margaret M. "Women's Educational Attainment and
      the Timing of Entry into Parenthood." AMERICAN
      SOCIOLOGICAL REVIEW 49 (August 1984): 491-511.
      Analysis data from a fifteen year follow-up of high school
      students, who were first interviewed in 1957-58 and again in 1973-
      74, to examine the relationship between women's educational
      attainment and the timing of their entry into parenthood. The
      findings suggest that educational attainment has a strong delaying
      effect on entry into parenthood and that the timing of entry into
      parenthood also has a smaller but still significant causal effect on
      educational attainment.

321. Martin, Anne, and Nancy R. Baenen. "School-Age Mothers'
      Attitudes Toward Parenthood and Father Involvement."
      FAMILY THERAPY 14 (1987): 97-103.
      Studied 60 adolescent mothers in order to ascertain: (1) their
      initial and present attitudes toward their parenthood; (2) which
      variables have the strongest influence on their attitudes about
      their pregnancy and parenthood and the change in these attitudes
      over time; and (3) the nature of the father's involvement as well
      as the young mothers' attitudes about this involvement. Even
      though some of the young mothers were initially unhappy about
      their pregnancies, over time their attitudes became more
      accepting and positive. Family support was an important
      influence on present attitudes and attitudinal change. Most of
      the young fathers were involved with their children on at least a
      weekly basis and most of the young mothers desired more father
      involvement.

322. Moore, Kristin A., and Linda J. Waite. "Early Childbearing and
      Educational Attainment." FAMILY PLANNING
      PERSPECTIVES 9 (September/October 1977): 220-225.

Examines data from the National Longitudinal Survey of the Education and Labor Market Experiences of Young Women to study the relationship between age at first birth and educational attainment. The findings support the hypothesis that the younger a woman is at first birth, the fewer years of education she will complete. While the relationship exists for both blacks and whites, it is much stronger for whites. These data do not indicate that the young mothers ever reach the same level of education as those who defer childbearing, but rather that they fall further and further behind.

323. Mott, Frank L., and Nan L. Maxwell. "School Age Mothers: 1968 and 1979." FAMILY PLANNING PERSPECTIVES (November/December 1981): 287-292.
Examines data from both the National Longitudinal Survey of Work Experience of Young Women and the National Longitudinal Surveys of Work Experience of Youth to compare the school status of young mothers in 1968 and 1979. The data indicate that young mothers were much more likely to remain in school during their pregnancies in 1979 than they were in 1968. In both years blacks were more likely to continue attending school than whites. In 1979 a larger proportion of young women returned to school after the birth of their child than was the case in 1968. Once again the percentages were higher in both years for blacks than they were for whites. In 1979 more young mothers were unmarried, their labor force participation and their unemployment rates were higher than they had been in the earlier year.

324. Mott, Frank L., and William Marsiglio. "Early Childbearing and Completion of High School." FAMILY PLANNING PERSPECTIVES 17 (September/October 1985): 234-237.

325. Rindfuss, Ronald R.; St. John, Craig; and Larry L. Bumpass. "Education and the Timing of Motherhood: Disentangling Causation." JOURNAL OF MARRIAGE AND THE FAMILY 46 (November 1984): 981-984.
Points out that the negative relationship between age at first birth and educational attainment is indisputable. The question is about the causal process. Do young women with high educational aspirations adopt various strategies to curtail their fertility or does an early first birth truncate educational

attainment? Attempts to explain the diverse findings of research addressing this issue.

326. Simkins, Lawrence. "Consequences of Teenage Pregnancy and Motherhood." ADOLESCENCE 19 (Spring 1984): 39-54.
    Reviews the literature concerned with adolescent sexual behavior with a focus on adolescent pregnancy and its consequences for both mother and child.

327. Teti, Douglas M., and Michael E. Lamb. "Socioeconomic and Marital Outcomes of Adolescent Marriage, Adolescent Childbirth and Their Co-occurrence." JOURNAL OF MARRIAGE AND THE FAMILY 51 (February 1989): 203-212.
    Draws upon data from the June 1980 Current Population survey conducted by the Bureau of the Census. Found that the co-occurrence of adolescent childbirth and adolescent marriage is associated with different economic and marital outcomes than either of these events alone. Adolescent childbirth alone, adolescent childbirth with later marriage, and adolescent childbirth coupled with adolescent marriage had economic outcomes that were similar and more negative than those associated with adolescent marriage alone. Marital instability was greater among those who married as adolescents without giving birth than it was among those where adolescent marriage and childbirth co-occurred. Some differences by race were found in the marital stability of those who gave birth as adolescents and then married later in life.

328. Teti, Douglas M.; Lamb, Michael E.; and Arthur B. Elster. "Long Range Socioeconomic and Marital Consequences of Adolescent Marriage in Three Cohorts of Adult Males." JOURNAL OF MARRIAGE AND THE FAMILY (August 1987): 499-506.
    Examines the long term consequences of adolescent marriage in three male cohorts using data collected by the United States Bureau of the Census. Found that black and white males who married as adolescents had fewer years of completed education, less earned income, greater levels of marital disruption and lower status occupations than same race aged peers who did not marry until they were adults.

3. *Subsequent Fertility and Family Structure*

329. Ford, Kathleen. "Second Pregnancies Among Teenage Mothers." FAMILY PLANNING PERSPECTIVES 15 (November/December 1983): 268-272.
Examines data from the National Survey of Family Growth (NSFG) to describe the contraceptive use and pregnancy experience of adolescent mothers in the year following their first birth. Finds that most (82%) sexually active teenage mothers were using contraceptives in the year following the birth of their first child. Black mothers and lower income mothers had lower rates of contraceptive use. There was a 17 percent probability of a pregnancy during the year following a first birth for all adolescent mothers. The rate was nearly twice as high for those with low incomes. Most of the births which occurred during this year were unintentional.

330. Kellam, Sheppard G.; Adams, Rebecca G.; Brown, Hendricks C.; and Margaret E. Ensminger. "The Long-Term Evolution of the Family Structure of Teenage and Older Mothers." JOURNAL OF MARRIAGE AND THE FAMILY 44 (August 1982):539-554.
Presents the results of a longitudinal study which compares the changes over 15 years in the family structure of teenage and older mothers who in 1966-67 had a natural child in the first grade in schools located in Woodlawn, a poor urban black community on the south side of Chicago. The emphasized finding is the extent of mother aloneness which characterizes the family structure of those who became mothers as teenagers. Teenage mothers often started child rearing as the only adult in the household. There is also a high probability that they will become over time the only adult and that this status will be long lasting. Less social participation and less assistance with child rearing are both associated with the trend toward mother aloneness.

331. Millman, Sara R., and Gerry E. Hendershot. "Early Fertility and Lifetime." FAMILY PLANNING PERSPECTIVES 12 (May/June 1980): 139-149.
Claims to be the first study to describe changes over time in the relationship between age at first birth and life time fertility. Does this by inquiring into the average number of children born during five year intervals and calculating expected completed

fertility, by race and age at first birth for four five year birth cohorts of women in the United States. Adolescent mothers are still likely to have more children than those who postpone childbearing, but these differences are not as great as they used to be. There is also a pattern of convergence between black women and white women.

332. Mott, Frank L. "The Pace of Repeated Childbearing Among Young American Mothers." FAMILY PLANNING PERSPECTIVES 18 (January/February 1986): 5-12.

333. Whelan, Elizabeth Murphy. "Estimates of the Ultimate Family Status of Children Born Out-of-Wedlock in Massachusetts, 1961-1968." JOURNAL OF MARRIAGE AND THE FAMILY 34 (November 1972): 635-646.

The birth certificates of illegitimate children were studied in order to estimate the final family status of children born out-of-wedlock in Massachusetts. A notation on the birth certificate that a "legal correction" had been made was construed as evidence that the child had been legitimated or adopted. Linkage of the birth certificate with a post-natal marriage certificate was interpreted as a indication that the child had gained a father or substitute father following birth. The bulk of Massachusetts children born out-of-wedlock to white mothers and a considerable minority of those born to nonwhite women appear to have been afforded a two parent family shortly after birth as a result of adoption, legitimation or a post-natal marriage.

4. *Early Marriage*

334. Bahr, Steven, and Richard J. Galligan. "Teenage Marriage and Marital Stability." YOUTH AND SOCIETY 15 (June 1984): 387-400.

Uses a subsample of 259 young men drawn from the young men's cohort of the National Longitudinal Survey of Labor Market Experience to follow a cohort of first marriages from the time of the marriage through at least five years. While five separate hypotheses are stated about the relationship between age at marriage and marital dissolution the major goal of this analysis is to test one of them. Basically, this hypothesis states that the relationship between age at marriage and marital stability will decrease but not disappear when educational level and unemployment are controlled. The findings indicate that during the early years of marriage level of education and steadiness of employment account for some of the apparent relationship between age at marriage and marital dissolution.

335. Bartz, Karen W., and F. Ivan Nye. "Early Marriage: A Propositional Formulation." JOURNAL OF MARRIAGE AND THE FAMILY 32 (May 1970): 258-268.
Reviews the empirical literature concerned with the causes and consequences of early marriage. The research literature yields 23 empirical propositions concerned with the causes of young marriage and three concerned with consequences. The empirical propositions are then reduced first to theoretical propositions and then to derived propositions. Three of the derived propositions concern the causes of young marriage and three concern consequences. It is argued that the theoretical propositions are a special case of exchange theory. Finally the implications for future research are discussed.

336. Burchinal, Lee G. "Trends and Prospects for Young Marriages in the United States." JOURNAL OF MARRIAGE AND THE FAMILY 27 (May 1965): 243-245.
Organizes data around a review of rates, factors affecting young marriage decisions, characteristics and outcomes of young marriages and implications. Between 1950-1964 young marriage rates remained stable suggesting a balance between those factors which promote and those which inhibit youthful marriages. The former include the idealization of marriage, earlier and more ardent dating, and elevated levels of intimacy. The latter includes increasing high school attendance as well as greater post-high-school education, increased employment among women and rising expectations about marriage. Young marriages generally involve young females and their slightly older husbands. A large proportion involve premarital pregnancy and those from the lower or working class. The divorce rates for youthful marriages are more than twice as high as those for post twenties marriages and those involved in them have offered negative evaluations. Fourteen variables demonstrated by research or inferred to be related to the outcome of young marriages are presented. Suggestions are provided about how various social agencies and institutions can influence both the rates and outcomes of these marriages.

337. Furstenberg, Frank F., Jr. "Premarital Pregnancy and Marital Instability." JOURNAL OF SOCIAL ISSUES 32 (1976): 67-86.

Utilized data from a subsample of a larger longitudinal study to examine how four conditions, personality stability, insufficient preparation for marriage, lack of economic resources and rapid subsequent fertility affect the stability of marriages created after a pregnancy has occurred. The data come from 203 adolescents who married after becoming pregnant and 90 of their classmates. The data fail to confirm the notion that the dissolution of these marriages result either from rapid additional childbearing or a unique set of cultural values held by women who become pregnant premaritally. The results do support the argument that premarital pregnancy disrupts the courtship process and abbreviates the necessary preparation for marriage. The data most strongly support the economic hypothesis, suggesting that these marriages often fail because the husband cannot support the family.

338. Kerckhoff, Alan C., and Alan A. Parrow. "The Effects of Early Marriage on the Educational Attainment of Young Men." JOURNAL OF MARRIAGE AND THE FAMILY 41 (February 1979): 97-107.

Assesses the influence of early marriage on the educational attainment of five cohorts of white and two cohorts of black young men using data from the young men's sample of the National Longitudinal Surveys of Labor Market Experience. The findings indicate that for both races early marriages lead to lower educational attainment among those who were still in high school. However, since individuals of the same age can differ in terms of educational attainment the findings also indicate that studies of the relationship between age at marriage and educational attainment must also begin to take into account prior educational attainment as well as age.

339. Kiernan, Kathleen E. "Teenage Marriage and Marital Breakdown: A Longitudinal Study." POPULATION STUDIES 40 (March 1986): 35-54.

Uses data from a longitudinal study of a cohort of British women born in 1946 to examine whether women who marry as adolescents differ from those who marry at later ages and whether there are any traits that distinguish between teenage marriages which survive and those which break down. The life histories of the women in this cohort demonstrate that adolescent brides have the least privileged backgrounds, educational and occupational careers. In terms of background those teenage brides whose marriages have been dissolved by the time they reach their 30s and those whose marriages remain intact are quite similar.

340. Lowe, George D., and David D. Witt. "Early Marriage as a Career Contingency: The Prediction of Educational Attainment." JOURNAL OF MARRIAGE AND THE FAMILY (August 1984): 689-698.

Uses data from the combined General Social Surveys for 1977, 1978, 1980 and 1982 to examine the utility of a new definition of early marriage, to assess its antecedents and its effect on the educational attainment of men and women. The index of early marriage, the number of years prior to age 22 that a person is when he or she first marries, is seen as superior to age at first marriage as a measure. So defined, early marriage is found to have an important effect on educational attainment. Women, because of an inclination to marry early, are found to be more susceptible to the relationship.

341. Lowrie, Samuel H. "Early Marriage: Premarital Pregnancy and Associated Factors." JOURNAL OF MARRIAGE AND THE FAMILY 27 (February 1965): 49-56.

Uses public records on marriages, births and divorces along with questionnaires returned by some of 1,850 brides to determine the proportion of brides pregnant at the time of their marriage, what other factors are associated with early or premarital pregnancies, and what proportion of the marriages are breaking down. Nearly 90 percent of the pregnant brides were minors. Pregnancy is inversely related to education. No relationship was found between age dating begins and pregnancy. Pregnancies were related to short or no engagement and unhappy parental homes

342. McLaughlin, Steven D.; Grady, William R.; Billy, John O.G.; Landale, Nancy S.; and Linda D. Winges. "The Effects of the Sequencing of Marriage and First Birth During Adolescence." FAMILY PLANNING PERSPECTIVES 18 (January/February 1986): 12-18.

343. Moore, Kristin A., and Linda J. Waite. "Marital Dissolution,
     Early Motherhood and Early Marriage." SOCIAL FORCES
     60 (September 1981): 20-40.
     Draws upon data from the National Longitudinal Study of the
     Labor Market of Experiences of Young Women to examine the
     nature of the relationship between early parenthood, early
     marriage and marital instability. Finds that especially for white
     women, marriage before the age of 19 significantly increases the
     probability of separation or divorce even when the effects of age
     at first birth and for various social, economic and demographic
     characteristics have been taken into account. Among whites,
     there was no relationship between age at first birth and marital
     dissolution, but among blacks an early first birth was related to
     greater marital instability.

344. Moss, Joel J. "Teenage Marriage: Crossnational Trends and
     Sociological Factors in the Decision of When to Marry."
     ACTA SOCIOLOGICA 8 (1964): 98-117.
     Hopes to stimulate more research on adolescent marriages cross
     culturally by reviewing a set of conference papers concerned with
     the topic. Compares demographic data for the countries reported
     on which shows an overall decline in age at marriage since 1890
     and that teenage marriages are less stable. Categorizes the
     conceptual frameworks used in dealing with the topic in terms of
     whether they give emphasis to personality, cultural or social
     systems. Points out, for example, that in the United States it is
     personality factors which are given priority, while in the European
     studies the institutional factors are accentuated.

345. O'Connell, Martin, and Carolyn C. Rogers. "Out-of-Wedlock
     Births, Premarital Pregnancies and Their Effect on Family
     Dissolution." FAMILY PLANNING PERSPECTIVES 16
     (July/August 1984): 157-162.
     Uses data from June 1980 and June 1982 Current Population
     Surveys to assess the effect of premarital pregnancies and births
     on family formation and dissolution. Concludes that the
     probability of a marriage following either a premarital conception
     or a premarital birth has declined. Women who marry after a
     conception or birth have a higher probability of separation and
     divorce than women who marry without being either pregnant or
     a mother.

346. Teachman, Jay D. "Early Marriage, Premarital Fertility and Marital Dissolution: Results for Blacks and Whites." JOURNAL OF FAMILY ISSUES 4 (March 1983): 105-126. Uses data from the 1973 National Survey of Family Growth to inquire into the simultaneous influence of age at first marriage and premarital fertility status on subsequent marital dissolution for both black and white women first married between 1950 and 1970. Results, using multivariate proportional hazards models, indicate that: (1) premarital births, but not pregnancies, increase the risk of marital dissolution; (2) higher age at first marriage reduces the risk of marital separation and divorce, up to ages 22-24 for whites and ages 20 for blacks. The probability of marital disruption increases slightly after age 25 for both whites and blacks. Black women have higher probabilities of marital disruption at all ages at first marriages; (3) blacks are less responsive than whites to the effects of premarital birth or young age at first marriage; and (4) older age at first marriage somewhat offsets the destabilizing effects of a premarital birth.

347. Waite, Linda J.; Haggstrom, Gus W.; and David E. Kanouse. "The Consequences of Parenthood for the Marital Stability of Young Adults." AMERICAN SOCIOLOGICAL REVIEW 50 (1985): 850-857. Uses data from the National Longitudinal Survey of the Class of 1972 to examine the consequences of parenthood for those who married and bore a child before age 25. The results indicate that, over the short run, the entry into parenthood has a positive effect on the marital stability of young adults.

5. *Parenting and Child Outcomes*

348. Bolton, F.G., and R.H. Laner. "Maternal Maturity and Maltreatment." JOURNAL OF FAMILY ISSUES 2 (December 1981): 485-508. Analyzes data from 4400 cases of child maltreatment reported to an Arizona county to compare three groups of mothers in terms of demographic and dynamic stress. The groups were: (1) those less than 20 at the time of their involvement in the reported incident; (2) those over twenty at the time of the incident who had become mothers before age 20; and (3) those mothers over 20 who had not given birth before that age. The youngest

mothers lived alone under conditions of extreme poverty and tended to be neglectful rather than abusive. They also tended to be minority group members. The presence of a male was not an important variable. The dynamics leading to the incident were quite similar across the groups.

349. Bolton, Frank G., Jr.; Charlton, J.K.; D.S. Gai; Laner, R.H.; and S.M. Shumway. "Preventive Screening of Adolescent Mothers and Infants: Critical Variables in Assessing Risk for Maltreatment." JOURNAL OF PRIMARY PREVENTION 5 (Spring 1985): 17-25.

Describes a study in which a population of 750 adolescent mothers was screened and 190 of them characterized as presenting an extreme risk for child abuse. Within 12 to 27 months following the birth of their children 10 percent had been reported for suspected child abuse. These 18 mothers were then compared to the others in terms of pregnancy and childbirth experience, maternal and child health, previous experience with violence, attitudes toward the child and demographic, social and environmental conditions. The adolescent most likely to be an early child maltreater was the one who deferred verification of the pregnancy and responded to it with anger while her social network responded to it with indifference. These young mothers tended to be in poor physical health and to have experienced family disruption and violence. Her environment was characterized by isolation from friends and family, insufficient financial resources, and constant unrelieved child care demands. Argues that the problem could be reduced through identification and intervention.

350. Bolton, Frank G.; Laner, Roy H.; and Sandra P. Kane. "Child Maltreatment Risk Among Adolescent Mothers: A Study of Reported Cases." AMERICAN JOURNAL OF ORTHOPSYCHIATRY 50 (July 1980): 489-504.

Analyzed data from 4,851 child maltreatment cases reported in one Arizona county to determine if adolescent mothers have a higher incidence of child maltreatment than older mothers. Reported maltreatment cases involving a woman who both gave birth to and was involved in abusing a child before her twentieth birthday accounted for 6.4 percent of the cases. More than a third of the cases involved a woman who gave birth as an adolescent but whose reported abuse did not occur until after the age of twenty. Children who had been born while their mother was still a teenager accounted for 61.7 percent of reported victims. Black and Hispanic mothers were over-represented in the officially reported cases of adolescent pregnancy and child maltreatment. All of the mothers had incomes below the poverty level but adolescent mothers were the poorest. Among whites the majority of both teenage and older mothers were married, while among blacks the reverse was true. The dynamics associated with abuse were different for the adolescent and older mothers.

351. Brooks-Gunn, J., and Frank F. Furstenberg, Jr. "The Children of Adolescent Mothers: Physical, Academic, and Psychological Outcomes." DEVELOPMENTAL REVIEW 6 (1986): 224-251.
Reviews the literature concerned with the children of adolescent parents with an emphasis on how little is actually known. Points out, for example, that most research in this area is conducted on black, urban, poor unwed mothers. These studies, overall, fail to separate the effect of maternal age itself from that of its covariates. The research that does exist suggests that: (1) intellectual differences between the children of adolescent and older mothers become more pronounced as the children develop; (2) behavioral differences are observed at earlier ages; and (3) male children, at least in the earlier ages, are more affected than girls.

352. Crockenberg, Susan. "Predictors and Correlates of Anger Toward and Punitive Control of Toddlers by Adolescent Mothers." CHILD DEVELOPMENT 58 (1987): 964-975.
Uses data on 21 mothers between 17 and 21 and their two year old children. Finds that the maternal behavior of adolescents is a function of both the mother's developmental history and her current social support. Angry and punitive parenting was associated with low current support from the partner and rejection during childhood. There was no relationship found between maternal behavior and the temperamental characteristics of the child at three months.

353. Daniel, Jessica; Hampton, Robert; and Eli Newberger. "Child Abuse and Accidents in Black Families: A Controlled Comparative Study." AMERICAN JOURNAL OF ORTHOPSYCHIATRY 53 (October 1983): 645-653.
Analyzes data on 1209 children (cases) under the age of four who were hospitalized with a diagnosis of abuse, neglect, accident,

ingestion or failure to thrive and on 209 controls who were hospitalized for acute onset conditions such as pneumonia. Across all categories no differences were found in race or sex. Age did differ with those who were diagnosed as abused and neglected being younger than the accident victims. Abuse victims came largely from poor families, four out of five of which were welfare dependent. A subsample of black children was also compared with their controls. Black families who abuse their children appear to be poor, socially isolated, and involved in stressful relationships with and among kin. The children who were accident victims were more likely to have families characterized by maternal depression and poor mobility.

354. De Lissovoy, V. "Child Care by Adolescent Parents."
     CHILDREN TODAY 2 (1973): 22-25.
     Examines child care practices in 48 adolescent couples from rural Pennsylvania. Found the young parents to be intolerant, impatient, insensitive, irritable and prone to use physical punishment on their children. The young parents were also found to be unacquainted with the developmental norms for the infant and young child.

355. Elster, Arthur B.; McAnarney, Elizabeth R.; and Michael E.
     Lamb. "Parental Behavior of Adolescent Mothers."
     PEDIATRICS 71 (April 1983): 494-503.
     Reviews the literature concerned with adolescent parenting. The first set of studies reviewed are those which look at the parental behavior of adolescents. Argues that taken together the results of these studies suggest that there are qualitative differences in the parental behavior of adolescent and older mothers with younger mothers showing a preference for stimulating their children physically rather than verbally. Then discusses those factors which may account for these differences in parental behavior including stress and coping, social support, adolescent cognitive development and characteristics of the infant. Discusses the conflicting findings in regard to the relationship between age of mother and child abuse and the cognitive development of the child. Also discusses the methodological flaws of existing research.

356. Franklin, Donna L. "The Impact of Early Childbearing on
     Developmental Outcomes: The Case of Black Adolescent
     Parenting." FAMILY RELATIONS 37 (July 1988): 268-274.

Discusses changes over time in black family structure with an emphasis on the increase in female headed families and the proportions of them which are headed by adolescent mothers. Reviews the research literature concerned with the developmental outcomes for children born to adolescent mothers. Discusses the implications of these research findings for intervention strategies designed to improve outcomes for young mothers and their children. Ends by discussing the additional research which is needed in this area.

357. Gullo, Dominic. "A Comparative Study of Adolescent and Older Mothers' Knowledge of Infant Abilities." CHILD STUDY JOURNAL 18 (1988) 223-231.
    Compares the knowledge of infant abilities in a group of 20 adolescent mothers (10 white, 6 black and 4 Hispanic) to that of a group of older white middle class mothers. In each of four behavioral domains (motor, social, cognitive and language development) older mothers were better predictors of infant abilities. When first and second year behaviors were analyzed separately, older mothers continued to be better predictors of infant development during the first year but there was no difference between the two groups of mothers in their ability to predict infant ability during the second year of life.

358. Jones, Freda A.; Green, Vicki; and David Krause. "Maternal Responsiveness of Primiparous Mothers During the Postpartum Period: Age Differences." PEDIATRICS 65 (March 1980): 579-584.
    Found, on the basis of the study of 40 mothers, that age influences maternal readiness. In this study the mothers 19 years of age and older demonstrated more maternal responsiveness toward their newborn infants than mothers 18 years of age and younger. Suggests that 19 may be the pivotal age at which a mother develops maternal readiness.

359. Kinard, E. Milling, and Lorraine V. Klerman. "Teenage Parenting and Child Abuse: Are they Related?" AMERICAN JOURNAL OF ORTHOPSYCHIATRY 50 (July 1980): 481-488.
    Discusses three methodological problems which confound any bid to evaluate the relationship between child abuse and adolescent parenting. Then reviews and/or reanalyses four data sets which depict the methodological difficulties and shed light on

the problem. The three methodological problems discussed include those associated with defining maternal age, identifying the actual perpetrator, and identifying appropriate control groups. The results of the four data sets examined are conflicting. They suggest, however, that the apparent relationship between adolescent motherhood and child abuse may be spurious or at least confounded by the covariation of each of these variables with social class.

360. Leventhal, John M. "Risk Factors for Child Abuse: Methodologic Standards in Case Control Studies." PEDIATRICS 68 (November 1981): 684-690.
Presents seven methodological standards for case control studies: (1) choice of specific control group; (2) nonbiased assembly of cases; (3) nonbiased assembly of controls; (4) spectrum of abuse described; (5) risk factor defined; (6) equal detection of abuse; and (7) adjustments for susceptibility factors. Twenty two case control studies published in English between January 1955 and December 1979 which investigated the prematurity or low birth weight of the child and/or young age of the mother were then assessed in terms of how well they fit these seven standards. None of the studies met all seven standards.

361. Levine, Lauren; Coll-Garcia, Cynthia T.; and William Oh. "Determinants of Mother-Infant Interaction in Adolescent Mothers." PEDIATRICS 75 (January 1985): 23-29.
Compares the mother-infant interaction of 15 primiparous white females 17 years old and younger to that of 15 older white first time mothers. Maternal age was not related to differences in maternal behaviors during face to face interaction. Maternal age was related to how the mothers behaved in a teaching situation with their infants. The relationship between age and teaching behavior may, however, be explained by their covariation with other variables including less schooling, lower ego development, less social support and the stress of being an adolescent mother.

362. McCarthy, James, and Ellen S. Radish. "Education and Childbearing Among Teenagers." FAMILY PLANNING PERSPECTIVES 14 (May/June 1982): 154-155.
Uses the June 1980 Current Population Survey to compute the mean number of years of school completed by women categorized in terms of their present age and their age at first birth. Women who bore children early have clearly increased the number of

years of schooling they complete. However, since other groups of women have also increased the level of their completed education, the gap between them has not closed.

363. McLaughlin, F. Joseph; Sandler, Howard M.; Sherrod, Kathryn; Vietze, Peter and Susan O'Connor. "Social Psychological Characteristics of Adolescent Mothers and Behavioral Characteristics of Their First Born Infants." JOURNAL OF POPULATION 2 (Spring 1979): 69-73.

Studied the child rearing attitudes, perceptions of infant temperament and mother child interactions of 225 primiparous adolescent mothers and 80 mothers who first gave birth after their adolescence. On most of the measures used there was very little difference between the two groups of mothers. Age of mother was not related to maternal attitudes, maternal perception of child, or the neonatal behavior of infants. The older a mother was the more time she was likely to spend out of contact with her infant and the more time she spent vocalizing during her interactions with the infant.

364. Parks, Peggy L., and Vincent L. Smeriglio. "Parenting Knowledge Among Adolescent Mothers." JOURNAL OF ADOLESCENT HEALTH CARE 4 (1983): 163-167.

Reports on a comparison of 80 primiparous mothers (45 adolescent and 35 older) in terms of their parenting knowledge. There was a high level of parenting knowledge in both groups, and no significant difference was found between the adolescent and the older group.

365. Philliber, Susan, and Elizabeth H. Graham. "The Impact of the Age of Mother on Mother-Child Interaction Patterns." JOURNAL OF MARRIAGE AND THE FAMILY 43 (February 1981): 109-115.

Utilizes data on 282 urban, black and Hispanic women who had their first child at a New York hospital in 1975 to examine the relationship between age of mother and various dimensions of parenting. The number of months the mother had been on welfare was more consistently related to the mother-child interaction variables than was age of mother.

366. Ragozin, Arlene; Basham, Robert B.; Crnic, Keith; Greenberg, Mark T.; and Nancy M. Robinson. "Effects of Maternal Age

on Parenting Role." DEVELOPMENTAL PSYCHOLOGY 18 (1982): 627-634.

Employs data on 105 mother-infant pairs to examine the relationship between maternal age and parenting attitudes and behaviors. Found that, overall, there is a linear relationship between age and maternal attitudes and behavior. The results offered no support for the popular notion that the negative effects of adolescent parenthood simply fade away after age 20 or that late parenthood had inherent detrimental effects.

367. Reis, Janet. "Child-Rearing Expectations and Developmental Knowledge According to Maternal Age and Parity." INFANT MENTAL HEALTH JOURNAL 9 (Winter 1988): 287-305.

368. Reis, Janet S., and Elicia J. Herz. "Correlates of Adolescent Parenting." ADOLESCENCE 22 (Fall 1987): 599-609.

Uses data on a self selected sample of 177 adolescent mothers in an attempt to ascertain what factors are associated with their parenting skills as measured by the Home Observation Measurement of the Environment instrument. Three of the six independent variables studied were statistically significant predictors of HOME scores: age, race and punitive attitudes toward child rearing and discipline. Together these three variables explained 20 percent of the variation in HOME scores. The older, white adolescent mother with less punitive child rearing attitudes achieved the higher scores.

369. Roosa, Mark W. "A Comparative Study of Pregnant Teenagers' Parenting Attitudes and Knowledge of Sexuality and Child Development." JOURNAL OF YOUTH AND ADOLESCENCE 12 (1983): 213-223.

Compares the knowledge that three groups of females (90 never pregnant teens, 50 pregnant teens, and 31 older mothers) have in terms of child development and sexuality. Also compares the attitudes of the two groups of teens. Found that in terms of attitudes and knowledge base there was no significant difference between the pregnant and never pregnant teens. The older mother knew more about child development but the teens knew more about sexuality.

370. Vukelich, Carol, and Deborah S. Kliman. "Mature and Teenage Mothers: Infant Growth Expectations and Use of Child

Development Information Sources." FAMILY RELATIONS 34 (April 1985): 189-196.
Employs data on 19 single adolescent mothers and 45 more mature mothers to compare their infant growth expectations and use of child development information sources. Compares the two groups in terms of level of information, sources of information and the factors that influence both. The findings indicate that adolescent mothers have significantly less knowledge of child development than the mature mothers. Concludes that occupation, age and educational level affect a mother's expectations for the development of her infant and the sources of information that she uses. There is a large body of information about child development that mothers do not have.

371. Wise, Susan, and Frances K. Grossman. "Adolescent Mothers and Their Families: Psychological Factors in Early Attachment." AMERICAN JOURNAL OF ORTHOPSYCHIATRY 50 (July 1980): 454-488.
Employs data on 30 adolescent mothers and their infants who had few medical and/or psychological problems to examine the correlates of adjustment to motherhood. Found that the young mothers' ego strength, measured by her accommodation to pregnancy, and the temperament and pediatric status of the infant were more strongly related to adjustment to motherhood than her feminine identification or her relationship with family, friends or the infant's father.

372. Zeanah, Charles H.; Keener, Marcia A.; and Thomas F. Anders. "Adolescent Mothers Prenatal Fantasies and Working Models of Their Infants." PSYCHIATRY 49 (August 1986): 193-203.
Utilizes data on 24 adolescent mother-infant pairs to describe the fantasies and working models they developed of their unborn infants. Not only did the adolescent mothers in this study develop solid and graphic images of their infants during late pregnancy but these images were not totally transformed by one month of postnatal experience.

373. Zeanah, Charles H.; Keener, Marcia A.; Anders, Thomas F. and Catherine C. Viera-Baker. "Adolescent Mothers' Perceptions Of Their Infants Before and After Birth." AMERICAN JOURNAL OF ORTHOPSYCHIATRY 57 (July 1987): 351-360.

Describes a study in which 21 adolescent mothers were asked to rate the temperament of their infants both pre and post natally. Several aspects of how the mothers rated the temperaments of their four month old infant were predicted by how they rated them before the child was born. The results are interpreted as contributing to the growing body of evidence that parents develop reasonably stable working models of their infants before they are born which are only partially recast by experiences with the infant during the first few months of its life.

374. Zuravin, Susan J. "Unplanned Pregnancies, Family Planning Problems, and Child Maltreatment." FAMILY RELATIONS 36 (April 1987): 135-139.

Uses data on 518 Baltimore single mothers to examine two questions. (1) Is there a positive relationship between number of unplanned pregnancies and child abuse and child neglect? (2) Do abusive and neglectful mothers have unplanned pregnancies because they failed to use a birth control method or because they fail to use their selected method correctly? The findings suggest that overall, the number of unplanned pregnancies conceived by a very low income woman (measured by receipt of AFDC) is predictive of both child abuse and child neglect independent of a woman's demographic characteristics. Unplanned pregnancies resulting from both failure to use a contraceptive and those resulting from a contraceptive failure are both typical of abusive as well as of neglectful mothers. The number of unplanned pregnancies is more predictive of neglect than abuse and unplanned pregnancies due to failure to contracept are more typical of neglectful than abusive mothers.

375. Zuravin, Susan J. "Child Maltreatment and Teenage First Births: A Relationship Mediated by Chronic Sociodemographic Stress?" AMERICAN JOURNAL OF ORTHOPSYCHIATRY 58 (January 1988): 91-103.

Tests the hypothesis that chronic stress mediates the delayed relationship between adolescent motherhood and child abuse and neglect using data on 518 welfare dependent single mothers. The stressors measured were excessive live births, low educational attainment, and a life history of unemployment. The findings support the hypothesis and indicate that the number of live births is the most important mediator for both abuse and neglect.

6. *Coping and Family Support*

376. Bright, Priscilla D. "Adolescent Pregnancy and Loss."
MATERNAL CHILD NURSING JOURNAL 16 (Spring
1987): 1-12.

377. Colletta, Nancy D., and Carol H. Gregg. "Adolescent Mothers'
Vulnerability to Stress." JOURNAL OF NERVOUS AND
MENTAL DISEASE 169 (1981): 50-54.
Investigates variations in the reaction to stress in a sample of 64
black adolescent mothers. The greatest amount of variation was
explained by total social support. Those young mothers with the
highest levels of total social support reported lower levels of
stress. Self esteem explained the second highest amount of
variance. Those young mothers with high levels of self esteem
reported lower levels of stress. Coping style was the third most
important variable with those young mothers who used direct
action reporting lower levels of stress than those who used other
coping styles.

378. Colletta, Nancy Donahue; Hadler, Susan; and Carol Hunter
Gregg. "How Adolescents Cope With the Problems of Early
Motherhood." ADOLESCENCE 16 (Fall 1981): 499-512.
Uses data on 64 black adolescent mothers selected in a
nonrandom fashion to measure the problems they encounter, the
coping responses they utilize, how their coping styles are related
to stress and their locus of control and self-esteem. Found that
when faced with task oriented problems the most common coping
response was to ask for assistance. Conflicts with institutions
evoked a range of coping responses while interpersonal problems
tended to be dealt with through avoidance. Lower levels of stress
were associated with more active support systems, higher levels
of self esteem and direct action coping.

379. Flaherty, Mary Jean, Sr.; Facteau, Lorna; and Patricia Garver.
"Grandmother Functions in Multigenerational Families: An
Exploratory Study of Black Adolescent Mothers and Their
Infants." MATERNAL AND CHILD NURSING
JOURNAL (Spring 1987): 61-73.

380. Furstenberg, Frank F., Jr. "Burdens and Benefits: The Impact of Early Childbearing on the Family," JOURNAL OF SOCIAL ISSUES 36 (Winter 1980): 64-87.
    Summarizes the results of two longitudinal surveys in order to present an overview of the assistance offered to first time adolescent mothers by their families of origin. Then looks at the clinical case studies of 15 families (nine black, three white and three Hispanic) in order to present a microscopic view of the family support process. The data on this very small sample resulted in the delineation of what the author calls the "imperatives of childbearing." These imperatives are presented as; incorporating the child into the family, the division of labor and the repositioning of the family. The families in the study showed a great deal of variation in how they responded to these imperatives. Different responses have both benefits for and can impose burdens on the mother's family of origin

381. Furstenberg, Frank F., Jr., and Albert G. Crawford. "Family Support: Helping Teenage Mothers to Cope." FAMILY PLANNING PERSPECTIVES 10 (November/December 1978): 322-333.
    Uses data from the first four waves of the Baltimore study to explore some of the issues involved in understanding how the family, as a unit, may be involved in helping the young mother to cope with adolescent parenthood. Finds that family assistance is related to the marital status and residence patterns of the young mother. Among the young mothers who never married a clear relationship is found between residential patterns and economic outcome. The mothers who continued to live with their parents were somewhat more likely to return to school and to graduate from high school. A much larger proportion were employed and fewer were dependent upon public assistance. Argues that the relationship between family assistance and economic achievement is probably reciprocal. Those who receive family assistance are more likely to make economic progress and those who want to advance are more likely to seek aid from their families.

382. Held, Linda. "Self Esteem and Social Networks of the Young Pregnant Teenager." ADOLESCENCE 16 (Winter 1981): 905-912.
    Describes the self esteem of and the support offered by social networks to 62 pregnant teenagers who were participants in five

different programs. The small sample was 56 percent black, 27 percent white, and 16 percent Mexican American. The self esteem scores do not support the idea that pregnant adolescents, as a group, have lower than normal self esteem scores. The blacks in the sample had higher self-esteem scores than the other two groups. The social network data gathered measures how the mothers to be perceived a supplied list of significant others felt about the pregnancy, i.e., whether they felt it was good or bad. Blacks tended to rate the pregnancy least highly. The few Mexican Americans in the sample along with their mothers rated the pregnancy least harshly. The blacks in the sample were more likely to be in school and to plan to return to school.

383. Nathanson, Madelaine; Baird, Allen; and Jay Jemail. "Family Functioning and the Adolescent Mother: A Systems Approach." ADOLESCENCE 21 (Winter 1986): 827-841.
Attempts to assess how interpersonal functioning within the family system affects the adaptation of adolescent mothers in the postpartum period. Some of the findings include that in family systems characterized as enmeshed there is a greater chance that the young mother will remain in the parental home, but such families also tend to have an adverse effect on her relationship with the father of the infant. The relationship between the young parents was also adversely affected in those family systems characterized by a great deal of differentiation between children, those in which conflict went unresolved, and by what was described as ineffective executive functioning. The researchers appear to assume that the most effective adaptation for the young mother to make is the formation of a nuclear dyad. As they say about how she is able to perform academically, this is a very complex issue which deserves further study.

384. Presser, Harriet B. "Sally's Corner: Coping With Unmarried Motherhood." JOURNAL OF SOCIAL ISSUES 36 (Winter 1980): 107-129.
Analyzes data on 69 unmarried women who constituted a subsample of a randomly selected sample of first time New York mothers. Each member of the subsample was interviewed three times: in 1973, 1974, and 1976. The paper discusses the unique characteristics of these unwed mothers, the significant extent to which the birth of their child led to expanded role responsibilities, the assistance they get or don't get from the child's father, their family and friends as well as the welfare system. The

contraceptive behavior of the mothers as well as their additional
fertility is analyzed. Three case studies are presented to show
variations in coping strategies.

385. Stevens, Joseph H., Jr. "Black Grandmothers and Black
     Adolescent Mothers' Knowledge About Parenting."
     DEVELOPMENTAL PSYCHOLOGY 20 (1984): 1017-1025.
     Uses data on 55 low income black families with adolescent
     daughters who were mothers and 46 with adolescent daughters
     who were neither pregnant nor parenting. Addressed the
     following questions: (1) Are black grandmothers more
     knowledgeable about child development than their daughters are?
     (2) Do grandmothers exhibit more appropriate parenting
     behavior than their daughters? (3) Is there a relationship
     between the grandmothers' knowledge about children and their
     daughters' knowledge? (4) To whom do black adolescent
     mothers turn for information about and help with child rearing?
     The data indicated that grandmothers with more knowledge also
     had daughters with more knowledge but only when the daughter
     was a parent. The presence of a young infant in the household
     seemed to provide the context for the grandmother to share her
     knowledge. The grandmothers were more responsive and less
     punitive in child rearing behavior than their adolescent daughters.

386. Townsend, Janet K., and John Worobey. "Mother and
     Daughter Perceptions of the Relationship: The Influence of
     Adolescent Pregnancy Status." ADOLESCENCE 22
     (Summer 1987): 487-496.
     Examines how 95 mother-daughter pairs perceive their
     relationship with each other and assess how the perceived
     relationship is affected by whether the adolescent daughter is
     pregnant or not. Found no significant difference in how the
     mother-daughter relationship was perceived by those in the
     pregnant and nonpregnant groups. Did find a strong correlation
     between the views of mothers and daughters on the nature of
     their relationship.

387. Unger, Donald G., and Lois Pall Wandersman. "The Relation
     of Family and Partner Support to the Adjustment of
     Adolescent Mothers." CHILD DEVELOPMENT 59 (August
     1988): 1056-1060.
     Uses data from 87 low SES adolescent primiparas to explore
     the relationship between family and partner support and the

adjustment of adolescent mothers. Both types of support were related to the young mother's overall level of reported life satisfaction. Since 75 percent of the young mothers were living with their families, their perceptions of family support were related to their concern about daily living and finances. Partner support was related to parenting behavior as measured by HOME.

7. Social Costs

388. Burt, Martha. "Estimating the Public Cost of Teenage Childbearing." FAMILY PLANNING PERSPECTIVES 18 (September/October 1986): 221-226.

389. Darity, William A., Jr., and Samuel L. Myers Jr. "Does Welfare Dependency Cause Female Headship? "The Case of the Black Family." JOURNAL OF MARRIAGE AND THE FAMILY (November 1984): 765-779.
    Uses a Granger-Sims statistical causality test, applied to data from the Current Population Surveys and Social Security Administration data for the years 1955 to 1980, which demonstrates that female headship is not caused by the attractiveness of welfare. Statistically, the force behind the increase in black female headed households appears to be a decline in the supply of black males.

390. Moles, Oliver C. "Predicting Use of Public Assistance: An Empirical Study." WELFARE IN REVIEW 7 (November/December 1969): 13-19.
    Uses data from interviews conducted early in 1963 with a random sample of 1,021 mothers of 5th and 6th grade school children in 12 inner city school districts to examine social and psychological variables which may explain why some low income parents but not others seek and obtain public assistance. Variables included in the study were are : (1) eligibility factors; (2) knowledge of public assistance; (3) attitudes towards public assistance; (4) initiative and aspirations; (5) alternatives to public assistance; (6) history of family poverty; and (7) length of residence in a location. City welfare records were used to determine which families were Aid to Families With Dependent Children (AFDC) recipients. Thirty one families were receiving

AFDC, 28 AFDC families were matched with 28 non AFDC families. Only two important and statistically significant differences were found: (1) intact recipient families were headed by men who recently worked fewer hours than the men in the nonrecipient groups; and (2) recipient mothers tended to be less fatalistic than the others.

391. Moore, Kristin A. "Teenage Childbirth and Welfare Dependency." FAMILY PLANNING PERSPECTIVES 10 (July/August 1978): 233-235.
    Employs data collected by the United States Bureau of the Census in its March 1976 Current Population Survey of approximately 50,000 households to estimate the cost of adolescent childbearing to the government through the Aid to Families with Dependent Children (AFDC) program. The analysis described here deals with women 14-30 years of age in 1976 who lived in a household with their own children. The data indicate that in 1975 the government disbursed 9.4 billion to households through AFDC. About half of this, 4.65 billion, was paid to households containing women who became mothers as adolescents.

392. Moore, Kristin A., and Robert F. Wertheimer. "Teenage Childbearing and Welfare: Preventive and Ameliorative Strategies: FAMILY PLANNING PERSPECTIVES 16 (November/December 1984): 285-289.
    Reports the results of an analysis which uses seven computer simulations to ascertain the effect of each scenario on the proportion of women 20-24 years of age in 1990 who will require welfare assistance. The first scenario is a baseline which assumes that current adolescent fertility patterns continue to 1990. Scenarios 2-4 involve what are termed preventive strategies which assume (2) no births to unmarried women under 18, (3) fewer births to women under age 20, and (4) fewer births to women under age 18. Scenarios 5-7 involve strategies which would improve the conditions of those who are already mothers; (5) involves smaller completed family size, (6) increased marriage, and (7) increased education. The three preventive strategies result in an estimated 22-48 percent reduction below the baseline figures. The three ameliorative strategies on the other hand produce estimated reductions of only 6-12 percent. It is pointed out that the due to the relatively low earnings of women, increasing education has the smallest potential impact.

B. Chapters in Books

393. Belmont, Lillian; Cohen, Patricia; Dryfoos, Joy; Stein, Zena and Susan Zayac. "Maternal Age and Children's Intelligence." TEENAGE PARENTS AND THEIR OFFSPRING. Edited by Keith G. Scott, Tiffany Field, and Euan G. Robertson. New York: Grune and Stratton, 1981, pp. 177-194. Uses data from the Health Examination Survey (cycles II and III) and from the Collaborative Perinatal Project to assess the nature of the relationship between maternal age and the intelligence of children when a wide variety of social and economic factors are taken into account. Concludes that there is virtually no depression in the intelligence of the offspring of adolescent mothers which is directly attributable to maternal age.

394. Bierman, Babette R., and Rosalie Streett. "Adolescent Girls as Mothers: Problems in Parenting." PREGNANCY IN ADOLESCENCE: NEEDS, PROBLEMS, AND MANAGEMENT. Edited by Irving R. Stuart and Carl F. Wells. New York: Van Nostrand Reinhold Company, 1982, pp. 407-426. Uses clinical observations and conversations with hundreds of young women who have participated in the Johns Hopkins Center for Teenaged Parents and Their Infants to discuss the problems encountered when becoming a mother while still an adolescent.

395. Chilman, Catherine S. "Never Married, Single, Adolescent Parents." VARIANT FAMILY FORMS. Edited by Catherine S. Chilman, Elam W. Nunnally, and Fred M. Cox. Beverly Hills: Sage Publications, 1988, 17-38.

396. Darabi, Katherine; Graham, Elizabeth H.; and Susan Gustavas Philliber. "The Second Time Around: Birth Spacing among Teenage Mothers." PREGNANCY IN ADOLESCENCE: NEEDS, PROBLEMS, AND MANAGEMENT. Edited by Irving R. Stuart and Carl F. Wells. New York: Van Nostrand Reinhold Company, 1982, pp. 427-438. Uses data from 93 black and Hispanic adolescent mothers to identify those characteristics associated with having a second live birth within 30 months.

397. Field, Tiffany; Widmayer, Susan; Stoller, Sherilyn; and
     Mercedes de Cubas. "School-Age Parenthood in Different
     Ethnic Groups and Family Constellations: Effects on Infant
     Development." SCHOOL-AGE PREGNANCY:
     BIOSOCIAL DIMENSIONS. Edited by Jane B. Lancaster
     and Beatrix A. Hamburg. New York: Aldine De Gruyter,
     1986, pp. 263-272.

398. Fine, Paul, and Mary Pape. "Pregnant Teenagers in Need of
     Social Networks; Diagnostic Parameters." PREGNANCY IN
     ADOLESCENCE: NEEDS, PROBLEMS, AND
     MANAGEMENT. Edited by Irving R. Stuart and Carl F.
     Wells. New York: Van Nostrand Reinhold Company, 1982,
     pp. 80-106.
     Stresses the necessity of adequate diagnosis in order to help
     pregnant adolescents make decisions about pregnancy. Not only
     must the adolescent's stage of development be taken into account
     but also the nature of the relationships with and within her family
     and other social networks.

399. Fineman, Jo Ann B., and Marguerite A. Smith. "Object Ties
     and Interaction of the Infant and Adolescent Mother."
     ADOLESCENT PARENTHOOD. Edited by Max Sugar.
     New York: SP Medical and Scientific Books, 1984, pp. 119-
     140.
     Focuses on the psychoanalytic problem of the earliest
     development of object relations experienced by the infants of low
     income black mothers.

400. Friedman, Stanford B., and Sheridan Phillips. "Psychosocial
     Risk to Mother and Child as a Consequence of Adolescent
     Pregnancy." PREMATURE ADOLESCENT PREGNANCY
     AND PARENTHOOD. Edited by Elizabeth McAnarney.
     New York: Grune and Stratton, 1983, pp. 269-278.
     Argues that while it certainly appears obvious that pregnant
     and parenting adolescents suffer many psychological, social, and
     school problems, there is little or no real evidence. Suggests that
     the problems do exist result from a combination of how
     pregnancy and parenthood complicate the already difficult tasks
     of identity development during adolescence and the lack of
     economic and social support.

401. Furstenberg, Frank F., Jr., and Albert G. Crawford. "Social Implications of Teenage Childbearing." ADOLESCENT PREGNANCY: PERSPECTIVES FOR THE HEALTH CARE PROFESSIONAL. Edited by Peggy B. Smith and David M. Mumford. Boston: G.K. Hall, 1980, pp. 48-76.
Reviews the literature on the social consequences of adolescent childbearing for the young parents, their offspring and for the family of orientation.

402. Furstenberg, Frank F., Jr. "Implicating the Family: Teenage Parenthood and Kinship Involvement." TEENAGE PREGNANCY IN A FAMILY CONTEXT. Edited by Theodora Ooms. Philadelphia: Temple University Press, 1981, pp. 131-164.
Describes the role of the family in supporting the young mother as she adjusts to her unplanned parenthood. Also discusses the impact of the process of unplanned parenthood on the family.

403. Gelles, Richard J. "School-Age Parents and Child Abuse." SCHOOL-AGE PREGNANCY: BIOSOCIAL DIMENSIONS. Edited by Jane B. Lancaster and Beatrix A. Hamburg. New York: Aldine De Gruyter, 1986, pp. 347-359.

404. Hamburg, Beatrix. "Subsets of Adolescent Mothers: Developmental, Biomedical and Psychosocial Issues." SCHOOL-AGE PREGNANCY: BIOSOCIAL DIMENSIONS. Edited by Jane B. Lancaster and Beatrix A. Hamburg. New York: Aldine De Gruyter, 1986, pp. 115-145.

405. Kinard, E. Milling, and Lorraine V. Klerman. "Effects of Early Parenthood on the Cognitive Development of Children." PREMATURE ADOLESCENT PREGNANCY AND PARENTHOOD. Edited by Elizabeth McAnarney. New York: Grune and Stratton, 1983, pp. 253-266.
Uses data from cycle II of the Health Examination Survey to assess the relationship between parental age and the intellectual development of children. Concludes that the data do not support the assumption that the children of adolescent mothers are at a significantly increased risk for considerable deficiencies in intellectual development.

406. Klerman, Lorraine V. "The Economic Impact of School-Age Child Rearing." SCHOOL-AGE PREGNANCY:

BIOSOCIAL DIMENSIONS. Edited by Jane B. Lancaster and Beatrix A. Hamburg. New York: Aldine De Gruyter, 1986, pp. 361-377.

407. Ladner, Joyce. "The Impact of Teenage Pregnancy on the Black Family." BLACK FAMILIES. Edited by Harriette Pipes McAdoo. Beverly Hills: Sage Publications, 1988, 296-297.

408. Lancaster, Jane B., and Beatrix A. Hamburg. "The Biosocial Dimensions of School-Age Pregnancy." SCHOOL-AGE PREGNANCY: BIOSOCIAL DIMENSIONS. Edited by Jane B. Lancaster and Beatrix A. Hamburg. New York: Aldine De Gruyter, 1986, pp. 3-13.

409. Lieberman, E. James. "The Psychological Consequences of Adolescent Pregnancy and Abortion." ADOLESCENT PREGNANCY AND CHILDBEARING: FINDINGS FROM RESEARCH. Edited by Catherine S. Chilman. U. S. Department of Health and Human Services, 1980, pp. 207-220.
Discusses the psychological consequences of adolescent pregnancy and abortion based upon an understanding of adolescence as a stage of development. The outcomes discussed range from suicidal behaviors and postpartum psychosis to lost educational and economic opportunities.

410. Mayfield, Lorraine. "Early Parenthood Among Low Income Girls." THE BLACK FAMILY: ESSAYS AND STUDIES. Edited by Robert Staples. Belmont, CA.: Wadsworth Publishing Co., 1986, pp. 211-223.

411. McCarthy, James, and Ellen Radish. "Education and Childbearing among Teenagers." PREMATURE ADOLESCENT PREGNANCY AND PARENTHOOD. Edited by Elizabeth McAnarney. New York: Grune and Stratton, 1983, pp. 279-292.
Reviews the literature concerned with the relationship between early parenthood and educational attainment.

412. Moore, Kristan A. "Government Policies Related to Teenage Family Formation and Functioning: An Inventory." TEENAGE PREGNANCY IN A FAMILY CONTEXT.

Edited by Theodora Ooms. Philadelphia: Temple University Press, 1981, pp. 165-212.
Identifies and describes approximately 35 programs, located in five federal agencies, that affect either family functioning or formation.

413. Moore, Kristin A.; Hofferth, Sandra L.; Wertheimer, Richard F.; Waite, Linda J.; and Steven B. Caldwell. "Teenage Childbearing: Consequences for Women, Families, and Government Welfare Expenditures." TEENAGE PARENTS AND THEIR OFFSPRING. Edited by Keith G. Scott, Tiffany Field, and Euan G. Robertson. New York: Grune and Stratton, 1981, pp. 35-54.
Uses data from the National Longitudinal Survey of the Labor Market Experience of Young Women and the Panel Study of Income Dynamics to trace the social and economic consequences of adolescent childbearing. Finds that adolescent childbearing precipitates a chain of events which undermine economic well being. The factors in this chain of events include lower educational attainment, higher subsequent fertility, lower household income and marital instability. Also discusses the high costs to society.

414. Ooms, Theodora. ""Family Involvement, Notification, and Responsibility: A Personal Essay." TEENAGE PREGNANCY IN FAMILY CONTEXT. Edited by Theodora Ooms. Philadelphia: Temple University Press, 1981, pp. 371-398.
Presents a personal summary of the policy implications of a family impact perspective on policies and programs related to adolescent pregnancy.

415. Osofsky, Howard J., and Joy D. Osofsky. "Adolescent Adaptation to Pregnancy and Parenthood." PREMATURE ADOLESCENT PREGNANCY AND PARENTHOOD. Edited by Elizabeth McAnarney. New York: Grune and Stratton, 1983, pp. 195-206.
Discusses the potential for problems and conflicts when adolescents, who have yet to resolve the developmental task of identity formation, become parents. Emphasizes the importance of both inner resources and social support for successful adaptation.

416. Lawrence, Ruth A. "Early Mothering by Adolescents."
PREMATURE ADOLESCENT PREGNANCY AND
PARENTHOOD. Edited by Elizabeth McAnarney. New
York: Grune and Stratton, 1983, pp. 219-230.
Points out that relatively little research has been conducted on
the mothering behaviors of adolescents. The research which has
been done indicates that there are differences in how some
adolescent mothers behave and how older mothers behave.
Argues that if mother-infant interaction is found to have an effect
on the long term development of infants and if mothering can be
taught, then every effort should be make to teach mothering skills
to adolescents.

417. Petersen, Anne, and Lisa Crockett. "Pubertal Development and
Its Relation to Cognitive and Psychosocial Development in
Adolescent Girls: Implications for Parenting. SCHOOL-
AGE PREGNANCY: BIOSOCIAL DIMENSIONS. Edited
by Jane B. Lancaster and Beatrix A. Hamburg. New York:
Aldine De Gruyter, 1986, pp. 147-175.

418. Presser, Harriet B. "Social Consequences of Teenage
Childbearing." ADOLESCENT PREGNANCY AND
CHILDBEARING: FINDINGS FROM RESEARCH.
Edited by Catherine S. Chilman. U. S. Department of Health
and Human Services, 1980, pp. 249-266.
Uses data on 408 women drawn from those who had a first
birth in New York City in July of 1970, 1971, or 1972, to assess
the social consequences of adolescent motherhood primarily in
terms of what it means for the assumption of other roles by the
young mother.

419. Sahler, Olle Jane Z. "Adolescent Mothers: How Nurturant Is
Their Parenting?" PREMATURE ADOLESCENT
PREGNANCY AND PARENTHOOD. Edited by Elizabeth
McAnarney. New York: Grune and Stratton, 1983, pp. 219-
230.
Argues that assessing the capabilities of any individual
adolescent to mother should be based on stage of development
rather than chronological age. Indicates that those who are in
the late stage of adolescence will be more ready to assume
parental responsibility than those in the early or middle stages.
Discusses the importance of the extended family in making up for
the deficits of individual adolescents.

420. Shouse, Judith Weatherford. "Psychological and Emotional Problems of Pregnancy in Adolescence." THE TEENAGE PREGNANT GIRL. Edited by Jack Zackler and Wayne Brandstadt. Springfield, Illinois: Charles C. Thomas, 1975, pp. 161-186.
Uses case studies to describe how the emotional and psychological stress of adolescence and pregnancy combine.

421. Spacks, Patricia Meyer. "The Wages of Sin: Adolescent Mothers in Nineteenth Century Fiction." ADOLESCENT PARENTHOOD. Edited by Max Sugar. New York: SP Medical and Scientific Books, 1984, pp. 3-20.
Reviews the treatment of the adolescent mother in the novels of Austen, Eliot, Gaskell and Scott.

422. Sugar, Max. "Infants of Adolescent Mothers: Research Perspectives." ADOLESCENT PARENTHOOD. Edited by Max Sugar. New York: SP Medical and Scientific Books, 1984, pp. 101-118.
Emphasizes the "at risk" nature of infants born to adolescent mothers and the importance of properly structured interventions to reduce the realization of these risks.

423. Super, Charles M. "A Developmental Perspective on School-Age Parenthood." SCHOOL-AGE PREGNANCY: BIOSOCIAL DIMENSIONS. Edited by Jane B. Lancaster and Beatrix A. Hamburg. New York: Aldine De Gruyter, 1986, pp. 379-386.

424. Trussell, T. James. "Economic Consequences of Teenage Childbearing." ADOLESCENT PREGNANCY AND CHILDBEARING: FINDINGS FROM RESEARCH. Edited by Catherine S. Chilman. U. S. Department of Health and Human Services, 1980, pp. 221-248.
Discusses the impact of early motherhood on the young mother in terms of such things as her educational attainment and labor force participation rates as well as the costs of the phenomenon to society.

C. Books

425. Bolton, Frank G. THE PREGNANT ADOLESCENT. Beverly
     Hills, CA: Sage Publications, 1980.
     Describes the process by which the pregnant adolescent comes
     to be at high risk for child maltreatment and the methods that
     may be utilized to reduce this risk. The early chapters describe
     the adolescent pregnancy problem and the parallels between the
     development of the adolescent pregnancy and the potential child
     mistreater. What follows from this description is the author's
     sense of methods which will help to reduce risks generated by
     participation in either, or both, of these environments.

426. Frank, Daniel B. DEEP BLUE FUNK AND OTHER
     STORIES: PORTRAITS OF TEENAGE PARENTS.
     Chicago: The Ounce of Prevention Fund, 1983.
     Describes the results of a participant-observation research
     project set in a community center for pregnant and parenting
     adolescents in a black neighborhood of largely white Evanston,
     Illinois. The adolescents are allowed to speak for themselves
     about the many different roles they play. The concerns of their
     parents are also raised.

427. Furstenberg, Frank F., Jr. UNPLANNED PARENTHOOD:
     THE SOCIAL CONSEQUENCES OF TEENAGE
     CHILDBEARING. New York: The Free Press, 1976.
     Presents a five year follow-up of 403 adolescent mothers and
     their first born children designed to document the consequences
     of early childbearing on the transition to adulthood. The early
     childbearers are compared to their class mates who postponed
     childbearing. The study demonstrated that adolescent
     motherhood has more negative consequences for some women
     than for others, as a significant minority of the young mothers
     made a successful transition to adulthood. The differences in the
     young mothers' adaptation to adulthood is explained in terms of
     the prenatal program in which they all participated, characteristics
     of the young parents, support offered to them by family and
     friends and the services provided to them by welfare agencies in
     the city of Baltimore.

428. Furstenberg, Frank F., Jr.; Brooks-Gunn, J.; and S. Philip
Morgan. ADOLESCENT MOTHERS IN LATER LIFE.
New York: 1987.
Traces the life histories of approximately 300 adolescent
mothers and their children over a seventeen year period. Using
data from interviews and case studies the differential impact of
early childbearing are portrayed.

429. Kamerman, Sheila B., and Alfred J. Kahn. MOTHERS
ALONE: STRATEGIES FOR A TIME OF CHANGE.
Dover, Mass.: Auburn House Publishing Co., 1988.
Surveys what is known, overall, about single mothers. Offers
some historical perspectives. Looks at four different but
overlapping groups of mothers, including adolescent mothers.
Reviews existing policies and programs and makes
recommendations for the future.

430. Moore, Kristan A.; Simms, Margaret; and Charles L. Betsey.
CHOICE AND CIRCUMSTANCE: RACIAL
DIFFERENCES IN ADOLESCENT SEXUALITY AND
FERTILITY. New Brunswick: Transaction Books, 1986.
Begins by pointing out that as a proportion of all births, early
and unmarried child bearing is more common among blacks than
among other groups in the United States. Black Americans, in
fact, have higher fertility than adolescents in any other developed
country. Addresses how this differential can be explained. Found
that several factors independently predict early fertility including
lack of information, poorly educated parents, school dropout,
poor employment prospects, and single parent families. Most
importantly argues that these factors are concentrated in the
neighborhoods in which black adolescents live and argues that the
"aggregate" influence of these factors may be "greater" than the
simple sum of the separate effects. Lists a number of policy
recommendations including: better sex education, broadly defined;
greater availability of contraceptive services; efforts to explain for
young people the relationship between early childbearing and the
attainment of educational and occupational aspirations. Black
youth and their families already have high aspirations in these
areas but need to find ways to implement them. Researchers are
urged to study families that are successfully rearing children in
the midst of poverty, crime and disorganization. Uncovering the
factors which underline their success would provide a foundation
on which to build effective strategies.

431. Moore, Kristan A., and Martha R. Burt. PRIVATE CRISES, PUBLIC COST: POLICY PERSPECTIVES ON TEENAGE CHILDBEARING. Washington, D.C.: The Urban Institute Press, 1982.
     Discusses the prevalence of childbearing in the United States over time and how it has varied by age, race, and marital status. Reviews the literature on the social, economic, and medical consequences of adolescent parenthood. Explores policy options to reduce public dependency and increase the life chances of adolescents and their children.

432. Ooms, Theodora. (Ed.) ADOLESCENT PREGNANCY IN A SOCIAL CONTEXT. Philadelphia: Temple University Press, 1981.
     Contains papers from the Family Impact Seminars which apply a family impact perspective to an examination of how policies on adolescent pregnancy affect families. Makes recommendations for policies that are more supportive of families and extends family impact analysis. Contains items 031, 269, 402, 410, 412, 414, 661, 662, 699.

433. Osofsky, Howard J. THE PREGNANT TEENAGER. Springfield, IL: Charles C. Thomas Publisher, 1968.
     Describes the problems facing pregnant adolescents and calls for social programs to help curtail those problems.

434. Sugar, Max. (Ed.) ADOLESCENT PARENTHOOD. New York: SP Medical and Scientific Books, 1984.
     Presents chapters concerned with the adolescent mother and her offspring which take into account the groups that make up her environment including the extended family and service providers as well as the broader social and cultural groups to which they each belong. Contains items 086, 090, 171, 278, 399, 421, 561, 648, 656, 672, 574, and 698.

435. Vincent, Clark E. UNMARRIED MOTHERS. New York: Free Press of Glencoe, 1961.
     Studies more than one thousand unwed California mothers and compares them to more than two hundred single never pregnant women.

IX. MEDICAL AND PHYSIOLOGICAL CONSEQUENCES

A. Articles

436. Amaro, Hortensia; Zuckerman, Barry; and Howard Cabral. "Drug Use Among Adolescent Mothers: Profile of Risk." PEDIATRICS 84 (July 1989): 144-151.

437. Anzar, Ramon, and Alwyn E. Bennett. "Pregnancy in the Adolescent Girl." AMERICAN JOURNAL OF OBSTETRICS AND GYNECOLOGY 81 (May 1961): 943-940.
    Presents the results of a study of pregnancy in 1,137 adolescent patients of 16 years of age and under who received obstetric care at two hospitals in Cleveland. The young patients exhibited an increase in the incidence of severe toxemia, especially in the girls of 15 years of age and under. Among the young patients there was also a higher percentage of prolonged labors as compared to a control group of adult primiparous patients. The overall conclusion, however, was that pregnancy and delivery of the adolescent girl is reasonably safe.

438. Bailey, L.B.; Mahan, C.S.; and D. Dimperio. "Folacin and Iron Status in Low Income Pregnant Adolescent and Mature Women." AMERICAN JOURNAL OF CLINICAL NUTRITION 33 (September 1980): 1997-2001.
    Reports the findings of a research project which involved measuring the folacin and iron status and hematocrit levels of 269 pregnant low income subjects at the time of their first visit to the prenatal clinic. The study included 70 adolescents (18 or less) and 199 mature women. It was found that within this population, folacin deficiency was much more prevalent than iron deficiency. The serum iron concentration in the adolescent women was significantly higher than that in the older women.

439. Baldwin, Wendy, and Virginia Cain. "The Children of Teenage Parents." FAMILY PLANNING PERSPECTIVES 12 (January/February 1980): 34-43.
    Reviews studies sponsored by the Center for Population Research U.S. Department of Health, Education and Welfare on the effects of adolescent childbearing on the development of the child. Argues that while phenomena such as low-birth weight and perinatal infant mortality have been found to be almost entirely functions of the quality of prenatal care received by the teenage

mother, even an infant born healthy may ultimately suffer from young parental age. The analyses examined indicate deficiencies in the cognitive development of children, especially males, born to adolescents. Many of these effects are the results of the socioeconomic consequences of early childbearing. Less consistent effects are found in the children's social and emotional development and school adjustment. The children born to adolescents are more likely to spend part of their childhood in one parent households and to have children themselves while still adolescents. Family structure may be a mediating factor with detrimental outcomes most likely to occur when the child is raised without the father's presence or without help from the teenager's parents.

440. Battaglia, Frederick C.; Frazier, Todd; and Andre E. Hellegers. "Obstetric and Pediatric Complications of Juvenile Pregnancy." PEDIATRICS 32 (November 1963): 902-910.
    Analyzes data on 636 girls 14 or younger who were obstetrical patients at Johns Hopkins Obstetrical Clinic between 1936 and 1960. Compares the outcomes for this group with all obstetrical patients and to those 15-19. The youngest age group had significantly higher levels of perinatal mortality, toxemia, prematurity and contracted pelvis.

441. Beardslee, William R.; Zuckerman, Barry S.; and Hortensia Amaro. "Depression Among Adolescent Mothers: A Pilot Study." DEVELOPMENTAL AND BEHAVIORAL PEDIATRICS 9 (April 1988): 62-66.

442. Bochner, Kurt. "Pregnancies in Juveniles." AMERICAN JOURNAL OF OBSTETRICS AND GYNECOLOGY 83 (January 1962): 269--271.
    Compares the pregnancies of 272 patients between the ages of 12 and 16 and 658 patients between the ages of 20 and 29. The juvenile patients were similar in most respects to the older patients. The principal differences included increased frequency of toxemia, contracted pelvis and prolonged labor in the adolescent primipara. There were no major differences in terms of spontaneous births, forceps or breech deliveries or caesarean sections. The adolescents who had previously borne children experienced few problems of any kind.

443. Briggs, Richard M.; Herren, Reginald; and William Thompson. "Pregnancy in the Young Adolescent." AMERICAN JOURNAL OF OBSTETRICS AND GYNECOLOGY 84 (August 1982): 436-441.
Examines how young pregnant adolescents compare with older unmarried women under identical environmental and obstetric care conditions. Compared young adolescent mothers (16 or younger) to an older group of mothers who were on the average 25.4 years old. The data examined covered a ten year period. The sample was 90 percent white and 100 percent unmarried. It included 204 women who were 16 or younger and 105 members who were 21 or older. The study confirms the fact that pregnancy in the young adolescent presents no more significant maternal complications than that in the older group. The antepartum care was a significant factor in keeping complication rates down.

444. Carey, William Baldwin; McCann-Sanford, Thurma; and Ezra C. Davidson Jr. "Adolescent Age and Obstetric Risk." SEMINARS IN PERINATOLOGY 5 (January 1981): 9-17.
Discusses the problems associated with giving birth at a very young age. The factors discussed include prematurity, low birth weight, pregnancy induced hypertension, nutrition, psychological dimensions, drug abuse/alcoholism, and sexually transmitted diseases.

445. Coates, John B. "Obstetrics in the Very Young Adolescent." AMERICAN JOURNAL OF OBSTETRICS AND GYNECOLOGY 108 (September 1970): 68-72.
Compares 137 Negro mothers 14 years of age and under to 2,968 primigravidas more than 14 years old in order to establish: (1) if obstetric complications occur more frequently in the very young Negro primigravida; (2) if age alone is a significant predictor of fetal outcome; and (3) what maternal and fetal complications in the study population are associated with other complications. The findings were that several complications occurred more frequently in the younger age group, including acute toxemia, uterine dysfunction, one day fever, and cardiovascular system anomalies. The complications studied which appeared similar in both groups included contracted pelvis, cesarean section, anemia, abnormal presentation, prolonged labor, antepartum and postpartum haemorrhagia, prematurity and perinatal mortality. Complications associated with each other in

the young teenagers included uterine dysfunction with idiopathic bilirubinemia.

446. Committee on Adolescence, American Academy of Pediatrics. "Care of Adolescent Parents and Their Children." PEDIATRICS 83 (January 1989): 138-140.

447. Committee on Adolescence, American Academy of Pediatrics. "Adolescent Pregnancy." PEDIATRICS 83 (January 1989): 132-134.

448. Culp, Rex E.; Appelbaum, Mark I.; Osofsky, Joy D.; and Janet A. Levy. "Adolescent and Older Mothers: Comparison Between Perinatal Maternal Variables and Newborn Interaction Measures." INFANT BEHAVIOR AND DEVELOPMENT 11 (July 1988): 353-362.

449. Darabi, Katherine; Graham, Elizabeth; Namerow, Pearila B.; Philliber, Susan G.; and Phyllis Varga. "The Effect of Maternal Age on the Well-being of Children." JOURNAL OF MARRIAGE AND THE FAMILY (November 1984): 933-936.

Uses data from hospital records and interviews with 282 mothers and their 2.5 to 4 year-old first-born children to examine the effects of maternal age on 21 measures of child well-being and on four composite scales of those measures (neonatal outcome, child health and development, mother-child interaction and nutritious food in the home) while limiting the variation in socioeconomic status and ethnicity. Slightly more than half of the sample was Hispanic, largely Dominican and Puerto Rican, and the remainder was black. There were only two significant differences by age of mother: gestational age and opportunities for stimulation.

450. Dott, Andrew B., and Arthur T. Fort. "Medical and Social Factors Affecting Early Teenage Pregnancy." AMERICAN JOURNAL OF OBSTETRICS AND GYNECOLOGY 125 (June 1976): 532-536.

Compares the outcome of pregnancies in the 414 girls younger than 15 who gave birth in Louisiana in 1972 to those that occurred to all other women. Argues that the poor outcome of early adolescent pregnancies are the result of a combination of medical management, physiological immaturity, poverty, and race.

451. Duenhoelter, Johann H.; Jimenez, Jaun M.; and Gabriele
     Baumann. "Pregnancy Performance of Patients Under 15
     Years of Age." OBSTETRICS AND GYNECOLOGY 46
     (July 1975): 49-52.
     Reports the pregnancy performance of 471 girls under 15 who
     delivered between 1968 and 1972 and compares this performance
     to that of the same number of patients 19-25 using the matched
     pairs method. On the average, the study group experienced
     sexual maturation as measured by age at menarche 18 months
     earlier than the control group. Of the complications studied only
     pregnancy induced hypertension and pelvic inlet contraction
     occurred more frequently in the younger group.

452. Dwyer, John G. "Teenage Pregnancy." AMERICAN
     JOURNAL OF OBSTETRICS AND GYNECOLOGY 118
     (February 1974): 373-376.
     Examines data on 231 pregnant teenagers (12-16) between 1966
     and 1971 in order to determine whether the adolescent obstetric
     patient is more likely to experience complications due to intrinsic
     factors such as physical and emotional immaturity or extrinsic
     factors such as prenatal care and socioeconomic status. No
     significant differences were found between these adolescents when
     they were grouped into those 12-14 and those 15-16. Overall
     these young mothers did not appear to experience higher rates of
     low birth weight and/or premature infants.

453. Elster, Arthur B., and Elizabeth R. McAnarney. "Medical and
     Psychosocial Risks of Pregnancy and Childbearing During
     Adolescence." PEDIATRIC ANNALS 9 (March 1980):
     89-94.
     Reviews the reports of previous research which addresses the
     question of what are the consequences of those 14 years and
     younger bearing children? Concludes that the very young
     adolescent who may not be physiologically mature has a greater
     risk of bearing low-weight babies and having medical
     complications. The very young adolescent is at high risk of having
     a repeat pregnancy, and there appears to be a relationship
     between parity and morbidity. Pregnancy is described as
     interfering with the normal psychosocial development of teens and
     leading to lower education and unsatisfactory occupational
     outcomes. The research reviewed also suggests that the children
     of adolescent mothers may not receive adequate parenting due to
     her immaturity. This less than adequate parenting may well have

negative consequences for the child's cognitive development.
While the available evidence does not support the contention that
adolescent parents are more likely to become child abusers, they
do seem to be at high risk of neglecting the children. Briefly
discusses the problems and stresses experienced by adolescent
fathers. Offers recommendations for further research.

454. Erkan, Kilinc A.; Rimer, Bobby; and Oscar C. Stine. "Juvenile
     Pregnancy Role of Physiologic Maturity." MARYLAND
     STATE MEDICAL JOURNAL 20 (March 1971): 50-52.
     Reviews data from the medical charts of girls 12-15 years old
     and experiencing their first pregnancy to ascertain the relationship
     between physiological maturity (as measured by the time between
     menarche and conception) and pregnancy complications. Finds
     that low birth weight may be more related to physiological
     maturity than to chronological age. The adolescent mother who
     conceives within 24 months of menarche has twice as many low
     birth weight infants as her more physically mature counterpart.
     The differences in preeclampsia rates were not statistically
     significant.

455. Field, Tiffany M.; Widmayer, Susan; Stringer, Sharon; and
     Edward Ignatoff. "Teenage Lower Class Black Mothers and
     Their Preterm Infants: An Intervention and Developmental
     Follow-Up." CHILD DEVELOPMENT 51 (1980): 426-436.
     Investigates the simultaneous contribution of adolescent
     parenting and preterm birth to the delayed development of infants
     by studying five groups of 150 lower class black women and their
     children. Also attempts to evaluate an early intervention strategy.
     Finds that having both the reproductive risk of being premature
     and the caretaking risk of having an adolescent mother put the
     infant at higher risk of developmental delay than either of the
     factors alone. Found that the intervention strategy had both
     benefits and costs. The preterm infants of adolescent mothers
     who received the intervention, for example, had greater gains in
     weight and length, lower blood pressures, and higher scores on a
     mental test than their control counterparts. The mothers in the
     intervention group, however, had higher blood pressures than
     their counterparts in the control group, which may have been
     indicative of the anxiety produced by the intervention.

456. Frisancho, A. Roberto; Matos, Jorge; and Pam Flegel. "Mat-
     ernal Nutritional Status and Adolescent Pregnancy Outcome."

AMERICAN JOURNAL OF CLINICAL NUTRITION 38
(November 1983): 739-746.

Uses data on 1,256 adolescent mothers who received obstetric
services at the Maternal Hospital of Lima, Peru, to investigate
the factors influencing the birth weight of their children. The
findings indicate that neither the physiological immaturity of the
young mother nor prematurity in terms of short gestation are the
primary determinant of low birth weight among children born to
adolescent mothers. The findings do support the hypothesis that
among teenagers who are still in rapid growth the nutritional
requirements for pregnancy are greater than they are among adult
women. The implications are that adolescent women who are
pregnant may need increased nutrition in order to both sustain
their own growth and supply the needs of the fetus. The ideal
amount of weight which should be gained during a pregnancy
then appears to be greater for adolescents than for adult women.

457. Frisancho, A. Roberto; Matos, Jorge; and Laura A. Bollettino.
"Influence of Growth Status and Placental Function on Birth
Weight of Infants Born to Still-Growing Teenagers."
AMERICAN JOURNAL OF CLINICAL NUTRITION 40
(October 1984): 801-807.

Uses maternal height as the criterion by which 412 adolescent
mothers, 13-15, who received obstetrical services from the
Maternal Hospital of Lima Peru were divided into those who
were still growing and those who were not. The findings indicate
that among young adolescents prenatal growth is influenced by
differences in maternal growth status so that those adolescents
who have completed their expected growth have larger newborns
than those who are still growing. It is unclear whether this results
from the fact that the still growing adolescent is competing with
the fetus for nutrition or that the immature female is simply not
able to deliver the needed nutrients to the unborn child.

458. Garn, Stanley M. and Audrey S. Petzoldt. "Characteristics of
the Mother and Child in Teenage Pregnancy." AMERICAN
JOURNAL OF DISEASES OF CHILDREN 137 (April
1983): 365-368.

Addresses whether low birth weight and other unwanted
outcomes of adolescent pregnancies result from low maternal age,
low maternal weight or physiological immaturity using data on
more than 14,000 teenage pregnancies. Argues that some of the
negative outcomes from adolescent pregnancies are the result of

the smaller size of teenagers rather than simply their younger age or developmental immaturity. Also points out that while adolescents do tend to have babies with lower birth weights that the scores on the five minute Apgar and the eight-month Bayley indicate that teenage pregnancies are not biological disasters.

459. Garn, Stanley M.; LaVelle, Marquisa; Pesick, Shelly D.; and Stephen A. Ridella. "Are Pregnant Teenagers Still in Rapid Growth?" AMERICAN JOURNAL OF DISEASES OF CHILDREN 138 (January 1984): 32-34.

Addresses the question of whether adolescent mothers, especially the youngest of them, are still in a period of rapid growth while they are pregnant using longitudinal analysis of 1,601 teenage girls, followed up through two or three pregnancies. The findings provided no evidence that the larger pregnancy weight gains observed in younger adolescent mothers were attributable to rapid growth. These data were congruent with the time elapsed between menarche and the first pregnancy and failed to support popular explanations for the higher weight gains in pregnancy. Argues that a more likely explanation of the high weight gain in younger adolescent mothers is fluid retention and fluid volume rather than additional body mass.

460. Graham, David. "The Obstetric and Neonatal Consequences of Adolescent Pregnancy." BIRTH DEFECTS 17 (1981): 49-67.

Compares the obstetric experience of 745 adolescent and more than 2,000 older mothers during 1979 at The Johns Hopkins Hospital. Presents a review of the recent literature on adolescent pregnancy.

461. Grazi, Richard; Redheendran, Ramakreshan; Mudaliar, Nirmala; and Robin M. Bannerman. "Offspring of Teenage Mothers." JOURNAL OF REPRODUCTIVE MEDICINE 2 (1982): 89-96.

Examines the records of 925 infants born to adolescent mothers at the Buffalo Children's Hospital between 1976 and 1978 to determine whether there is an excess of chromosomal abnormalities in the infants of adolescent mothers and to provide information on the incidence of nonchromosomal congenital anomalies. When compared to a published control population teenage mothers were found to have a significantly higher frequency of congenitally malformed infants. Mothers 17 and under had higher rates of low birth weight and perinatal death.

No chromosomal anomalies were found among the infants in this population.

462. Hoff, Charles; Wertelecki, Wladimir; Zansky, Shelley; Reyes, Elena; Dutt, James; and Alfred Stumpe. "Earlier Maturation of Pregnant Black and White Adolescents." AMERICAN JOURNAL OF DISEASES OF CHILDREN 139 (October 1985): 981-986.
Reports on a survey which was made of the menarcheal age and anthropometry of 1,844 lower income, nulliparous female patients receiving prenatal care in Mobile, Alabama. No differences were found between black and white patients in height and maximum pregnant weight. Younger adolescents (12 to 14) of both races were taller and heavier before their pregnancies than National Center for Health Statistics standards and had a significantly greater weight for height. Body habitus and menarcheal age were congruent with reports that younger adolescents who are pregnant tend to have matured earlier than older pregnant adolescents and adults. Compared with their age group in the Collaborative Perinatal Study of the National Institute of Neurological Communicative Disorders and Stroke, the patients were larger and had larger weight gains during pregnancy. These findings may reflect the improvements in social assistance and prenatal care available to lower income women over the two decades between the studies.

463. Horon, Isabelle L.; Strobino, Donna M.; and Hugh M. MacDonald. "Birth Weights Among Infants Born to Adolescent and Young Adult Women." AMERICAN JOURNAL OF OBSTETRICS AND GYNECOLOGY 146 (June 1983): 444-449.
Investigates the relationship between maternal age and birth weight using a sample of 422 primigravid patients 15 and younger and a control group of the same size composed of women between 20 and 24. The most important finding was that when race and gravidity were controlled there was no significant difference in the weights of children born to older and younger mothers, even though the adolescents tended to have shorter gestations. There were some differences between the two groups. The older mothers were less likely to be clinic patients, more likely to be married, and more likely to live in more affluent neighborhoods. The younger mothers tended to begin prenatal

care later in their pregnancies, were shorter, and had lower pregnancy weights.

464. Israel, S. Leon, and Theodore B. Woutersz. "Teenage Obstetrics." AMERICAN JOURNAL OF OBSTETRICS AND GYNECOLOGY 85 (March 1963): 659-668.
Analyzes data on 3,995 adolescent pregnancies that occurred in 1958 in 10 hospitals and compares them to the 36,714 births to women over 20 occurring in the same hospitals. There were no differences between the older and younger patients in terms of fetal, neonatal or perinatal mortality. There were also no differences between the two groups in the rates of abnormal presentation, transfusions, lacerations, hemorrhage, intercurrent disease or dystocia. The adolescent mothers were delivered by cesarean section less often than the older mothers. The problems which occurred more often in the younger mothers were pre-eclampsia, anemia, one day fever, puerperal morbidity and labors lasting more than 20 hours. Points out that blacks have more obstetric complications than whites.

465. Lawrence, Ruth, and T. Allen Merritt. "Infants of Adolescent Mothers: Perinatal, Neonatal and Infancy Outcomes." SEMINARS IN PERINATOLOGY 5 (January 1981): 19-32.
Reviews data from various sources to address the nature of the relationship between adolescent pregnancy and medical risk. Concludes that when race and socioeconomic status are controlled age is not a crucial factor unless the mother is 14 or younger. Points out that the mothering skills and child rearing practices of adolescent mothers have yet to be adequately evaluated.

466. Lieberman, Ellice; Ryan, Kenneth J.; Monson, Richard R.; and Stephen C. Schoenbaum. "Risk Factors Accounting for Racial Differences in the Rate of Premature Birth." THE NEW ENGLAND JOURNAL OF MEDICINE 317 (September 1987): 317-743.
Utilized data on 8,903 women in a hospital based cohort to examine the higher rate of prematurity in black women. Found that among the medical factors studied only the maternal hematocrit explained a substantial amount of the variation in prematurity. Four social factors were also examined: being younger than 20, unmarried, welfare dependent, and not being a high school graduate. The number of these social factors which characterized a woman was highly predictive of prematurity.

When all four factors were considered simultaneously race was no longer a factor in prematurity.

467. Lobl, Michele; Welcher, Doris; and E. David Mellits.
"Maternal Age and Intellectual Functioning of Offspring."
JOHNS HOPKINS MEDICAL JOURNAL 128 (June 1971):
347- 361.
Utilizes data on 3,263 obstetrical patients to examine the nature of the relationship between maternal age at birth and intellectual functioning of the child at age four. Found that the children of mothers younger than 15 and the first born children of women 35 and over were at high risk. Black children were found to score significantly lower on the measure of intelligence than white children. Among whites there was no significant difference by gender, but among blacks, females scored significantly higher than males. These differences were influenced by maternal age.

468. Makinson, Carolyn. "The Health Consequences of Teenage Fertility." FAMILY PLANNING PERSPECTIVES 17 (May/June 1985): 132-139.
Reviews the literature concerned with the consequences of adolescent pregnancy and birth for the mother and the child in the United States, Canada, Britain, France and Sweden. Points out that most of the research indicates that many of the negative outcomes associated with adolescent pregnancy are not directly attributable to young adolescent age but rather are social and economic in origin.

469. Mangold, William D. "Age of Mother and Pregnancy Outcome in the 1981 Arkansas Birth Cohort." SOCIAL BIOLOGY 30 (Summer 1983): 205-210.
Examines the relationship between age of the mother and pregnancy outcome in 11,810 nulliparous women who gave birth in 1978 in Arkansas. Data from the linked birth and death records indicate that when socioeconomic status and access to medical care are controlled there is no significant relationship between age of mother and infant mortality or birth weight.

470. McAnarney, Elizabeth R. "Young Maternal Age and Adverse Neonatal Outcomes." AMERICAN JOURNAL OF THE DISEASES OF CHILDREN 141 (October 1987): 1053-1059.

471. McAnarney, Elizabeth R., and Henry A. Thiede. "Adolescent
     Pregnancy and Childbearing: What We Have Learned in a
     Decade of Study and What Remains to be Learned."
     SEMINARS IN PERINATOLOGY 5 (January 1981): 91-103.
     Reviews the literature concerned with both the medical and
     physiological consequences of adolescent pregnancy and parenting
     and that which is concerned with psychosocial outcomes. Also
     describes comprehensive programs which have been designed to
     cope with these problems. In terms of health outcomes it is
     reported that adolescent mothers, even those less than 15 years
     of age are not at greater obstetrical risk when race,
     socioeconomic status, and legitimacy status are taken into
     account. In fact, the newer data suggest that medically the best
     time for a woman to bear a child is between 16 and 19 years of
     age.

472. McCormick, Marie C.; Shapiro, Sam; and Barbara Starfield.
     "High Risk Young Mothers: Infant Mortality and Morbidity in
     Four Areas in the United States, 1973-1978." AMERICAN
     JOURNAL OF PUBLIC HEALTH 74 (January 1984): 18-23.
     Employs data from four regions of the country to assess changes
     in the infant mortality and morbidity rates for adolescent mothers
     between 1973 and 1978. Finds that the infants of two groups of
     mothers, 18-19 year old multiparas and those 17 or younger, are
     at high risk of experiencing health problems. The infants of
     young mothers, largely because of their low birth weights, are at
     high risk of unfavorable outcomes during the neonatal period.
     Even when birth weight is controlled, these infants continue to
     experience health problems into the postnatal period largely
     because their mothers are poor and not well versed in the
     requirements of parenthood.

473. Mednick, Birgitte R.; Baker, Robert L.; and Brian Sutton-Smith.
     "Teenage Pregnancy and Perinatal Mortality." JOURNAL
     OF YOUTH AND ADOLESCENCE 8 (September 1979):
     343-357.
     Sets out to explain why the results of two large scale university
     hospital studies show that adolescents have lower rates of
     perinatal mortality than women in their twenties while studies of
     the general population show the reverse. Finds that the university
     hospitals provide a high quality of care to all patients, while the
     medical care received by adolescents in the general population is,
     because of their poverty, uneven in quality. This difference in the

quality of care given in the divergent situations is seen as being responsible for the differences in results.

474. Menken, Jane. "The Health and Social Consequences of Teenage Childbearing." FAMILY PLANNING PERSPECTIVES 4 (July 1972): 45-53.
    Focuses on the medical aspects of adolescent childbearing using data from the National Natality Survey and the National Infant Mortality Study. Found that mothers under 15 and their infants are at higher risk in all categories. Lists various medical and social consequences of early motherhood, all of which are seen to be negative.

475. Miller, Michael E., and C. Shannon Stokes. "Teenage Fertility, Socioeconomic Status and Infant Mortality." JOURNAL OF BIOSOCIAL SCIENCE 17 (April 1985): 147-155.
    Examines the relationship between socioeconomic status and infant mortality and the role played by adolescent fertility using data from counties within the United States covering the five year period 1971-1975. Found that there continues to be an inverse relationship between the socioeconomic status of areal populations and their rate of infant mortality. Also found that adolescent births are a mediating link between socioeconomic status and neonatal but not postneonatal mortality. Argues that the usual division of infant mortality into the neonatal and postneonatal periods may be too unrefined to actually measure the effects of the socioenvironmental context in contemporary American society.

476. Naeye, Richard L. "Teenaged and Pre-Teenaged Pregnancies: Consequences of the Fetal Maternal Competition for Nutrients." PEDIATRICS 67 (January 1981): 146-150.
    Analyzes data on 13,830 black mothers and their infants in order to determine if the negative obstetric risk associated with pregnancy outcome in the young adolescent results from a competition between the growing adolescent and the fetus for nutrition. Found that the fetuses of 10-16 year old mothers grow more slowly than those of older mothers suggesting that there is competition for nutrition. The children of young mothers were found to make up for this growth difference by age seven. However, the most significant result of the nutritional competition may be fetal or neonatal deaths. Suggests that those who argue

that pregnant adolescents have higher optimal weight gains than older mothers may in fact be on the right track.

477. Newman, John F., and William L. Graves. "Neonatal Mortality and Socioeconomic Status in a Metropolitan County." SOCIOLOGICAL SYMPOSIUM 8 (Spring 1972): 37-49. Examined the nature of the relationship between four variables (mother's age, parity, socioeconomic status, race) and neonatal mortality using data from a large metropolitan county in the South. All four of the independent variables were found to be correlated with neonatal mortality at the zero-order level. However, none were significantly related when each of the others was controlled. Age and parity combinations were found to be critical. The moderate to high risk groups were: (1) all ages at parity three and beyond; (2) women under twenty at all parities; and (3) mothers over 30 at parity 0.

478. Norr, Kathleen F.; Roberts, Joyce E.; and Uwe Freese. "Early Postpartum Rooming in and the Maternal Attachment Behavior in a Group of Medically Indigent Primiparas." JOURNAL OF NURSE MIDWIFERY 34 (March/April 1989): 85-91.

479. Roosa, Mark W. "Maternal Age, Social Class, and the Obstetric Performance of Teenagers." JOURNAL OF YOUTH AND ADOLESCENCE 13 (August 1984): 365-374. Examines the interaction of maternal age, social class, and obstetric and neonatal outcome using data from lower and middle-income adolescents (15-19) and lower and middle-income women (20-30) all of whom were first time mothers. Rather than the frequently reported influence of mother's age what was found was a "complex" interaction between maternal age and social class which "suggested" that the most "at risk" group was older low income mothers, while the group at least risk was the middle income adolescent. Suggests that to assess the risk of negative obstetric and neonatal outcome on the basis of age or class alone is much too simplistic to be very useful.

480. Roosa, Mark W.; Fitzgerald, Hiram E.; and Nancy A. Carlson. "Comparison of Teenage and Older Mothers: A Systems Analysis." JOURNAL OF MARRIAGE AND THE FAMILY 44 (May 1982): 367-377.

Presents a model for examining the relationship between maternal age and the development of the child using data on 62 mothers and their children. Finds that socioeconomic status has the most widespread and powerful influence upon the predictors of infant development. When socioeconomic status is controlled young mothers and their children were weighted higher on predictors of infant mortality than older mothers and their children.

481. Rothenberg, Perila B., and Phyllis E. Varga. "The Relationship Between Age of Mother and Child Health and Development." AMERICAN JOURNAL OF PUBLIC HEALTH 71 (August 1981): 810-817.

Employs data on 282 Black and Hispanic mothers who gave birth to their first child in a New York City Hospital in 1975 to investigate the nature of the relationship between maternal age and children's health and development at birth and at age three. Found no difference between the children of teenage and older mothers in terms of either prematurity or low birth weight. Perhaps surprisingly, even when other variables were controlled, the children of adolescent mothers received higher Apgar scores than those of older mothers. Even at age three the children of adolescent mothers were not characterized by more negative health outcomes or lower cognitive development. All of the children in the study were seen to be at high risk due primarily to low socioeconomic status.

482. Smith, Peggy; Weinman, Maxine; and L. Russell Malinak. "Adolescent Mothers and Fetal Loss, What Experience." PSYCHOLOGICAL REPORTS 45 (1984): 775-778.

Attempts to verify the existence of a higher rate of neonatal loss in multiparous adolescents and to examine the behavioral and medical outcomes associated with adolescent pregnancy by comparing the medical records of 73 gravida I and 93 gravida III patients between 13 and 19 years of age. There were no significant differences between the two groups in terms of infant birth weights, Apgar scores or premature births. However, when fetal loss was considered only 45 percent of the gravida III women had all three children living while 95 percent of the first time mothers had a living child. The first time mothers were also more likely to have received prenatal care and less likely to have problems with their babies. Argues that the data indicate that gravida III mothers are at greater risk of fetal death, that their earlier experiences may not have taught them the value of prenatal care and that their subsequent contraceptive failures may be related to the fact that when discharged from the hospital it may be without their first choice of a contraceptive method.

483. Stevens-Simon, Catherine, and Elizabeth R. McAnarney. "Adolescent Maternal Weight Gain and Low Birth Weight: A Multifactional Model." AMERICAN JOURNAL OF CLINICAL NUTRITION 47 (1988): 948-953.
Summarizes the literature concerned with the relationship between adolescent maternal weight gain and infant birth weight. Argues that the recommendation that adolescents should have larger weight gains during pregnancy may be premature. Argues for the importance of using a multifactorial model in reformulating weight gain guidelines for pregnant adolescents. Other factors considered to be important are: incomplete maternal growth, reproductive immaturity, diminished maternal size, nutritional deficiencies, socioeconomic and behavioral factors, and maternal emotional stress.

484. Sweeney, Patrick J. "A Comparison of Low Birth Weights, Perinatal and Infant Mortality Between First and Second Births to Women 17 Years Old and Younger." AMERICAN JOURNAL OF OBSTETRICS AND GYNECOLOGY 160 (June 1989): 1361-1367.

485. Swenson, Ingrid; Erickson, Deanne; Ehlinger, Edward; Swaney, Sheldon; and Gertrude Carlson. "Birth Weight, Apgar Scores, Labor and Delivery Complications and Prenatal Characteristics of Southeast Asian Adolescent and Older Mothers." ADOLESCENCE 21 (Fall 1986): 711-722.
Compares selected maternal characteristics and pregnancy outcomes of Hmong and other Southeast Asian refugees, Caucasian and black adolescents. The Southeast Asians had relatively favorable pregnancy outcomes in spite of significantly later entry into prenatal care, lower weight gains and hematocrit levels. Argues that the almost complete absence of smoking and alcohol use in the Asian populations may contribute to these favorable outcomes. Finds the level of smoking in the white mothers high enough to suggest specific intervention.

486. Thompson, Robert J.; Cappleman, Mary W.; and Kathleen A. A. Zeitschel. "Neonatal Behavior of Infants of Adolescent

Mothers." DEVELOPMENTAL MEDICINE AND CHILD NEUROLOGY 21 (1979): 474-482.

Describes the results of administering the Brazleton Neonatal Assessment Scale to 60 infants between two and five days after birth. Half of the infants had mothers under 18 and they were rated less able to respond to social stimuli, less alert, less capable of controlling motor behavior and of performing integrated motor activities. Argues that the interaction of these characteristics of the newborn with the young mother's inadequate capacity to parent may lead to problems which could be the focus of programs designed to provide stimulation to such infants.

487. Wicklund, Kristine; Moss, Sheila; and Floyd Frost. "Effects of Maternal Education, Age, and Parity on Fatal Infant Accidents." AMERICAN JOURNAL OF PUBLIC HEALTH 74 (October 1984): 1150-1152.

Analyzes data drawn from linked birth and death certificates in North Carolina and Washington from 1968 to 1980 to examine the maternal characteristics which are correlates of fatal infant accidents. Finds that both maternal age and education are inversely related to fatal infant accidents while parity is positively related.

488. Zackler, Jack; Andelman, Samuel L.; and Frank Bauer. "The Young Adolescent as an Obstetric Risk." AMERICAN JOURNAL OF OBSTETRICS AND GYNECOLOGY 103 (February 1969): 305-312.

Compares 2,403 pregnancies in patients 15 and younger who were treated in a special program by the Chicago Board of Health Clinics (CBH) and 4,400 patients treated elsewhere between January 1, 1965 and June 30, 1967. The goal of the study was to determine whether the care provided to the young patients by CBH was effective in meeting the needs of the young mothers. Detailed comparisons were made between Negro mothers in both groups. Hebdomadal and neonatal mortality rates as well as prematurity rates were higher in those not receiving care from CBH. There was no difference in the rate of toxemia. It was concluded that the young mothers who receive care from CBH were not at high obstetric risk.

489. Zuckerman, Barry; Alpert, Joel J.; Dooling, Elizabeth; Hingson, Ralph; Kayne, Herbert; Morelock, Suzette; and Edgar

Oppenheimer. "Neonatal Outcome: Is Adolescent Pregnancy a Risk Factor?" PEDIATRICS 71 (April 1983): 489-493.
Uses data from hospital records on 275 adolescent mother-infant pairs and 423 non-adolescent mother-infant pairs to explore whether infants born to adolescents have poorer birth outcomes and if so, what other factors besides being an adolescent are predictive of those outcomes. The findings support the hypothesis that for primiparous women, factors other than young age (16 years or less) are associated with low birth weight and other negative neonatal outcomes.

B. Chapters in Books

490. Barnett, Alva P. "Sociocultural Influences on Adolescent Mothers." BLACK FAMILY: ESSAYS AND STUDIES. Edited by Robert Staples. Belmont, CA: Wadsworth, 1987, pp. 154-163.

491. Broman, Sarah H. "Longterm Development of Children Born to Teenagers." TEENAGE PARENTS AND THEIR OFFSPRING. Edited by Keith G. Scott, Tiffany Field, and Euan G. Robertson. New York: Grune and Stratton, 1981, pp. 195-226.
Uses data from the Collaborative Perinatal Project of the National Institute of Neurological Disorders and Stroke to identify risks to mother and child associated with adolescent pregnancy. Concludes that for most of the characteristics examined the differences by age were smaller than those in terms of ethnicity and socioeconomic characteristics. Prenatal care appears to offset any biological deficits, and environmental deficits in early childhood can be offset by intervention strategies.

492. Carey, William Baldwin; McCann-Sanford, Thurma; and Ezra C. Davidson, Jr. "Adolescent Age and Obstetric Risk." PREMATURE ADOLESCENT PREGNANCY AND PARENTHOOD. Edited by Elizabeth McAnarney. New York: Grune and Stratton, 1983, pp. 109-118.
Discusses the common complications of adolescent pregnancy and childbirth and stresses the need for care during pregnancy.

493. Cooper, Elizabeth. "Prenatal Care for the Pregnant
     Adolescent." PREGNANCY IN ADOLESCENCE: NEEDS,
     PROBLEMS, AND MANAGEMENT. Edited by Irving R.
     Stuart and Carl F. Wells. New York: Van Nostrand Reinhold
     Company, 1982, pp. 66-79.
     Discusses the most common complications of adolescent
     pregnancy and emphasizes the importance of prenatal care based
     on a multidisciplinary model implemented by a multidisciplinary
     team.

494. Field, Tiffany. "Early Development of the Preterm Offspring of
     Teenage Mothers." TEENAGE PARENTS AND THEIR
     OFFSPRING. Edited by Keith G. Scott, Tiffany Field, and
     Euan G. Robertson. New York: Grune and Stratton, 1981,
     pp. 145-176.
     Employs data on 150 experimental and control infants to assess
     the effect of prematurity and adolescent mothering on the early
     development of infants and to test an intervention.

495. Garn, Stanley M.; Pesick, Shelly D.; and Audrey S. Petzoldt.
     "The Biology of Teenage Pregnancy: The Mother and the
     Child." SCHOOL-AGE PREGNANCY: BIOSOCIAL
     DIMENSIONS. Edited by Jane B. Lancaster and Beatrix A.
     Hamburg. New York: Aldine De Gruyter, 1986, pp. 77-93.

496. Handwerker, Lisa B., and Christopher H. Hodgman.
     "Approach to Adolescents by the Perinatal Staff."
     PREMATURE ADOLESCENT PREGNANCY AND
     PARENTHOOD. Edited by Elizabeth McAnarney. New
     York: Grune and Stratton, 1983, pp. 311-328.
     Argues that perinatal care will be most effective and rewarding
     when the staff understands the nature of adolescent development,
     their own biases and attitudes toward adolescents, and how to
     communicate with them.

497. Hardy, Janet B. and E. David Mellits. "Relationship of Low
     Birth Weight to Maternal Characteristics of Age, Parity,
     Education and Body Size." THE EPIDEMIOLOGY OF
     PREMATURITY. Edited by Dwayne M. Reed and Fiona J.
     Stanley. Baltimore: Urban and Schwarzenberg, 1977, pp. 105-
     117.

498. Hollingsworth, Dorothy R.; Kotchen, Jane Morley; and
     Marianne E. Felice. "Impact of Gynecological Age on
     Outcome of Adolescent Pregnancy." PREMATURE
     ADOLESCENT PREGNANCY AND PARENTHOOD.
     Edited by Elizabeth McAnarney. New York: Grune and
     Stratton, 1983, pp. 169-190.
     Reviews the literature and presents data from the University of
     Kentucky Young Mother's Program to arrive at the conclusion
     that it is economic deprivation rather than maternal age which is
     responsible for the risks faced by the infants of adolescent
     mothers.

499. Jacobson, Marc. S., and Felix P. Heald. "Nutritional Risks of
     Adolescent Pregnancy and Their Management."
     PREMATURE ADOLESCENT PREGNANCY AND
     PARENTHOOD. Edited by Elizabeth McAnarney. New
     York: Grune and Stratton, 1983, pp. 119-136.
     Synthesizes what is known or inferred about prenatal nutritional
     needs and care in adolescent pregnancy.

500. Kafatos, Anthony G.; Christakis, George; and Marianna
     Fordyce. ""Nutrition and Early Teenage Pregnancy."
     TEENAGE PARENTS AND THEIR OFFSPRING. Edited
     by Keith G. Scott, Tiffany Field, and Euan G. Robertson.
     New York: Grune and Stratton, 1981, pp. 103-130.
     Reviews the literature concerned with nutrition and adolescent
     pregnancy outcomes and concludes that there is a relationship
     between the nutritional status of the pregnant adolescent, the
     weight of the newborn, perinatal and infant mortality, and
     maternal morbidity and mortality. The risks appear to be greater
     when the adolescent is still physically immature, that is when the
     pregnancy occurs close to the age of menarche or during the
     adolescent growth spurt. Those of low socioeconomic status, who
     are more likely to be malnourished, are at higher risk.

501. King, Janet, and Howard N. Jacobson. "Nutrition and
     Pregnancy in Adolescence." THE TEENAGE PREGNANT
     GIRL. Edited by Jack Zackler and Wayne Brandstadt.
     Springfield, Illinois: Charles C. Thomas, 1975, pp. 134-160.
     Points out the disjuncture between the dietary habits of
     adolescents and their nutritional needs which is increased by the
     requirements of pregnancy.

502. Lawrence, Ruth A., and T. Allen Merritt. "Infants of
     Adolescent Mothers: Perinatal, Neonatal, and Infancy
     Outcome." PREMATURE ADOLESCENT PREGNANCY
     AND PARENTHOOD. Edited by Elizabeth McAnarney.
     New York: Grune and Stratton, 1983, pp. 149-168.
     Reviews what is known about the outcomes for the infants of
     adolescent mothers. Concludes that when the role of race and
     socioeconomic status are taken into account age is not the critical
     factor unless the mother is 14 years of age and younger.

503. Menken, Jane. "The Health and Demographic Consequences of
     Adolescent Pregnancy and Childbearing." ADOLESCENT
     PREGNANCY AND CHILDBEARING: FINDINGS FROM
     RESEARCH. Edited by Catherine S. Chilman. U. S.
     Department of Health and Human Services, 1980, pp. 177-
     206.
     Summarizes trends in adolescent pregnancy, birth and abortion
     rates and what is known about the health outcomes of adolescent
     pregnancy and childbearing for both mother and child.

504. Monkus, Ellen, and Eduardo, Bancalari. "Neonatal Outcome."
     TEENAGE PARENTS AND THEIR OFFSPRING. Edited
     by Keith G. Scott, Tiffany Field, and Euan G. Robertson.
     New York: Grune and Stratton, 1981, pp. 131-144.
     Reviews studies concerned with the neonatal outcome of
     adolescent pregnancies and concludes that due to methodological
     problems it is very difficult to reach valid generalizations.
     Recommends that future studies be prospective rather than
     retrospective and that they use the newer neonatal technologies
     for determining gestational age.

505. Reedy, Nancy Jo. "Birth Alternatives for Adolescents."
     PREMATURE ADOLESCENT PREGNANCY AND
     PARENTHOOD. Edited by Elizabeth McAnarney. New
     York: Grune and Stratton, 1983, pp. 329-350.
     Describes what must be known about the alternatives to
     traditional hospital delivery room births and adolescent pregnancy
     in order to successfully combine the two.

506. Robertson, Euan Gordon. "Adolescence, Physiological Maturity
     and Obstetric Outcome." TEENAGE PARENTS AND
     THEIR OFFSPRING. Edited by Keith G. Scott, Tiffany

Field, and Euan G. Robertson. New York: Grune and
Stratton, 1981, pp. 91-102.
Reviews the literature concerned with the obstetric outcome of
adolescent pregnancies and concludes that when adequate
prenatal care is received the outcomes, in a physical way, can be
satisfactory.

507. Sacker, Ira M., and Sol D. Neuhoff. "Medical and Psychosocial
Risk Factors in the Pregnant Adolescent." PREGNANCY IN
ADOLESCENCE: NEEDS, PROBLEMS, AND
MANAGEMENT. Edited by Irving R. Stuart and Carl F.
Wells. New York: Van Nostrand Reinhold Company, 1982,
pp. 107-139.
Describes prematurity and toxemia as the major medical risk
factors in adolescent pregnancy. In terms of psychosocial
consequences mentions reduced income and education, repeat
pregnancies, child abuse and family instability.

508. Safro, Ivor L. "Adolescent Sexuality, Pregnancy and
Childbearing." ADOLESCENT PREGNANCY:
PERSPECTIVES FOR THE HEALTH CARE
PROFESSIONAL. Edited by Peggy B. Smith and David M.
Mumford. Boston: G.K. Hall, 1980, pp. 32-48.
Discusses the most common medical problems experienced by
pregnant adolescents, the nutritional needs of the pregnant
teenager and how these should be managed during the prenatal
period.

509. Sandler, Howard M.; Vietze, Peter M.; and Susan O'Connor.
"Obstetric and Neonatal Outcomes Following Intervention
with Pregnant Teenagers." TEENAGE PARENTS AND
THEIR OFFSPRING. Edited by Keith G. Scott, Tiffany
Field, and Euan G. Robertson. New York: Grune and
Stratton, 1981, pp. 249-264.
Uses data from the Nashville Comprehensive Child Care
Project. Argues that the provision of comprehensive health care
to pregnant adolescents may be able to eliminate the negative
repercussions in a number of areas. Also concludes that while
the child rearing attitudes and behaviors observed in the indigent
population studied may not be ideal, the infants of adolescent
mothers in this group are no worse off than the infants of older
mothers.

510. Selstad, Georgiana. "The Community Health Nurse and the
     Adolescent Family." THE TEENAGE PREGNANT GIRL.
     Edited by Jack Zackler and Wayne Brandstadt. Springfield,
     Illinois: Charles C. Thomas, 1975, pp. 187-202.
     Describes the role that any community nurse can play in school,
     clinic or community programs for adolescent families.

511. Stepto, Robert C.; Keith, Louis; and Donald Keith. "Obstetrical
     and Medical Problems of Teenage Pregnancy." THE
     TEENAGE PREGNANT GIRL. Edited by Jack Zackler
     and Wayne Brandstadt. Springfield, Illinois: Charles C.
     Thomas, 1975, pp. 83-133.
     Presents an over view of the physical and medical outcomes of
     pregnancy during adolescence and offers some guidelines for
     management.

     C. Books

512. Field, Tiffany, and Anita Sostek. INFANTS BORN AT RISK:
     PHYSIOLOGICAL, PERCEPTUAL, AND COGNITIVE
     PROCESSES. New York: Grune and Stratton, 1983.
     Presents research papers which explore the physiological,
     perceptual and cognitive processes that underlie the behavior and
     development of infants born at risk (defined arbitrarily as those
     who suffered perinatal medical complications that might
     contribute to later developmental delays or deficits). Among the
     conditions studied are anoxia, low birth weight, prematurity,
     respiratory distress syndrome, bronchopulmonary dysplasia, and
     Down's syndrome. The chapters are divided into three sections:
     the neonatal period, the infancy stage, and then childhood follow-
     up.

513. Scott, Keith G.; Field, Tiffany; and Euan G. Robertson.
     TEENAGE PARENTS AND THEIR OFFSPRING. New
     York: Grune and Stratton, 1981.
     Contains chapters which focus on the outcomes of adolescent
     pregnancy for the young mother and her child. Contains items
     019, 274, 276, 393, 413, 491, 494, 500, 504, 506, 509, 658, 659, 660,
     664, 668, and 694.

514. Smith, Peggy B., and David M. Mumford. ADOLESCENT
     PREGNANCY: PERSPECTIVES FOR THE HEALTH
     CARE PROFESSIONAL. Boston: G.K. Hall.
     Contains items 088, 092, 299, 401, 508, 644, 649, and 695.

X. ADOLESCENT FATHERS

A. Articles

515. Adams, Gina, and Karen Pittman. ADOLESCENT AND YOUNG ADULT FATHERS: PROBLEMS AND SOLUTIONS. Washington, D.C.: Children's Defense Fund's Adolescent Pregnancy Prevention Clearing House (May 1988).
Points out that the realities of life for young fathers are much more complex than the stereotype which sees them as uncaring victimizers of young women. Data are available to at least partially answer three frequently raised questions about young fathers: (1) how old are the fathers of the children of adolescent mothers; (2) what is known about young fathers' willingness to accept responsibility for their children; and (3) what factors seem to influence the support provided by young fathers? Two additional questions are also raised. What should be done for young fathers and what should be done for young families that, even with the father present or providing support, are still without sufficient income?

516. Applegate, Jeffrey S. "Adolescent Fatherhood: Developmental Perils and Potential." CHILD AND ADOLESCENT SOCIAL WORK 5 (Fall 1988): 205-217.
Employs a psychodynamic conceptual framework to illustrate some of the singular developmental difficulties associated with adolescent fatherhood. The formulations are designed to help clinicians in designing interventions to assist young men going through this period of "double jeopardy."

517. Barret, Robert L., and Bryan E. Robinson. "Teenage Fathers: Neglected Too Long." SOCIAL WORK 27 (November 1982): 484-488.
Offers a review of the limited, and often methodologically flawed, literature on teenage fathers. Points out that it is incorrect to assume that adolescent fathers wish to detach themselves from their female partner and totally abandon their child. Also gives recommendations on how services to unwed adolescent parents of both sexes can be improved by taking the young fathers into account.

518. Connolly, Lisa. "Boy Fathers." HUMAN BEHAVIOR 7 (January 1978): 40-43.

Argues that the reason the unwed natural teenage father is ignored and not offered supportive services is because he is blamed for creating the situation. Points out that while it is often assumed that the teen father isn't concerned, in actuality he is often forbidden to see the female he has impregnated. The adolescent father's right to equal protection was ratified in 1972 by the Supreme Court in the case of *Stanley vs. Illinois*. Reviews a 1971 book which is based on research conducted in Los Angeles with middle class Jewish teens, and a study of low income youth in Philadelphia. The findings of both studies are seen as similar in that they appear to refute the notion that the young father doesn't care. The young men in these studies were willing to go to counseling and wanted to be supportive of their girlfriends. Suggests that more programs should be established to offer counseling to these young men.

519. Cutright, Phillips. "Increasing Paternal Responsibility."
     FAMILY PLANNING PERSPECTIVES 17 (July/August):
     176-179.
     Argues that the rapid growth in the numbers of unsupported unwed mothers and their children since 1960 requires some innovative way of making fathers financially responsible for the children they produce out of wedlock. Further argues that paternity should be systematically determined at the time of birth and then an absent-parent tax, determined by clear and impartial rules, levied against the fathers of children born out of wedlock. This would provide a potentially powerful economic incentive for responsible male reproductive and parental behavior.

520. Earls, Felton, and Ben Siegel. "Precocious Fathers."
     AMERICAN JOURNAL OF ORTHOPSYCHIATRY 50
     (July 1980): 469-480.
     Reviews current knowledge about adolescent fathers, states the possible clinical benefits of involving them in the pregnancy experience and lists specific research questions which need to be addressed by mental health professionals. The clinical benefits listed include: (1) psychological preparation of the father for making responsible choices regarding fatherhood; (2) an increase in preventive knowledge; (3) the provision of counseling efforts to support the potential for interpersonal maturation as an outcome of the early parenthood crises; (4) provision of supportive services to prevent educational failure. The research needs include: (1) a nationally based demographic profile on adolescent fathers; (2) a

detailed understanding of the psychological correlates of adolescent fatherhood; (3) an understanding of the social context of adolescent fatherhood; (4) clarification of the relationship between procreation and sexually permissive environments; (5) the influence of pregnancy outcome on the sexual attitudes and activities of adolescent males; and (6) the likely impact of new types of male contraceptives.

521. Elster, Arthur B.; Lamb, Michael; and Nancy Kimmerly. "Perceptions of Fatherhood Among Adolescent Fathers." PEDIATRICS 83 (May 1989): 758-765.

522. Elster, Arthur B., and Susan Panzarine. "The Adolescent Father." SEMINARS IN PERINATOLOGY 5 (January 1981): 39-51.
Uses information from various sources to discuss: (1) the sexual behavior of adolescent males; (2) their knowledge of, attitudes about, and use of contraceptives; (3) the psychological characteristics of teenage fathers; (4) the consequences of the pregnancy for them; and (5) the implications for clinical intervention.

523. Elster, Arthur B., and Susan Panzarine. "Adolescent Pregnancy--Where Is the Unwed Teenage Father? PEDIATRICS 63 (May 1979): 824.
Argues, in a letter to the editor, that perhaps the key to reducing the risks associated with repeat pregnancies among adolescents is to devise programs that include the young father as well as the young mother. Cites three potential benefits from such services. One, they might increase the level of social support received by young mothers. Two, they might encourage the young fathers to assume more financial responsibility for his child. Three, they might help the young father to receive the level of social support he needs to deal with the pregnancy.

524. Elster, Arthur B., and Michael E. Lamb. "Adolescent Fathers: A Group Potentially at Risk for Parenting Failure." INFANT MENTAL HEALTH JOURNAL 3 (Fall 1982): 148-155.
Argues that adolescent fathers may be subject to stresses beyond those normally associated with the transition to fatherhood. The groups of stressors identified included: vocational educational worries; apprehensions about the health of the young mother and child; and anxiety about relationships,

especially those with parents and with the mate. Further, because of their immaturity the young fathers may be less able to cope adequately with the stressors. As a result of these stresses the young fathers may be less able to invest in their children emotionally or to respond sensitively to needs of the infant and thereby fail to adequately perform the father role.

525. Elster, Arthur B., and Susan Panzarine. "Unwed Teenage Fathers: Emotional and Health Educational Needs." JOURNAL OF ADOLESCENT HEALTH CARE 1 (1981): 116-120.
    Uses data on 16 adolescent males between 15 and 19 who were the fathers of children whose mothers were participants in an adolescent pregnancy program to assess the emotional and health education needs of unwed teenage fathers. The results of this analysis are interpreted to indicate that the young fathers who were having the most difficult time coping with the pregnancy were those who were less well adjusted and who had a negative initial reaction to the pregnancy. When asked questions about reproduction and contraception 11 of the 16 respondents answered 50 percent of them incorrectly. Overall the young men showed a great deal of interest in learning how to care for their children.

526. Elster, Arthur B., and Susan Panzarine. "Adolescent Fathers: Stresses During Gestation and Early Parenthood." CLINICAL PEDIATRICS 22 (October 1983): 700-703.
    Provides information on the nature of the stresses experienced by 20 adolescent fathers and how these stresses change over the course of the pregnancy. Argues that the social situation surrounding adolescent fatherhood produces a pattern of concerns that stress the young men whatever their race, marital status or socioeconomic status. Also finds that the intensity of the stressors change throughout the course of the pregnancy. The discovery of the pregnancy and the decision to continue the relationship led to the initial concerns about education and the ability to provide financially for a family. These stressors remained throughout the pregnancy. From the middle to the end of the pregnancy these young fathers were distressed about labor and delivery and the health of the mother and the child. In this sample the majority of the young parents married before the birth of the child arousing difficulty with relationships. At the lowest level of

intensity was concern about parenthood itself, such as discipline and child care.

527. Freeman, Edith M. "Teenage Fathers and the Problem of Teenage Pregnancy." SOCIAL WORK IN EDUCATION (Fall 1988): 36-52.
Reviews the literature which has assessed the needs of adolescent fathers. Summarizes the attitudes, knowledge and skills which act as obstacles to providing services to meet these needs. Suggests more appropriate intervention strategies.

528. Fry, P.S., and Robert J. Trifiletti. "Teenage Fathers: An Exploration of their Developmental Needs and Anxieties and the Implications for Clinical-Social Intervention and Services." JOURNAL OF PSYCHIATRIC TREATMENT AND EVALUATION 5 (1983): 219-227.
Explores the stresses and anxieties characteristic of adolescent fathers through data collected from 95 teenagers. These young men revealed in the interviews that they were experiencing high levels of emotional rejection, personal anxiety, feelings of self blame and feelings of guilt. The intensity of these feelings varied along with whether or not the couple married, the resolution decision, and whether or not the young man was involved in the decision making process. Argues that these young men are clearly in need of support and counseling services.

529. Gabbard, Glen O., and John R. Wolff. "The Unwed Pregnant Adolescent and Her Male partner." THE JOURNAL OF REPRODUCTIVE MEDICINE 19 (September 1977): 137-140.
Utilizes data on 100 adolescent mothers (17 or younger) who were interviewed one to three days after the birth of their first child to assess the nature of the association between the young mothers' relationship with the child's father and complications of labor and delivery. Found that even for the unmarried adolescent there was a high level of continued involvement with the father, but that there was no apparent relationship between continued interaction with the father and labor and delivery difficulties.

530. Gershenson, Harold P. "Redefining Fatherhood in Families with White Adolescent Mothers." JOURNAL OF MARRIAGE AND FAMILY 45 (August 1983): 591-599.

Relates the experiences of 30 primiparous white mothers who gave birth prior to age 20 with some of the men who were significant to them and their children (who were 12-27 months old at the time of the study). These men included husbands, former husbands and boyfriends and the child's grandfather or stepgrandfather. Describes the roles that these different men play in the life of the young mother and child, and her attitudes toward and relationships with these men. Argues that any discussion of adolescent parenting must take into account that more than one man can function as father to the child and that the concept of father should not be treated as though it were synonymous with either the male who impregnated the female or to the mother's spouse.

531. Hendricks, Leo E. "Suggestions for Reaching Unmarried Black Adolescent Fathers." CHILD WELFARE 62 (March/April 1983): 141-146.

Compares recent, first time, unwed black adolescent fathers in Tulsa, Oklahoma (20); Chicago, Illinois (27); and Columbus, Ohio (48). Describes what the young men see as their service needs and their feelings about their child and his or her mother. Makes recommendations about what service workers can do to reach this client population.

532. Hendricks, Leo E. "Unwed Adolescent Fathers: Problems They Face and Their Sources of Support." ADOLESCENCE 15 (Winter 1980): 862-869.

Employs data on 20 black unwed adolescent fathers to answer qualitative questions concerned with: who he is, what he is like, what his problems are, and the potential sources of support available to him in coping with his problems. It was found that the young father in this study was most likely to be an employed high school graduate who would turn to his parents, especially his mother for social support.

533. Hendricks, Leo E.; Robinson-Brown, Diane; and Lawrence E. Gary. "Religiosity and Unmarried Black Adolescent Fatherhood." ADOLESCENCE 19 (Summer 1984): 417-424.

Addresses the question of whether unmarried adolescent fathers are less religious than their nonfather peers using data gathered in face to face interviews with 48 fathers and 50 nonfathers selected in a nonrandom fashion. There were no significant differences between the fathers and nonfathers on the religiosity measures but it is noted that the fathers' religious involvement tended to be within media forms while the nonfathers religious involvement tended to be within institutionalized religious groups. The two groups were significantly different in terms of school status, employment status and contraceptive behavior with the fathers being less likely to be enrolled in any type of school, more likely to be employed and less likely to be contraceptors.

534. Hendricks, Leo E. "Outreach with Teenage Fathers: A Preliminary Report on Three Ethnic Groups." ADOLESCENCE 23 (Fall 1988): 711-720.
Uses cross sectional data on 56 recent, first time fathers (11 Anglo, 14 black, 21 Hispanic) to examine their sociodemographic background and their service needs. Makes suggestions about how these young fathers with their divergent individual and cultural needs can be reached initially and then retained in service programs.

535. Hendricks, Leo E., and Teresa Montgomery. "A limited Population of Unmarried Adolescent Fathers: A Preliminary Report of Their Views on Fatherhood and the Relationship with the Mothers of Their Children." ADOLESCENCE 18 (Spring 1983): 201-210.
Addresses the attitudes of 47 unmarried adolescent fathers toward fatherhood and their relationship with the mother of their first child. Most of the young fathers positively accept fatherhood and see their relationship with the mother as involving sentiments of love.

536. Hendricks, Leo; Howard, Cleopatra S.; and Patricia P. Caesar. "Help Seeking Behavior Among Selected Populations of Black Adolescent Fathers." AMERICAN JOURNAL OF PUBLIC HEALTH 71 (July 1981): 733-735.
Provides information on the help seeking behavior and service needs of 95 unwed adolescent fathers in three cities. A large majority of these young men reported that when they needed help with a problem they would turn to members of their families. Only two of them reported that they would seek help from an agency. If they did go to an agency they would want it to supply them with information on such things as sex education and child development, help with jobs and schools, and counseling to help them deal with family life. Argues that these young men clearly

need services but will probably only become involved with
agencies if they institute assertive outreach efforts.

537. Johnson, Cliff, and Andrew Sum. DECLINING EARNINGS
OF YOUNG MEN: RELATIONSHIP TO POVERTY,
TEEN PREGNANCY AND FAMILY FORMATION.
Washington, D.C.: Children's Defense Fund's Adolescent
Pregnancy Prevention Clearing House (May 1987).
Draws upon a variety of economic data to examine how the lack
of employment opportunities at an adequate wage makes it more
difficult for some young people to get a good start in the labor
market. Then traces the sequence of events that arise from the
new economic realities for young males: distinct declines in
employment and earnings, falling marriage rates and increasing
poverty among young families and their children.

538. Leashore, Bogart. "Human Services and the Unmarried Father:
The 'Forgotten Half." THE FAMILY COORDINATOR
(October 1979): 529-534.
Examines the attributes of unmarried fathers, their status in
the law and the social services provided for them. Suggests
improvements to the services offered this population from a policy
approach.

539. Lorenzi, M. Elisabeth; Klerman, Lorraine V.; and James F.
Jekel. "School Age Parents: How Permanent a Relationship?"
ADOLESCENCE 12 (Spring 1977): 3-22.
Reports on the nature of the relationship between 162
adolescent mothers and the fathers of their children based on
data collected from the young mother at several points in time.
While still pregnant 43 percent of the girls expected financial
assistance from the father. At 3 and 15 months after the birth
of the child 64 percent were in fact receiving monetary help, but
by 26 months this figure had diminished to 49 percent. Two years
after the birth 23 percent were married to the father, and another
23 percent were still seeing him regularly. The data are
interpreted to indicate that the relationships between these young
people were not casual. The implications of these relationships
including service needs are discussed.

540. Marsiglio, William. "Adolescent Fathers in the United States:
Their Initial Living Arrangements, Marital Experience and

Educational Outcomes." FAMILY PLANNING
PERSPECTIVES 19 (November/December 1987): 240-251.
Utilizes data from the National Longitudinal Survey of Labor
Market Experience of Youth to examine the living arrangements
and educational level of adolescent fathers. Found that seven
percent of the male respondents who were 20-27 years of age in
1984 fathered a child while still an adolescent. Half of these
young fathers lived with their child shortly after his or her birth
and one-third of them married within 12 months of conception.
Race was related to the probability of fathering a child, marrying
and residing with the child. Young black men were more likely
to have become fathers as adolescents and less likely to have lived
with the child. Ethnicity, social class and religion were also
important factors. Adolescent fathers were more likely to be high
school dropouts, though once again race was a significant factor
as was the young man's educational aspirations.

541. Marsiglio, William. "Commitment to Social Fatherhood:
Predicting Adolescent Males' Intentions to Live with Their
Child and Partner." JOURNAL OF MARRIAGE AND
THE FAMILY 50 (May 1988): 427-441.
Analyzes data collected from 325 high school males on how they
would react to an hypothetical pregnancy of a girl they had been
dating for a year. About 48 percent of the respondents reported
that they would be quite likely to live with their child and partner.
There were no significant differences between blacks and whites
in their reported intentions. The attitudinal and subjective norm
components of the Fishbein and Ajzen Model of Reasoned Action
together explained 32 percent of the variance in intentions. While
the subjective norm component was a significant predictor only
for whites, the attitudinal component was a powerful predictor for
blacks as well as whites.

542. Nakashima, Ida I., and Bonnie W. Camp. "Fathers of Infants
Born to Adolescent Mothers." AMERICAN JOURNAL OF
DISEASES OF CHILDREN 138 (May 1984): 452-454.
Uses data on 192 females who were younger than 17 at the time
of conception and their male partners, 138 of whom were 19 or
younger and 54 who were 20 or older. Describes the similarities
and differences possibly related to age, maturity or developmental
level in couples composed of adolescent mothers with male
partners of different ages. Demonstrates that a sizeable portion
of adolescent mothers are paired with older men and suggests

that such couples may require services which are different from those required by adolescent couples.

543. Pauker, Jerome D. "Fathers of Children Conceived Out of Wedlock: Pregnancy, High School, Psychological Test Results." DEVELOPMENTAL PSYCHOLOGY 4 (1971): 215-218.
Compares the ninth grade MMPIs and other information of 94 males reported to have later fathered children while still single and 94 matched controls. The results indicated very few differences between the two groups and do not support many of the broad characterizations of adolescent fathers found in earlier literature.

544. Rivara, Frederick P. "Parental Rights and Obligations of the Unwed Adolescent Father." AMERICAN JOURNAL OF THE DISEASES OF CHILDREN 140 (June 1986): 531-534.
Begins by summarizing the decisions of the Supreme Court which appear to mean that the state cannot discriminate against fathers who have taken an active interest in their children and whose paternity is not in doubt simply because they are not married to the mother. The law apparently makes no distinction based on the age of the father. Discusses the benefits and ways of establishing paternity including the role of the *guardian ad litem*, the statute of limitations and laboratory testing. Briefly explains the laws involving child support and enforcement as they relate to the adolescent father. Describes the rights of the father in custody disputes including the fact that the Supreme Court has ruled that a natural father is of equal standing with a mother in custody disputes, has constitutionally protected visitation rights and, depending upon the relationship he has established with the child, the right to be involved in adoption proceedings. Points out that health care professionals need to understand the legal rights and obligations of both adolescent parents.

545. Rivara, Frederick P.; Sweeney, Patrick J.; and Brady F. Henderson. "A Study of Low Socioeconomic Status, Black Teenage Fathers and Their NonFather Peers." PEDIATRICS 75 (April 1985): 648-656.
Compares 100 adolescent fathers to 100 nonfathers to ascertain whether significant differences existed between the two groups in terms of their attitudes toward the consequences of adolescent pregnancy and their knowledge and use of contraception and their

rate of abstinence. Drawing upon the Health Belief Model five hypotheses were stated: (1) teenage fathers would perceive the consequences of teenage pregnancy to be less serious than would their nonfather peers: (2) the nonfather peers would have a better understanding of the risks of pregnancy as indicated by (a) better knowledge about sex, contraception and pregnancy and (b) higher rates of pregnancy preventing behavior (contraceptive and abstinence); (3) the fathers would perceive the barriers to contraceptive use as greater and the benefits as less than would the members of the comparison group; (4) the fathers would come from families characterized by more disruption and conflict and (5) the adolescent fathers would be less well adjusted psychologically than their nonfather peers.

546. Rivara, Frederick P.; Sweeney, Patrick J.; and Brady F. Henderson. "Black Teenage Fathers: What Happens When the Child Is Born?" PEDIATRICS 78 (July 1986): 151-158.
Explores the changes in the lives of 100 black adolescent fathers and 100 black adolescent nonfathers from before the birth of the child to as long as 18 months after. Two of the most important conclusions are: (1) that even in this short period of time the fathers are already falling behind the nonfathers educationally and economically; and (2) that the majority of these young men continue to be involved in the lives of the mother and the child on a regular basis. Recommendations are made for including the young fathers in programs for adolescent parents and their children.

547. Robinson, Bryan E., and Robert L. Barret. "Self-Concept and Anxiety of Adolescent and Adult Fathers." ADOLESCENCE 22 (Fall 1987): 611-616.
Compares the self-concept and anxiety level of 12 unmarried adolescent fathers to those of 12 unwed older fathers. Found no significant difference between the self-concept or anxiety level of the two groups.

548. Robinson, Bryan E. "Teenage Pregnancy from the Father's Perspective." AMERICAN JOURNAL OF ORTHOPSYCHIATRY 58 (January 1988): 46-51.
Describes five myths about adolescent fathers and argues that current evidence does not support these myths. Reviews the existing evidence on sexual knowledge and behavior, attitudes toward marriage and childbearing, psychological variables and the

consequences of fatherhood. The implications for mental health practitioners are discussed.

549. Robinson, Bryan, and Robert L. Barret. "Locus of Control of Unwed Adolescent Fathers versus Adolescent NonFathers." PERCEPTUAL AND MOTOR SKILLS 56 (1983): 397-398.
The scores of 20 adolescent fathers on the Nowicki-Strickland Locus of control scale were compared to that of 20 adolescent nonfathers. There was no significant difference in the scores of the two groups. Adolescent fathers see themselves as much in control of their destiny as adolescent males who have not fathered children.

550. Rothstein, Arden A. "Adolescent Males, Fatherhood, and Abortion." JOURNAL OF YOUTH AND ADOLESCENCE 7 (1978): 203-214.
Describes in very psychoanalytic terms the results of a study of adolescent males who had accompanied their partner to an abortion clinic.

551. Sander, Joelle Hevesi, and Jacqueline L. Rosen. "Teenage Fathers: Working with the Neglected Partner." FAMILY PLANNING PERSPECTIVES 19 (May/June 1987): 107-110.
Describes a two year research and demonstration project, the Teen Father Collaboration, which was started in 1983. Argues that the project helped to erase some of the stereotypes of all adolescent fathers as neglecting their parental responsibility. Instead, many young fathers wanted to contribute to the financial support of their children but were unable to do so. The project often led to school or GED enrollment or completion and to employment. Emphasizes the need to have a good working knowledge of the community in which programs are based and an aggressive approach to recruiting young fathers into programs.

552. Vaz, Rosalind; Smolen, Paul; and Charlene Miller. "Adolescent Pregnancy: Involvement of the Male Partner." JOURNAL OF ADOLESCENT HEALTH CARE 4 (1983): 246-250.
Uses data on 52 unwed adolescent mothers and 47 of the fathers of their children to describe the nature and length of their relationship with each other, the role played by each partner in the pregnancy resolution decision and how satisfied they are with the decision, the psychosocial effects of the pregnancy on the male, involvement with health care providers and with the

families. Found that the majority of these young men maintain an ongoing relationship with the mother and child and that an even larger percentage had told their families about the pregnancy. Less than half the young men had played a significant role in the pregnancy resolution decision. They had been even more overlooked by the providers of health care, only 19 percent having discussed the pregnancy with a health care professional and only 9 percent having received information about birth control. Some of the young men seem to have experienced depression and social isolation as a result of their impending fatherhood. It is concluded that more energy should be put into identifying those young men who are interested and allowing them to participate in all aspects of the pregnancy process while making sure that they are offered the necessary social support.

553. Westney, Ouida E.; Cole, O. Jackson; and Theodosia L. Mumford. "Adolescent Unwed Prospective Fathers: Readiness for Fatherhood and Behaviors Toward the Mother and the Expected Infant." ADOLESCENCE 21 (Winter 1986): 901-911.
Uses data on 28 unmarried black adolescent fathers to describe their readiness for fatherhood, their interactions with their pregnant partners, and how they plan to behave toward the mother and child after birth. The data highlight how unprepared these teens are for fatherhood. Yet they do make some effort to be responsible. For example, 80 percent of them want to provide partial financial support to their children. The longer the prepregnancy relationship the more supportive the young man was of the young mother and the more he planned to be involved with the child.

554. Williams-McCoy, Janice E.; and Forrest B. Tyler. "Selected Psychological Characteristics of Black Unwed Adolescent Fathers." JOURNAL OF ADOLESCENT HEALTH CARE 6 (1985): 12-16.
Compares 24 unwed adolescent fathers to 27 unwed adolescent nonfathers in terms of locus of control, interpersonal trust, coping styles, and family history of unwed parenthood. No differences between the two groups were found in terms of locus of control or coping styles. The fathers, however, tended to be older, less trusting, and more likely to have been born out wedlock themselves.

B. Chapters in Books

555. Belsky, Jay, and Brent C. Miller. "Adolescent Fatherhood in the Context of the Transition to Parenthood." ADOLESCENT FATHERHOOD. Edited by Arthur B. Elster and Michael E. Lamb. Hillsdale, New Jersey: Lawrence Erlbaum Associates, 1986, pp. 107-122.
Hopes to sensitize the scientist practitioner to the potential role conflicts that confront the adolescent faced with the premature transition to the role of father. Presents the psychosocial implications of these conflicts and offers a rationale and model for addressing the needs of this population in clinical settings.

556. Bolton, Frank G., Jr., and Jay Belsky. "The Adolescent Father and Child Maltreatment." ADOLESCENT FATHERHOOD. Edited by Arthur B. Elster and Michael E. Lamb. Hillsdale, New Jersey: Lawrence Erlbaum Associates, 1986, pp. 123-140. Reviews the literature concerned with child maltreatment by adolescent parents.

557. Elster, Arthur B., and Leo Hendricks. "Stresses and Coping Strategies of Adolescent Fathers." ADOLESCENT FATHERHOOD. Edited by Arthur B. Elster and Michael E. Lamb. Hillsdale, New Jersey: Lawrence Erlbaum Associates, 1986, pp. 55-66. Explores the nature of the stresses that are perceived by adolescent fathers.

558. Marsiglio, William. "Teenage Fatherhood: High School Completion and Educational Attainment." ADOLESCENT FATHERHOOD. Edited by Arthur B. Elster and Michael E. Lamb. Hillsdale, New Jersey: Lawrence Erlbaum Associates, 1986, pp. 67-88. Presents data concerned with the calamitous effect of early fatherhood on the educational and occupational attainment of young men.

559. Elster, Arthur B., and Susan Panzarine. "Adolescent Fathers." PREMATURE ADOLESCENT PREGNANCY AND PARENTHOOD. Edited by Elizabeth McAnarney. New York: Grune and Stratton, 1983, pp. 231-252.

Discusses the sexual and contraceptive behavior of adolescent males, the psychosocial characteristics of adolescent fathers, the consequences of fatherhood for these young men, and the implications for practice.

560. Elster, Arthur B., and Michael E. Lamb. "Adolescent Fathers: The Understudied Side of Adolescent Pregnancy." SCHOOL-AGE PREGNANCY: BIOSOCIAL DIMENSIONS. Edited by Jane B. Lancaster and Beatrix A. Hamburg. New York: Aldine De Gruyter, 1986, pp. 177-190.

561. Herzog, James M. "Boys Who Make Babies." ADOLESCENT PARENTHOOD. Edited by Max Sugar. New York: SP Medical and Scientific Books, 1984, pp. 65-74.
Describes experiences with sexually active male adolescents including their paternal feelings, fantasies and actualities, which shed light on the developing nature of the sexuality.

562. Kahn, James S., and Frank G. Bolton, Jr. "Clinical Issues in Adolescent Fatherhood." ADOLESCENT FATHERHOOD. Edited by Arthur B. Elster and Michael E. Lamb. Hillsdale, New Jersey: Lawrence Erlbaum Associates, 1986, pp. 141-154.
Draws upon clinical experience to make suggestions about strategies which could be effective in programs offering services to young fathers.

563. Klinman, Debra G.; Sander, Joelle H.; Rosen, Jacqueline L.; and Karen R. Longo. "The Teen Father Collaboration: A Demonstration and Research Model." ADOLESCENT FATHERHOOD. Edited by Arthur B. Elster and Michael E. Lamb. Hillsdale, New Jersey: Lawrence Erlbaum Associates, 1986, pp. 155-170.
Describes the National Teen Father Collaboration.

564. Lamb, Michael E., and Arthur B. Elster. "Parental Behavior of Adolescent Mothers and Fathers." ADOLESCENT FATHERHOOD. Edited by Arthur B. Elster and Michael E. Lamb. Hillsdale, New Jersey: Lawrence Erlbaum Associates, 1986, pp. 89-106.
Reviews the literature concerned with parental behavior.

565. Montemayor, Raymond. "Boys as Fathers: Coping with the Dilemmas of Adolescence." ADOLESCENT

FATHERHOOD. Edited by Arthur B. Elster and Michael
E. Lamb. Hillsdale, New Jersey: Lawrence Erlbaum
Associates, 1986, pp. 1-18.
Presents an overview of key issues in the study of adolescence.

566. Teti, Douglas M., and Michael E. Lamb. "Sex-Role Learning
and Adolescent Fatherhood." ADOLESCENT
FATHERHOOD. Edited by Arthur B. Elster and Michael
E. Lamb. Hillsdale, New Jersey: Lawrence Erlbaum
Associates, 1986, pp. 19-30.
Discusses male sex role development during adolescence.

567. Sonenstein, Freya. "Risking Paternity: Sex and Contraception
Among Adolescent Males." ADOLESCENT
FATHERHOOD. Edited by Arthur B. Elster and Michael
E. Lamb. Hillsdale, New Jersey: Lawrence Erlbaum
Associates, 1986, pp. 31-54.
Reviews the research concerned with the sexuality of adolescent
males and their contraceptive behavior.

568. Vinovskis, Maris. "Young Fathers and Their Children: Some
Historical and Policy Perspectives." ADOLESCENT
FATHERHOOD. Edited by Arthur B. Elster and Michael
E. Lamb. Hillsdale, New Jersey: Lawrence Erlbaum
Associates, 1986, pp. 171-192.
Reviews historical changes in the perceptions of young fathers
and changes in society's reaction to them.

C. Books

569. Elster, Arthur B., and Michael E. Lamb. ADOLESCENT
FATHERHOOD. Hillsdale, New Jersey: Lawrence Erlbaum
Associates, 1986.
Offers a broad perspective on adolescent fatherhood. Contains
items 555-558, 562-568.

570. Robinson, Bryan E. TEENAGE FATHERS. Lexington, Mass.:
Lexington Books, 1988.
Synthesized the author's work with hundreds of adolescent
fathers by combining the results of original research with case
studies from clinical practice. Surveys the scope of the problem

by comparing the myths about adolescent fathers with the realities. Presents the neglected consequences of early fatherhood for young men. Discusses the problems social scientists face in studying this population and makes recommendations for future research. Describes programs designed for young fathers and makes suggestions about how young men can be included in the experience of childbirth and fathering.

XI. SERVICES

A. Articles

1. *Adolescent Family Planning*

571. Chaime, Mary; Eisman, Susan; Forrest, Jacqueline D.; Orr, Margaret Terry; and Aida Torres. "Factors Affecting Adolescents' Use of Family Planning Clinics." FAMILY PLANNING PERSPECTIVES 14 (May/June 1982): 126-139.
Attempts to identify the approaches which attract and retain the highest number of adolescent clients through survey data collected from family planning clinic directors, adolescent and adult clients, physicians and pharmacists. Finds that those clinics which are located in counties where about 75 percent of those at risk are served differ in many ways from those located in counties where only about 28 percent of those at risk are served. These are differences in clinic characteristics, including sources of funding, organization and visibility. There are also community differences in state laws about sex education and specificity in regard to parental consent.

572. Forrest, Jacqueline D.; Hermalin, Albert I.; and Stanley K. Henshaw. "The Impact of Family Planning Programs on Adolescent Pregnancy." FAMILY PLANNING PERSPECTIVES. 13 (May/June 1981): 109-116.
Estimates the effects of federally funded family planning services on adolescent pregnancies, abortions and births. Estimates that during the 1970s adolescents, due to their participation in family planning clinics, avoided 2.6 million pregnancies. Argues that in 1979 alone 417,000 adolescent pregnancies, 1.4 million abortions and nearly one million births were prevented.

573. Furstenberg, Frank F., Jr.; Shea, Judy; Allison, Paul; Herceg-Baron, Roberta; and David Webb. "Contraceptive Continuation Among Adolescents Attending Family Planning Clinics." FAMILY PLANNING PERSPECTIVES 15 (September/October 1983): 211-217.
Reports the results of a study of 445 adolescents (under 18) who in 1980 and 1981 made an initial visit to a federally funded family planning clinic in Philadelphia. The goal was to develop a method of reliably measuring their contraceptive continuation.

Three separate measures varying in rigorousness were constructed. Regardless of the measure used, most of the discontinuation in contraceptive method occurred in the first three months after the initial visit. The measures differed, however, in their ability to predict pregnancy and the characteristics of those who would be consistent contraceptors.

574. Furstenberg, Frank F., Jr.; Herceg-Baron, Roberta; Mann, Dorothy; and Judy Shea. "Parental Involvement: Selling Family Planning Clinics Short." FAMILY PLANNING PERSPECTIVES 14 (May/June 1982): 140-144.

Employs data collected from phone interviews with 336 directors of family planning programs receiving Title X funds in order to describe their efforts to involve parents. Finds that while policies which emphasize encouragement enhance parental involvement those which mandate parental notification often use it as a substitute for specific activities designed to achieve the desired goals. Argues that mandatory parental notification may in fact serve to reduce their actual involvement.

575. Gold, Rachel, and Jennifer Macias. "Public Funding of Contraceptive, Sterilization and Abortion Services, 1985." FAMILY PLANNING PERSPECTIVES 18 (November/December 1985): 259-264.

576. Johnson, Leanor Boulin, and Robert E. Staples. "Family Planning and the Young Minority Male." FAMILY COORDINATOR (October 1979): 535-543.

Discusses the importance of culturally relevant approaches to delivering family planning services in minority communities. Points out that while most service delivery systems focus attention on the adolescent female, it is often the young male who determines whether contraceptives will be used. Describes a project designed with these issues in mind which was implemented in Los Angeles in 1974.

577. Marsiglio, William. "Confronting the Teenage Pregnancy Issue: Social Marketing as an Interdisciplinary Approach." HUMAN RELATIONS 38 (1985): 983-1000.

Describes the basic elements of social marketing as: (1) marketing research, (2) product development, (3) use of incentives, and (4) facilitation. Explains how social marketing has been used in the area of international family planning programs. Briefly reviews the literature concerned with adolescents' knowledge of, attitudes toward and practices in regard to contraception. Argues that social marketing is a viable strategy for increasing responsible and effective contraceptive behavior among adolescents.

578. Namerow, Pearila Brickner; Philliber, Susan G.; and Marilyn Hughes. "Follow up Adolescent Family Planning Clinic Users." FAMILY PLANNING PERSPECTIVES 15 (July/August 1983): 172-176.

Describes a project designed to vigorously follow up adolescents attending a contraceptive clinic based in a New York hospital. While many of the young patients were concerned about confidentiality and were very mobile, the research suggests that a program of vigorous follow-up is feasible. Skill in soliciting telephone numbers through which the teens can be reached is an important asset to counselors in such a program.

579. Reis, Janet; Reid, Evelyn; Herr, Toby; and Elicia Herz. "Family Planning for Inner City Adolescent Males." ADOLESCENCE 22 (Winter 1987): 953-960.

Describes how a community health center changed its clinic registration practices and the approach of health care providers to help overcome some of the barriers experienced by male adolescents in obtaining contraceptives.

580. Torres, Aida; Forrest, Jacqueline D.; and Susan Eisman. "Telling Parents: Clinic Policies and Adolescents' Use of Family Planning and Abortion Services." FAMILY PLANNING PERSPECTIVES 12 (November/December 1980): 284-292.

Summarizes the findings of two national surveys carried out to ascertain: (1) the current parental notification policies of abortion and family planning programs; (2) the degree to which adolescents currently inform their parents about their decisions to use such services; and (3) what those who have not told their parents would do if such notification was required by law. Found that those agencies requiring parental notification serve a much smaller adolescent population than those who do not have such policies. Also found that a majority of adolescents already inform their parents about their use of contraceptive and abortion services. Estimates, however, that if parental notification were required by law most teens would not stop having sex. Instead,

estimates that the adolescents who are now contracepting
effectively would experience 33,000 more unplanned pregnancies
and that 42,000 of those now obtaining legal abortions would
either have unwanted births or illegal abortions.

581. Torres, Aida; Forrest, Jacqueline Darroch; and Susan Eisman.
      "Family Planning Services in the United States: 1978-1979."
      FAMILY PLANNING PERSPECTIVES 13 (May/June
      1981): 132-141.
      Presents an overview of family planning services in the United
      States in 1978-1979. Points out that in the years covered, 2,681
      agencies at 5,195 locations served 4.5 million women. Fifty-six
      percent of the 4.8 million adolescents at risk of unplanned
      pregnancy were served. The number of patients served has
      increased in each year since the late 1960s but since 1973 there
      has been little real increase in the amount of federal funds
      distributed to these programs. And in 1979 almost three-fourths
      of $323 million spent on these services came from the federal
      government. Describes in detail the services rendered and their
      geographical distribution. Describes the populations served and
      discusses the implications of proposed changes in federal funding
      policies.

582. Torres, Aida. "Does Your Mother Know?" FAMILY
      PLANNING PERSPECTIVES 10 (September/October
      1978): 280-282.
      Uses data from self-administered questionnaires filled out by
      2,054 family planning clinic patients under the age of 20. Finds
      that more than half of the young patients had parents who were
      already aware of the fact that they were receiving contraceptive
      care at a clinic. If parental notification were required by law
      these young people would continue attending the clinic as would
      twenty percent of those whose parents were not currently aware.
      The remainder of those whose parents were currently unaware of
      the clinic attendance would, by and large, not give up sex (only
      one percent chose this option). The remainder of this group
      would use non-clinic contraception (40%) or have sex without
      contraception (30%).

2. *Adolescent Pregnancy Prevention*

583. Allen, Mary Lee; Miller, Susan; and Joan Abbey. TEENS IN FOSTER CARE: PREVENTING PREGNANCY AND BUILDING SELF SUFFICIENCY. Washington, D.C.: Children's Defense Fund's Adolescent Pregnancy Prevention Clearing House (September 1987).

States that adolescents in foster care and other out of home situations are at high risk of and the least prepared for adolescent parenthood. Describes the results of a study of adolescents in foster care which was designed to learn what actions are being taken by state child welfare agencies in order to prevent adolescent pregnancy and to increase self sufficiency among teens who are already pregnant or parenting.

584. Black, Cheryl, and Richard R. DeBlassie. "Adolescent Pregnancy: Contributing Factors, Consequences, Treatment, and Plausible Solutions." ADOLESCENCE 78 (Summer 1985): 281-290.

Describes the magnitude of the adolescent pregnancy problem in American society and the negative consequences associated with it. Then discusses treatments and possible solutions to the problem in terms of how those in the helping professions respond. Discusses preventive measures including sex education, family life education and family planning. Also discusses group therapy, vocational programs and counseling.

585. Carnegie Corporation of New York. "Adolescent Pregnancy: Testing Prevention Strategies." CARNEGIE QUARTERLY 31 (Summer/Fall 1986): 1-7.

Describes a series of adolescent pregnancy prevention programs which are being tried by the Girls Clubs of America with support from the Carnegie Corporation. These programs attempt to intervene by widening a young person's view of life options and by providing them with opportunities. The programs are described as being too new to evaluate completely, but as having clearly been successful enough that they should be tried on a larger scale.

586. Children's Defense Fund. ADOLESCENT PREGNANCY: AN ANATOMY OF A SOCIAL PROBLEM IN SEARCH OF COMPREHENSIVE SOLUTIONS. Washington, D.C.:

Children's Defense Fund's Adolescent Pregnancy Prevention
Clearing House (January 1987).
Adapts a lecture given by CDF president Marian Wright
Edelman. Lists ten reasons to work toward the prevention of
adolescent pregnancy and nine barriers to prevention. Describes
what various community agencies and organizations can do to
prevent adolescent pregnancy as well as the prevention efforts of
CDF.

587. Children's Defense Fund. MAKING THE MIDDLE GRADES
     WORK. Washington, D.C.: Children's Defense Fund's
     Adolescent Pregnancy Prevention Clearing House (September
     1988).
     Examines the role that the middle grades can play in helping
     youngsters deal with the problems of early adolescence in such
     a way that they can become successful and productive adults.

588. Davidson, Ezra C. "An Analysis of Adolescent Health Care and
     the Role of the Obstetrician-Gynecologist." AMERICAN
     JOURNAL OF OBSTETRICS AND GYNECOLOGY 139
     (April 1981): 845-854.
     Analyzes data from two sources; the USC-Mendenhall Man-
     power Study and the 1979 American College of Obstetricians and
     Gynecologists survey. These data are analyzed to determine what
     specialists supply services to adolescent females as well as the
     types of services that are supplied. Argues that the health care
     delivery system has not adjusted with sufficient rapidity to the
     changing sexual behavior of American adolescents. Suggests that
     for some physicians, additional training or reorientation may be
     needed in order to prevent their judgmental attitudes about
     adolescent sexuality from influencing the quality of the care they
     provide.

589. Doty, Mary B., and Myramae King. "Pregnancy Prevention: A
     Private Agency's Program in Public Schools." SOCIAL
     WORK IN EDUCATION 7 (1985): 90-99.
     Argues that social workers need to develop programs to prevent
     adolescent pregnancies which focus on males as well as females.
     Describes a program for junior and senior high school students
     in New York City which involves drop-in centers and individual
     and group counseling for teens of both sexes.

590. Dryfoos, Joy. "School-Based Health Clinics: A New Approach to Preventing Adolescent Pregnancy?" FAMILY PLANNING PERSPECTIVES 17 (March/ April 1985): 70-82.

Describes 14 clinics offering comprehensive health services, including family planning, which are located near or in public high schools and junior high schools. Describes their staffing patterns, caseload, community environment and funding sources. Points out that these school based programs have been credited with improving the overall health of students, increasing their contraceptive utilization rates, lowering their fertility, and increasing their school attendance. Argues, however, that there have been very few reliable evaluation studies of them. Suggests that soundly constructed program evaluations are necessary if these programs are to retain financial and community support.

591. Edwards, Laura F.; Steinman, Mary E.; Arnold, Kathleen A.; and Erick Y. Hakanson. "Adolescent Pregnancy Prevention Services in High School Clinics." FAMILY PLANNING PERSPECTIVES 12 (January 1980): 6-14.

Describes the health clinic opened at a junior-senior high school in St. Paul, Minnesota, in 1973. Outlines the development of the program, the services it provides and attempts to evaluate its effectiveness. Points out that in the three years since the start of the program, one-fourth of the female students have sought family planning services and 87 percent of these have continued to contracept for three years. In addition, pregnancies have declined by 40 percent and fertility by 23 percent.

592. Fischman, Susan H., and Howard A. Palley. "Adolescent Unwed Motherhood: Implications for a National Family Policy." HEALTH AND SOCIAL WORK 3 (1978): 30-46.

Describes out-of-wedlock pregnancies and choosing to keep and rear the child among adolescents from poor families as a cultural adaptation to conditions of poverty. Argues that without a national policy to affect change in their economic, social and ecological situation there will be no incentive to change the culture supporting early unwed motherhood.

593. Gilchrist, Lewayne D., and Steven P. Schinke. "Coping With Contraception: Cognitive and Behavioral Methods With Adolescents." COGNITIVE THERAPY AND RESEARCH 7 (1983): 379-388.

Uses data on 107 middle class suburban adolescents divided into treatment and control groups to evaluate the efficiency of cognitive behavioral treatment when conducted in the natural environment with groups larger than 20 members. Found that the cognitive behavioral treatment can help adolescents acquire the skills needed to reduce unwanted pregnancies even when the treatment is given in large groups.

594. Goodwin, Norma J. "Unplanned Adolescent Pregnancy: Challenge for the 1980s." JOURNAL OF COMMUNITY HEALTH 11 (Spring 1986): 6-9.

Introduces the articles in a special issue devoted to "Black Adolescent Pregnancy." Argues that solid research and broad community input should form the basis for policy and program development.

595. Govan, Carrie; Savage, Barbara; and Karen Pittman. ADOLESCENT PREGNANCY: WHAT THE STATES ARE SAYING. Washington, D.C.: Children's Defense Fund's Adolescent Pregnancy Prevention Clearing House (March 1986).

Examines 16 state reports on adolescent pregnancy and reviews their findings as well as some of the recent actions taken by states in their attempt to prevent adolescent pregnancy. The report is intended as a reference for those who are interested in what states can do.

596. Guttmacher Institute. "The Unmet Need for Legal Abortion Services in the United States." FAMILY PLANNING PERSPECTIVES 5 (September/October 1975): 224-230.

Summarizes the results of a study designed to measure the responses of health institutions and professionals in the United States to the 1973 Supreme Court decision regarding abortion. Found that the health institutions in many areas of the country responded in such a limited fashion that they really can be seen as not responding at all. The overall result has been the establishment of abortion services that are differentially available in terms of geographical location, quality and cost.

597. Hardy, Janet B. "Preventing Adolescent Pregnancy: Counseling Teens and Their Parents." MEDICAL ASPECTS OF HUMAN SEXUALITY (July 1987): 32-46.

Describes the findings of a study to evaluate the effectiveness of a pregnancy prevention program carried out with the cooperation of the Baltimore school system. Several significant differences were found between the program participants and a control group. The program participants showed greater gains in knowledge related to reproduction and contraception, they were more likely to attend contraceptive clinics and to use the more effective means of birth control. Program participants also delayed the age at first intercourse. Among those girls who were exposed to the program for a full three years there was a significant decrease in pregnancy experience (30.1%) while in the comparison group there was a 57.6 percent increase. Notes that the program also had an impact on the incidence of sexually transmitted diseases.

598. Height, Dorothy I. "Changing the Patterns of Children Having Children." JOURNAL OF COMMUNITY HEALTH 11 (Spring 1986): 41-44.
Discusses the problems associated with adolescent pregnancy and describes how the problems have been approached in a rural Mississippi community through the joint efforts of a national organization and individual members of the community. Argues that it is through continued and intensive collective effort that the black community will be able to assess and meet its needs.

599. Johnson, Robert L. "Preventing Adolescent Pregnancy: Meeting the Comprehensive Range of Needs." JOURNAL OF COMMUNITY HEALTH 11 (Spring 1986): 35-49.
Argues that in order to provide comprehensive treatment for pregnant adolescents, potentially pregnant adolescents, and the adolescent male it must be recognized that their needs vary along with their stage of adolescent development. Describes the needs associated with early, middle and late adolescence.

600. Johnson, Kay A. BUILDING HEALTH PROGRAMS FOR TEENAGERS. Washington, D.C.: Children's Defense Fund's Adolescent Pregnancy Prevention Clearing House (May 1986).
Estimates the health status and needs of children aged 10-20, with an emphasis on those who are poor. Describes the types of health services that are most suitable to meeting those needs, evaluates the adequacy of health programs currently serving

adolescents and makes recommendations for improving the provision of health services for this group.

601. Miller, Susan and Karen Pittman. OPPORTUNITIES FOR PREVENTION: BUILDING AFTER-SCHOOL AND SUMMER PROGRAMS FOR YOUNG ADOLESCENTS. Washington, D.C.: Children's Defense Fund's Adolescent Pregnancy Prevention Clearing House (July 1987).

Examines the significant role that can be played by well designed community programs in meeting the academic, pre-vocational, physical, social and emotional needs of 10-15 year olds in the after-school, vacation and summer hours.

602. Nix, Lulu Mae; Pasteur, Alfred B.; and Myrtice A. Servance. "Focus Group of Study of Sexually Active Black Male Teenagers." ADOLESCENCE (Fall 1988): 741-751.

Describes the intensive group discussions of 20 adolescent males on the meaning of success, on being a teenager, on dating and sex. The young men were also asked to discuss what services they would like to see offered by a comprehensive program. Overall these adolescents recognized that success meant completing school. Yet they found that as teenagers they had a difficult time resisting the pressure put on them by their peers to become involved in "streetlife" activities. Overall they saw dating as an expensive prelude to sexual intercourse. The services they requested were: (1) job training and placement; (2) vocational counseling; (3) educational services; (4) medical services; (5) nutrition information; (6) day care for children; (7) training in parenting skills; (8) family planning; (9) counseling; and (10) recreational activities.

603. Pittman, Karen, and Carrie Govan. MODEL PROGRAMS: PREVENTING ADOLESCENT PREGNANCY AND BUILDING YOUTH SELF SUFFICIENCY. Washington, D.C.: Children's Defense Fund's Adolescent Pregnancy Prevention Clearing House (July 1986).

Describes a number of high quality and innovative programs and curricula that deal with adolescents' needs for information, services and motivation for preventing adolescent pregnancy and increasing the self sufficiency of youth. The programs described are not presented as definitive models but rather as examples of the range of innovative strategies.

604. Pittman, Karen; Adams, Gina; Adams-Taylor, Sharon; and
     Mary Morich. WHAT ABOUT THE BOYS? TEENAGE
     PREGNANCY PREVENTION STRATEGIES. Washington,
     D.C.: Children's Defense Fund's Adolescent Pregnancy
     Prevention Clearing House (July 1988).
     Contains descriptions of 27 programs that address the need
     young males have for information, counseling and services related
     to sexuality. Also presents the views of researchers and program
     experts on three areas of inquiry. How great are the gender
     differences in sexual and contraceptive attitudes and behavior
     and what is the origin of these differences? What is the
     relationship between the ability of young males to escape the
     responsibilities of fatherhood and their motivation to be sexually
     responsible? Given what is known what kinds of program efforts
     should be created for boys?

605. Pittman, Karen. PREVENTING ADOLESCENT
     PREGNANCY: WHAT SCHOOLS CAN DO. Washington,
     D.C.: Children's Defense Fund's Adolescent Pregnancy
     Prevention Clearing House (September 1986).
     Begins by presenting data which shows the strong relationship
     between "life options" and adolescent parenthood. Offers a
     definition of what youths need to increase their "life options" and
     explores the role of schools in the development of youth.
     Examines the current state of family life education in schools as
     well as the more recent intensive school based efforts that provide
     not only information but also counseling and comprehensive
     health services. Attempts to develop an agenda for the schools
     that meets the diverse needs of adolescents.

606. Pittman, Karen. ADOLESCENT PREGNANCY: WHOSE
     PROBLEM IS IT? Washington, D.C.: Children's Defense
     Fund's Adolescent Pregnancy Prevention Clearing House
     (January 1980).
     Explains that adolescent parenthood is a problem not because
     births to adolescents are increasing (they are not), but because
     adolescent parenthood interferes with and often hinders the
     adolescent's transition to adulthood. Answers the question of
     whose problem is adolescent pregnancy in two ways. First the
     high relative rate in the U.S. as compared to that in other
     industrialized countries is presented to emphasize the fact that it
     is the nation's problem. Then the rate for poor minority teens is
     compared to that for advantaged non minority adolescents to

demonstrate that in poor and minority communities the problem
is a crisis. Makes recommendations for prevention.

607. Randolph, Linda A., and Melita Gesche. "Black Adolescent
     Pregnancy: Prevention and Management." JOURNAL OF
     COMMUNITY HEALTH 11 (Spring 1986): 10-18.
     Presents a brief overview of the prevalence and problems
     associated with adolescent pregnancy and parenthood. Describes
     the Teen Pregnancy Initiative of the State of New York. Argues
     that better off members of the black community and health care
     professionals are the human capital needed to address the
     problem.

608. Schinke, Steven; Gilchrist, Lewayne; and Richard W. Small.
     "Preventing Unwanted Adolescent Pregnancy: A Cognitive-
     Behavioral Approach." AMERICAN JOURNAL OF
     ORTHOPSYCHIATRY 49 (January 1979): 81-88.
     Conceptualized the prevention of pregnancy among adolescents
     as involving four steps:(1) access to relevant reproductive and
     contraceptive information; (2) accurate perception,
     comprehension and storage of this information; (3)
     personalization and use of information in decision making; and
     (4) decision implementation through overt behavior.

609. Schinke, Steven P. "Adolescent Pregnancy: An Interpersonal
     Skill Training Approach to Prevention." SOCIAL WORK IN
     HEALTH CARE 3 (Winter 1977): 159-168.
     Summarizes the consequences of adolescent pregnancy and
     parenthood and the nature of strategies used in attempts at
     prevention. Then describes a pilot study undertaken to assess
     the feasibility of training sexually active adolescents in
     interpersonal communication skills as a way of reducing
     adolescent pregnancy.

610. Zabin, Laurie S.; Hirsch, Marilyn B.; Smith, Edward A.; Streett,
     Rosalie and Janet B. Hardy. "Evaluation of a Pregnancy
     Prevention Program for Urban Teenagers." FAMILY
     PLANNING PERSPECTIVES 18 (May/June 1986): 119-126.

3. *Pregnant and Parenting Teens*

611. Adams, Barbara N.; Brownstein, Carol A.; Rennalls, Ivy M.; and Madeline H. Schmitt. "The Pregnant Adolescent-A Group Approach." ADOLESCENCE 11 (Winter 1976): 467-485.

Describes the structure, leadership, content patterns, techniques and research questions which emerged from the group approach to pregnant adolescents developed by the Rochester Adolescent Maternity Project (RAMP).

612. Adler, Emily S.; Bates, Mildred; and Joan M. Merdinger. "Educational Policies and Programs for Teenage Parents and Pregnant Teenagers." FAMILY RELATIONS 34 (April 1985): 183-187.

Examines the adolescent pregnancy avoidance programs of public school systems in Rhode Island using the responses of 20 school officials to self-administered questionnaires. Finds that the communities of Rhode Island have a variety of programs for handling and educating pregnant teenagers; because in the absence of clear guidelines from the state, the local communities are responsible by default for setting their own policies.

613. Ambrose, Linda. "Misinforming Pregnant Teenagers." FAMILY PLANNING PERSPECTIVES 10 (January/February 1978): 51-57.

Concludes that there are few educational and informational sources available to either pregnant adolescents or adolescents who have recently given birth. The few materials available are inadequate to meet their needs. Especially lacking are materials that would help them avoid repeat pregnancies.

614. Baptiste, David A. "Counseling the Pregnant Adolescent Within a Family Context." FAMILY THERAPY 13 (1986): 162-176.

Argues that family focused crisis intervention is an effective approach to use in counseling pregnant adolescents and their families. This approach recognizes the interrelationship of the pregnant adolescent and her family and unlike approaches based on the individual does not increase the amount of stress on the family. Strategies are suggested which can allow families with pregnant adolescents to achieve a meaningful resolution of the crisis through an alliance between parents, adolescents and counselors.

615. Bernstein, Rose. "Gaps in Services to Unmarried Mothers." CHILDREN 10 (March/April 1963): 49-54.
Asks why there are gaps in services to unmarried mothers. How are services distributed to various subgroups of the population of unmarried mothers? Does every unmarried mother require social services? And why are certain services such as prenatal care underutilized? Argues that gaps in services are frequently associated with gaps in knowledge. Also argues that it is important to improve supportive services so that no unmarried mother is denied service because of her race or place of residence. Points out that assumptions about cultural background do in fact affect the distribution of services. In white middle class adolescents, for example, unmarried pregnancies are often seen as indicators of individual psychopathology and a great deal of emphasis is then placed on providing psychological counseling. On the other hand, beliefs about the acceptability of illegitimacy among Negroes are utilized to assume that such unmarried mothers do not require services such as shelter care. Yet when such services are available to them, they use them.

616. Blinn, Lynn M. "Phototherapeutic Intervention to Improve Self-Concept and Prevent Repeat Pregnancies Among Adolescents." FAMILY RELATIONS 36 (July 1987): 252-257.
Presents a logical justification for using phototherapy with pregnant adolescents as a means of reducing subsequent unwanted births. Argues that if, as other authors have argued, those adolescents with low self images are the most likely to have repeated pregnancies then using phototherapy to elevate their views of themselves should have an inhibiting effect on subsequent fertility. Describes an ongoing experiment designed to test this view.

617. Braen, Bernard B. "The Evolution of a Therapeutic Group Approach to School-Age Pregnant Girls." ADOLESCENCE 5 (Summer 1970): 171-186.

618. Brown, Shirley Vining. "Early Childbearing and Poverty: Implications for Social Services." ADOLESCENCE 17 (Summer 1982): 397-408.

Reports the results of an analysis of national survey data which demonstrated that current social services lack programs designed to directly improve the economic well being of adolescent mothers and their children even though it is widely known that economic problems are among the most pervasive of the negative outcomes associated with early childbearing. Discusses the needed restructuring of social service systems.

619. Burt, Martha R., and Freya Sonenstein. "Planning Programs for Pregnant Teenagers: First You Define the Problem."
PUBLIC WELFARE (Spring 1985):
Uses data on twenty one care programs funded by the Office of Adolescent Pregnancy Programs to offer guidelines for designing and delivering such services. Addresses such issues as location, structure and services as well as cost effectiveness.

620. Canada, Mary J. "Adolescent Pregnancy: Networking and the Interdisciplinary Approach." JOURNAL OF COMMUNITY HEALTH 11 (Spring 1986):58-62.
Describes the Brooklyn Teen Pregnancy Network which was developed out of a recognition that the magnitude of the adolescent pregnancy problem in Brooklyn required a borough wide coordinated response by agencies that serve adolescents. The goals of the network are to: (1) increase communication among agencies which provide services to pregnant, parenting and at risk adolescents and; (2) to encourage service use on the part of the hard to reach population.

621. Cartoof, Virginia G. "Postpartum Services for Adolescent Mothers Part 2." CHILD WELFARE. 18 (December 1979): 673-680.
Describes the experience of the Boston based Crittenton-Hastings House in extending its services from the prenatal to the postnatal period of 77 black, poor young mothers. The client was visited in her home at regular intervals and offered support with continuing her education, finding a job and using birth control. Argues that young mothers need educational programs that are challenging and interesting which contain built in work components. They also need centers to care for their children from infancy and which are located in the schools the young mothers attend. They also need some type of supervised living arrangements when they desire to leave the parental home. They need birth control methods with fewer unwanted side effects and

which are easier to use. They also clearly need comprehensive services not only during their pregnancies but for several years after their children are born.

622. Children's Defense Fund. CHILD CARE: AN ESSENTIAL SERVICE FOR TEEN PARENTS. Washington, D.C.: Children's Defense Fund's Adolescent Pregnancy Prevention Clearing House (March 1987).
Focuses on child care for the children of adolescent mothers. Reviews the standards for good programs and the obstacles to achieving them. Also describes several model programs and some different state initiatives. Points out that while not nearly enough is being done the growing activity in this area shows promise.

623. Furstenberg, Frank F., Jr.; Masnick, G.S.; and Susan A. Ricketts. "How Can Family Planning Programs Delay Repeat Teenage Pregnancies?" FAMILY PLANNING PERSPECTIVES 4 (July 1972): 54-60.
Uses data from the first three waves of a longitudinal study of the Adolescent Family Clinic at Baltimore's Mt. Sinai Hospital to illuminate how family planning service experiences affect the timing of subsequent births to adolescent mothers. Compares the subsequent fertility of program participants to those in the hospital's regular prenatal program. Finds that the risk of pregnancy fluctuates with changes in the life circumstances of adolescents. Argues that programs which deal with adolescents only in the prenatal and early postnatal periods have little effect on subsequent fertility. Suggests that programs which are effective must offer long term continuing care which is sensitive to the life changes and contraceptive problems experienced by participants.

624. Gallagher, Eugene, and Michael G. Farrall. "Adolescent Vicissitudes and Medical Judgement: A Case Study." ADOLESCENCE 87 (Fall 1987): 671-680.
Describes a very tragic case in which the pregnant adolescent died. Suggests that if her case had been handled differently she might have lived. The authors argue that this adolescent, Lisa, died because the social and medical services provided to her did not meet her needs. Social Services were too fragmented and mired in bureaucracy to provide for Lisa. The medical profession, it is argued, made decisions about Lisa's treatment on "technical" grounds which did not take into account the

vulnerability associated with her stage in life, especially her potential to be sexually active and pregnant.

625. Hardy, Janet B.; Welcher, Doris W.; Stanely, Jay; and Joseph R. Dallas. "Long-Range Outcome of Adolescent Pregnancy." CLINICAL OBSTETRICS AND GYNECOLOGY 21 (December 1978): 1215-1232.
    Describes the long range outcomes of adolescent pregnancy using data from the Johns Hopkins Child Development Study (JHCDS). The study first began in 1959 and included children born through the summer of 1965. Approximately 4,600 women and their children were included in the study. The children and their mothers were studied when the children were four, seven and 12 years old. Over all the outcomes of births to adolescent mothers are seen as having more negative outcomes for the child in terms of health and cognitive and social development. Briefly describes a program that was started in 1974 to reduce the negative consequences.

626. Klerman, Lorraine V. "Adolescent Mothers and Their Children: Another Population That Requires Family Care." HOME HEALTH CARE SERVICES QUARTERLY 3 (1982): 111-128.
    Describes the emergence of adolescent parenting as a problem. Points out that the adolescent mother has a dual set of developmental tasks. She must accomplish the goals for her own individual maturation and child rearing. Describes the kinds of familial and agency supports that the young mother requires if her child is to achieve optimal development and the adult generation is not to be severely penalized.

627. Klerman, Lorraine V. "Evaluating Service Programs for School-Age Parents Design Problems." EVALUATIONS AND THE HEALTH PROFESSIONS 1 (March 1979): 55-70.
    Critically analyzes published studies describing the accomplishments of programs designed to provide services to pregnant and parenting adolescents. Given that more than a thousand such programs existed by 1977, there are very few published evaluations. Those that do exist suffer from a number of methodological problems including the absence of control groups, poor response rates, concentration on minority populations, and on a limited number of outcome variables. The existing reports suggest that programs achieve short-term

reductions in the negative consequences associated with adolescent pregnancy and parenthood but their effects on long term consequences are limited.

628. Landy, Sarah and Susan Walsh. "Early Intervention with High Risk Teenage Mothers and Their Infants." EARLY CHILD DEVELOPMENT AND CARE 37 (1988): 27-46.

629. Lineberger, Mable Rowe. "Pregnant Adolescents Attending Prenatal Parent Education Classes: Self-Concept, Anxiety and Depression Levels." ADOLESCENCE 22 (Spring 1985): 179-193.

Uses data on 48 adolescents to examine the personality characteristics, self concept, anxiety and depression of pregnant and nonpregnant teens and to determine if there are differences in these characteristics between those who attend prenatal parenting classes and those who do not. Overall there were no differences in the personality characteristics of the three groups.

630. Magid, Tracey D.; Gross, Barbara Danzger; and Bernard J. Shuman. "Preparing Pregnant Teenagers for Parenthood." THE FAMILY COORDINATOR (July 1979): 359-362.

Describes a program designed to teach infant development and child rearing skills to pregnant and parenting school age adolescents. A recent graduate of the program and her infant visit the alternative school for pregnant adolescents where her interaction with her infant is observed by current program participants and developmental psychologists. An examination of evaluations filled out by 159 participants indicate that the focused discussions served to sensitize the young mothers-to-be to many child rearing issues including, the needs of young children, the reasons behind certain infant behaviors, the individual differences among infants, age appropriate play materials and scheduling patterns. Discusses the implications for training parents of all ages and social backgrounds.

631. Matin, Khadijah. "Adolescent Pregnancy: The Perspective of the Sisterhood of Black Single Mothers." JOURNAL OF COMMUNITY HEALTH 11 (Spring 1986): 49-53.

Describes the Sisterhood of Black Single Mothers and several of its programs which are designed to deal with adolescent pregnancy. The programs described include the Youth Awareness Project, the Fatherhood Collective, the Big Apple Project, and

Kianga House. Points out that the Sisterhood endeavors not only to meet the specific needs of pregnant and parenting adolescents but also acts as advocates, role models, and the proponents of a value system which is congruent with positive family development.

632. Nelson, Margaret K. "The Effect of Childbirth Preparation on Women of Different Social Classes." JOURNAL OF HEALTH AND SOCIAL BEHAVIOR 23 (December 1982): 339-352.
Employs data on 322 white women, 15-38 years old collected from questionnaires they filled out in their ninth month of pregnancy, interviews while they were still in the hospital and a second questionnaire six weeks after the birth. The focus of the investigation was the relationship between social class and preparation for childbirth. Found that taking classes as preparation for childbirth appears to have a greater effect on working-class women than middle-class women. The socialization for childbirth in these classes had different effects on working-class and middle-class women. Overall, working-class women became less amenable to certain types of medical intervention, while the middle-class ones became more accepting of medical routine.

633. Nelson, Brenda. "A Comprehensive Program for Pregnant Adolescents: Parenting and Prevention." CHILD WELFARE 63 (January/February 1989):
Describes the Teen Pregnancy Project which was initiated in 1981 in order to reduce the infant mortality rate. This project has evolved into a multiservice program. Its ability to deliver services, however, is tied into an aggressive outreach program which includes home visits to establish meaningful relationships with clients.

634. Osofsky, Howard J., and Joy D. Osofsky. "Adolescents as Mothers: Results of a Program for Low-Income Pregnant Teenagers with Some Emphasis upon Infants' Development." AMERICAN JOURNAL OF ORTHOPSYCHIATRY 40 (October 1970): 825-834.
Describes the effects of a service program for parenting adolescents and their infants. Argues that with programs like YMED medical complications, prematurity and perinatal mortality in adolescent mothers can be greatly reduced. Shows that subsequent fertility and educational failure can also be

reduced. Points out, however, that many residual problems remain both for the adolescent mother and her child.

635. Polit, Denise, and Janet R. Kahn. "Project Redirection: Evaluation of a Comprehensive Program for Disadvantaged Teenage Mothers." FAMILY PLANNING PERSPECTIVES 17 (July/August): 150-155.

Compares parenting adolescents who had been participants in Project Redirection to a control group of similar teens who were not program participants. The project was a comprehensive service program for pregnant and parenting adolescents designed to direct them away from a life path characterized by chronic dependency. Found that after one year project participants were more likely to be using contraceptives, more likely to be in school and less likely to have experienced a subsequent pregnancy. After two years, however, each of these differences had disappeared. Argues that what is most immediately implicated by the short term nature of positive outcomes is stronger interventions.

636. Polit, Denise. "Teenage Mothers Five Years Later: Project Redirection Followup." TEC NETWORKS: NEWSLETTER OF THE TOO-EARLY-CHILDBEARING NETWORKS OF PROGRAMS SPONSORED BY THE CHARLES STEWART MOTT FOUNDATION 19 (December 1988): 1-2.

Summarizes the results of the five year follow-up of participants in Project Redirection. Unlike the third year results summarized above the findings of this study show more positive program effects. Here the program participants were found to be working more hours per week and to have higher weekly earnings than the comparison group. The program participants were found to be more likely to have breast fed their babies and to currently be providing their children with a home environment that was more stimulating. Children of the program participants scored higher on tests of vocabulary and behavior than did children in the comparison group.

637. Romig, Charles A., and J. Graham Thompson. "Teenage Pregnancy: A Family Systems Approach." THE AMERICAN JOURNAL OF FAMILY THERAPY 16 (1988): 133-143.

Questions the basic assumptions underlying the services delivered to late adolescents experiencing an "unplanned" pregnancy. Presupposes the existence of a two-parent family system and sees the pregnancy as a symptom of family dysfunction. By becoming pregnant the adolescent stabilizes the existing problematic system rather than braving the "normal" disengagement process. Discusses how service providers must deal with this situation in order to help both the adolescent and her parents.

638. Sarrell, Philip M. "The University Hospital and the Teenage Unwed Mother." AMERICAN JOURNAL OF PUBLIC HEALTH 57 (August 1967): 308-313.

Describes a multidisciplinary program for unmarried adolescent mothers established in the Department of Obstetrics and Gynecology at the Yale University Hospital. Argues that even though the program has existed for only a short period of time and served only a small number of patients, positive outcomes are already apparent. The young women in the program have less complicated labors and deliveries than non program teens. Part of this benefit is seen as coming from the program of special education which program participants receive. It is considered to be extremely important that the low income Negro girls in the program receive prenatal, delivery, and postpartum services from the same obstetrician who is thereby able to develop an influential doctor patient relationship with them. The program is also credited with providing a center around which widespread community concern could coalesce.

639. Wallace, Helen W.; Weeks, John; and Antonio Medina. "Services for and Needs of Pregnant Teenagers in Large Cities in the United States, 1979-80." PUBLIC HEALTH REPORTS 97 (November/December 1982): 583-588.

Summarizes the third in a series of national surveys of the needs and services for pregnant and parenting adolescents and their offspring in United States cities with populations of more than 100,000. Since the 1976 survey only five of these cities have established new programs for these populations. It is not clear whether the major problem is lack of funding or the attitudes of the cities' responsible adult population. Areas in which a significant amount of need continues to be unmet include health supervision and medical care, education, social services, vocational assistance, financial aid, infant day care, family life education, family planning and abortion services.

640. Weatherley, Richard A.; Perlman, Sylvia B.; Levine, Michael H.; and Lorraine V. Klerman. "Comprehensive Programs for Pregnant Teenagers and Teenage Parents: How Successful Have They Been?" FAMILY PLANNING PERSPECTIVES 18 (March/April 1986): 73-78.

641. Zellman, Gail. "Public School Programs for Adolescent Pregnancy and Parenthood: An Assessment." FAMILY PLANNING PERSPECTIVES 14 (January/February 1982): 15-21.

Reports the finding of a study in which 367 interviews were conducted with state officials, school staff, and pregnant and parenting adolescents from 11 school districts around the country. The conclusions reached were the following. The school districts deal with teen pregnancy in a very passive and limited fashion, often only to the extent required to be in compliance with the law. The administrators tend to believe that special programs are very expensive yet do not seek external funding or innovative arrangements. When special programs do come into existence, it is often because of the persistence of a single individual. Once a special program is put into place it tends to be seen as the only local response necessary. While the quality of the programs is uneven most meet some of the needs of the target population but none meet all of the needs.

642. Smith, Peggy B.; Nenney, Susan W.; Weinman, Maxine L.; and David M. Mumford. "Factors Affecting Perception of Pregnancy Risk in the Adolescent." JOURNAL OF YOUTH AND ADOLESCENCE 11 (1982): 207-215.

Uses data on 104 low income adolescent mothers to evaluate the effectiveness of a prenatal education class presented in a maternity clinic. Found that the young mothers are successful in utilizing short term content such as instructions in well baby care and birth control. However, they have more difficulty in retaining and utilizing information for the intermediate (such as correct notions of child development) and long term time span, such as vocational or educational reentry.

B. Chapters in Books

1. *Adolescent Family Planning*

643. Feldman, Margaret, and Catherine S. Chilman. Contraceptive and Abortion Services for Adolescents." ADOLESCENT SEXUALITY IN A CHANGING AMERICAN SOCIETY. by Catherine S. Chilman. New York: John Wiley and Sons, 1983, pp. 251-274.

644. Ingersoll, Ralph W. "Administrative Concerns." ADOLESCENT PREGNANCY: PERSPECTIVES FOR THE HEALTH CARE PROFESSIONAL. Edited by Peggy B. Smith and David M. Mumford. Boston: G.K. Hall, 1980, pp. 14-22.
Discusses how an administrator should approach the questions of adolescent pregnancy and presents information designed to address the questions that administrators often raise.

645. Jaffe, Frederick S., and Joy Dryfoos. "Fertility Control Services for Adolescents: Access and Utilization." ADOLESCENT PREGNANCY AND CHILDBEARING: FINDINGS FROM RESEARCH. Edited by Catherine S. Chilman. U. S. Department of Health and Human Services, 1980, pp. 129-176.
Discusses the changes in recent years in the use of family planning services by adolescents using the 1971 Johns Hopkins study as a baseline.

646. Kreipe, Richard. "Prevention of Adolescent Pregnancy: A Developmental Approach." PREMATURE ADOLESCENT PREGNANCY AND PARENTHOOD. Edited by Elizabeth McAnarney. New York: Grune and Stratton, 1983, pp. 37-60.
Emphasizes the shaping of responsible adolescent behavior in the context of development factors based upon the supposition that responsible adolescent behavior will prevent more pregnancies than either the prescribing of contraceptives or the proscribing of adolescent sexuality. Also talks about traditional approaches to prevention in terms of their level.

647. Ktsanes, Virginia. "The Teenager and the Family Planning
     Experience." ADOLESCENT PREGNANCY AND
     CHILDBEARING: FINDINGS FROM RESEARCH.
     Edited by Catherine S. Chilman. U. S. Department of Health
     and Human Services, 1980, pp. 83-100.
     Summarizes the findings of three studies concerned with the
     largely poor black adolescents who received services from the
     Louisiana Family Planning Program.

648. Smith, Peggy B. "Reproductive Health Care for Teens."
     ADOLESCENT PARENTHOOD. Edited by Max Sugar.
     New York: SP Medical and Scientific Books, 1984, pp. 159-
     180.
     Describes the development of family planning services for teens,
     the basic challenges they face, and how they can be made more
     effective.

649. Smith, Peggy B. "Programs for Sexually Active Teens."
     ADOLESCENT PREGNANCY: PERSPECTIVES FOR
     THE HEALTH CARE PROFESSIONAL. Edited by Peggy
     B. Smith and David M. Mumford. Boston: G.K. Hall, 1980,
     pp. 77-97.
     Reviews the variety of programs that have been instituted to
     deal with the problem of adolescent pregnancy. Points out that
     most of them deal with problems after the fact and largely ignore
     the role of the male.

2. *Adolescent Pregnancy Prevention*

650. Crawford, Albert G., and Frank F. Furstenberg, Jr. "Teenage
     Sexuality, Pregnancy, and Childbearing." HANDBOOK OF
     CHILD WELFARE. Edited by Joan Laird and Ann
     Hartman. New York: The Free Press, 1985, pp. 532-559.
     Explores many of the issues concerned with adolescent
     childbearing in contemporary American society with an emphasis
     on prevention.

651. Cutright, Phillips. "Teenage Illegitimacy: The Prospect for
     Deliberate Change." THE TEENAGE PREGNANT GIRL.
     Edited by Jack Zackler and Wayne Brandstadt. Springfield,
     Illinois: Charles C. Thomas, 1975, pp. 47-82.

Argues that attempts to prevent illegitimate births among adolescents must involve abortion on demand as well as the availability of contraceptives.

652. Davis, Kingsley. "A Theory of Teenage Pregnancy in the United States." ADOLESCENT PREGNANCY AND CHILDBEARING: FINDINGS FROM RESEARCH. Edited by Catherine S. Chilman. U. S. Department of Health and Human Services, 1980, pp. 309-339.
Describes the trends in adolescent childbearing, restates the problem, lists the questions that a theory of adolescent childbearing in the United States must provide answers to. Concludes with the idea that the solution to the problem lies not in providing contraception and abortion to children but in restructuring the institution underlying male-female relationships and returning to the family responsibility for its children.

653. Furstenberg, Frank F., Jr., Jr. "The Social Consequences of Teenage Parenthood." ADOLESCENT PREGNANCY AND CHILDBEARING: FINDINGS FROM RESEARCH. Edited by Catherine S. Chilman. U. S. Department of Health and Human Services, 1980, pp. 267-309.
Adapts the discussion of the Baltimore study presented in several articles.

654. Gilchrist, Lewayne D., and Steven Paul Schinke. "Counseling with Adolescents About Their Sexuality." ADOLESCENT SEXUALITY IN A CHANGING AMERICAN SOCIETY. by Catherine S. Chilman. New York: John Wiley and Sons, 1983, pp. 251-274.

655. Greydanus, Donald E. "The Health System's Responsibility to the Adolescent at Risk." PREGNANCY IN ADOLESCENCE: NEEDS, PROBLEMS, AND MANAGEMENT. Edited by Irving R. Stuart and Carl F. Wells. New York: Van Nostrand Reinhold Company, 1982, pp. 48-65.
Argues that all health care professionals should provide adolescents and their parents with counseling about developing sexuality and contraception. Describes the contraceptive methods which would be introduced in the counseling sessions and evaluates their potential effectiveness when used by adolescents.

3. *Pregnant and Parenting Teens*

656. Anastasiow, Nicholas. "Preparing Adolescents in Childbearing:
     Before and After Pregnancy." ADOLESCENT
     PARENTHOOD. Edited by Max Sugar. New York: SP
     Medical and Scientific Books, 1984, pp. 141-158.
     Describes programs designed to respond to teenage sexuality
     which deal either with preventing adolescent pregnancies or
     attempting to train the young parents how to raise their child.

657. Authier, Karen, and Jerry Authier. "Intervention with Families
     of Pregnant Adolescents." PREGNANCY IN
     ADOLESCENCE: NEEDS, PROBLEMS, AND
     MANAGEMENT. Edited by Irving R. Stuart and Carl F.
     Wells. New York: Van Nostrand Reinhold Company, 1982,
     pp. 290-313.
     Discusses a family systems approach to dealing with the
     pregnant adolescent which takes into account the mutually
     interdependent nature of her adaptation to and resolution of the
     crises of pregnancy and her family's.

658. Badger, Earladeen. "Effects of Parent Education Program on
     Teenage Mothers and Their Offspring." TEENAGE
     PARENTS AND THEIR OFFSPRING. Edited by Keith G.
     Scott, Tiffany Field and Euan G. Robertson. New York:
     Grune and Stratton, 1981, pp. 283-316.
     Describes the implementation of the Infant Stimulation Mother
     Training Project for welfare dependent adolescent mothers begin
     at Cincinnati General Hospital at the instigation of the staff of the
     Cincinnati Infant Care Program. Describes the structure of the
     program and its effectiveness. Points out, however, that it
     represents only the start of the type of support communities must
     offer adolescent mothers and their offspring if they are to escape
     the poverty trap.

659. DeRose, Ann M. "Identifying Needs, Gaining Support for and
     Establishing an Innovative School Based Program for
     Pregnant Adolescents." PREGNANCY IN
     ADOLESCENCE: NEEDS, PROBLEMS, AND
     MANAGEMENT. Edited by Irving R. Stuart and Carl F.
     Wells. New York: Van Nostrand Reinhold Company, 1982,
     pp. 337-362.

Describes the establishment of a school based program for pregnant adolescents in a rural or semirural setting.

660. Eisman, Howard D., and Frederick L. Covan. "The Emotionally Disturbed Pregnant Adolescent." PREGNANCY IN ADOLESCENCE: NEEDS, PROBLEMS, AND MANAGEMENT. Edited by Irving R. Stuart and Carl F. Wells. New York: Van Nostrand Reinhold Company, 1982, pp. 314-336.
Discusses the added complications to the problems of adolescent pregnancy when dealing with young women who in addition to being pregnant are emotionally disturbed using five case histories.

661. Forbush, Janet Bell, with Teresa Maciocha. "Adolescent Parent Programs and Family Involvement." TEENAGE PREGNANCY IN A FAMILY CONTEXT. Edited by Theodora Ooms. Philadelphia: Temple University Press, 1981, pp. 254-276.
Reports on the type and level of family involvement in twenty one programs offering services to pregnant adolescents. Overall the agencies have very little specific information of the types of support offered to pregnant adolescents by their families. Most agencies also had not built family involvement into their programs.

662. Furstenberg, Frank F., Jr.; Herceg-Baron, Roberta; and Jay Jemail. "Bringing in the Family: Kinship Support and Contraceptive Behavior." TEENAGE PREGNANCY IN A FAMILY CONTEXT. Edited by Theodora Ooms. Philadelphia: Temple University Press, 1981, pp. 345-370.
Traces the intellectual origins of a program designed to involve family members in the provision of family planning services to adolescents (the Kinship Support Program) and provides some preliminary observations on its implementation.

663. Gedan, Sharon. "Abortion Counseling with Adolescents." NURSING OF CHILDREN AND ADOLESCENTS. Compiled by Andrea B. O'Connor. New York: The American Journal of Nursing Co., 1975, pp. 234-239.

664. Hardy, Janet B.; King, Theodore M.; Shipp, Denese A.; and Doris Welcher. "A Comprehensive Approach to Adolescent

Pregnancy." TEENAGE PARENTS AND THEIR
OFFSPRING. Edited by Keith G. Scott, Tiffany Field and
Euan G. Robertson. New York: Grune and Stratton, 1981,
pp. 265-282.
Describes the multiple risks associated with unsupported
adolescent pregnancies and the supports offered by a
comprehensive hospital based program, the Johns Hopkins
Adolescent Pregnancy Program. Reports the extent to which the
program ameliorates the negative consequences.

665. Howard, Marion. "Bring About Change: A National Overview
with Respect to Early Childbearing and Childrearing." THE
TEENAGE PREGNANT GIRL. Edited by Jack Zackler
and Wayne Brandstadt. Springfield, Illinois: Charles C.
Thomas, 1975, pp.
Discusses change in the treatment of and services for pregnant
and parenting teens and the relationship between that change and
a research utilization and information sharing project.

666. Jekel, James F., and Lorraine V. Klerman. "Comprehensive
Service Programs for Pregnant and Parenting Adolescents."
PREMATURE ADOLESCENT PREGNANCY AND
PARENTHOOD. Edited by Elizabeth McAnarney. New
York: Grune and Stratton, 1983, pp. 295-310.
Reviews the history and current situation of efforts to provide
comprehensive services to pregnant and parenting teens.

667. Jekel, James F., and Lorraine V. Klerman. "Appraising Your
Program." THE TEENAGE PREGNANT GIRL. Edited by
Jack Zackler and Wayne Brandstadt. Springfield, Illinois:
Charles C. Thomas, 1975, pp. 292-300.
Presents the what, why, when and how of evaluating programs
for pregnant and parenting teens.

668. Klerman, Lorraine V. "Programs for Pregnant Adolescents and
Young Parents: Their Development and Assessment."
TEENAGE PARENTS AND THEIR OFFSPRING. Edited
by Keith G. Scott, Tiffany Field and Euan G. Robertson.
New York: Grune and Stratton, 1981, pp. 227-248.
Describes the proliferation of special services for sexually active,
pregnant, and parenting adolescents. Points out the problems
which such services encounter and makes recommendations for

changes that are needed in service provision and policy approaches if adolescent pregnancy is to be prevented.

669. Klerman, Lorraine V.; Jekel, James F.; and Catherine S. Chilman. ADOLESCENT SEXUALITY IN A CHANGING AMERICAN SOCIETY. by Catherine S. Chilman. New York: John Wiley and Sons, 1983, pp. 167-179.

670. Lightman, Ernie, and Benjamin Schlesinger. "Pregnant Adolescents in Maternity Homes: Some Professional Concerns." PREGNANCY IN ADOLESCENCE: NEEDS, PROBLEMS, AND MANAGEMENT. Edited by Irving R. Stuart and Carl F. Wells. New York: Van Nostrand Reinhold Company, 1982, pp. 363-385.
Describes the decrease in the proportion of pregnant adolescents using the services of traditional maternity homes and profiles pregnant adolescents in Canadian maternity homes.

671. Miller, Shelby H. "The Child Welfare League of America's Adolescent Parents Projects." EVALUATING FAMILY PROGRAMS. Edited Heather Weiss and Francine H. Jacobs. New York: Aldine De Gruyter, 1988, pp. 371-388.
Describes the evaluation of a program for low income, urban, minority teens who were pregnant or parenting. The program was an adaptation of a program which had originally been utilized with a largely white clientele.

672. Ooms, Theodora. "The Family Context of Adolescent Parenting." ADOLESCENT PARENTHOOD. Edited by Max Sugar. New York: SP Medical and Scientific Books, 1984, pp. 215-228.
Presents the social, scientific, and clinical bases for approaching adolescent pregnancy from a family perspective. Argues that the most effective programs for dealing with the problems of adolescent mothers and their children will be those which build upon, supplement, and support the efforts of families rather than replace them.

673. Ryan, Lee, and Ruth Sharpe. "A Comprehensive Service Program for School-Age Pregnant Girls." THE TEENAGE PREGNANT GIRL. Edited by Jack Zackler and Wayne Brandstadt. Springfield, Illinois: Charles C. Thomas, 1975, pp. 259-284.

Describes a comprehensive program for poor pregnant girls implemented in Chicago. Describes the impact of the program on the immediate crisis faced by the teen and her family and highlights the importance of ongoing, continuous evaluation.

674. Salguero, Carlos; Schlesinger, Nancy; and Edilma Yearwood. "A Mental Health Program for Adolescent Parents." ADOLESCENT PARENTHOOD. Edited by Max Sugar. New York: SP Medical and Scientific Books, 1984, pp. 181-196.
Describes the Teen Pregnancy and Parenting Program developed by the mental health department of a neighborhood health center. Discusses how some of its goals were reached and how other programs can benefit from its experience.

675. Walker, Deborah Klein, and Anita M. Mitchell. "Using an Impact Evaluation Model With Too-Early-Childbearing Programs." EVALUATING FAMILY PROGRAMS. Edited Heather Weiss and Francine H. Jacobs. New York: Aldine De Gruyter, 1988, pp. 407-425.
Describes the use of an impact evaluation model to evaluate programs for pregnant and parenting teens funded by the Charles C. Mott Foundation.

676. Weatherley, Richard, and Virginia G. Cartoof. "Helping Single Adolescent Parents." VARIANT FAMILY FORMS. Edited by Catherine S. Chilman, Elam W. Nunnally, and Fred M. Cox. Beverly Hills: Sage Publications, 1988, 39-55.

677. White, Myrtle; Chevalier, Dorothy; and Ruth T. Gross. "Staffing of Teenage Programs and Attitudes of Staff." THE TEENAGE PREGNANT GIRL. Edited by Jack Zackler and Wayne Brandstadt. Springfield, Illinois: Charles C. Thomas, 1975, pp. 285-291.
Describes how programs for pregnant teens should be structured and staffed with particular attention paid to the attitudes that staff must have toward their young clients if their service is to be beneficial.

C. Books

678. Bedger, Jean E. TEENAGE PREGNANCY: RESEARCH
RELATED TO CLIENTS AND SERVICES. Springfield,
Illinois: Charles C. Thomas, 1980.

679. Cheetham, Juliet. UNWANTED PREGNANCY AND
COUNSELING. London: Routledge and Kegan Paul, 1977.
Discusses from a sociological perspective the relationship
between unwanted pregnancy and the changing roles of men and
women and the function of the family. Also discusses the
psychological aspects and provides guidelines for counselors.

680. Children's Defense Fund. ADOLESCENT PREGNANCY
CHILD WATCH. Washington, D.C.: Children's Defense
Fund, 1984.
Is a manual for helping local citizens and communities create
child Watch projects. Contains a description of the Adolescent
Pregnancy Child Watch, its goals and a detailed statement of the
problem. Details the organization of the projects, the activities
which occur in them and outlines the responsibilities of the
director and the volunteers. Also outlines some follow-up
activities for writing and disseminating final reports and making
effective use of the media. Describes the data collection and
analysis needs. Finally contains several appendices including; a
glossary, examples of effective programs, a list of coalitions
concerned with the problem and a list of federal programs.

681. Corbett, Margaret-Ann, and Jerrilyn H. Meyer. THE
ADOLESCENT AND PREGNANCY. Boston: Blackwell
Scientific Publications, 1987.
Is a text book directed at clinicians who manage the health care
of adolescents.

682. Miller, Shelby H. CHILDREN AS PARENTS: FINAL
REPORT ON A STUDY OF CHILDBEARING AND
CHILD REARING AMONG 12 TO 15 YEAR OLDS. New
York: Research Center Child Welfare League of America,
1983.
Reports on a study designed to: (1) describe in detail adolescent
mothers aged 15 and younger; (2) assess the development of these
young mothers and their children during the first two years of the

child's life; and (3) to determine whether and in what ways younger adolescent mothers differ from their older peers. Overall, two-thirds of the adolescents in the study were, at 18 months postpartum, doing well on many of the measured outcomes: school continuation, contraceptive use or sexual abstinence, routine medical care for self and child, average or advanced developmental level for the child, financial stability, stable child care and living arrangements, and reasonably strong informal support networks. These findings are seen as related to the services that have been provided to the young mothers. That another third are not doing quite so well on these measures is seen as showing how much more work in this area needs to be done. It is also argued that all of these young mothers need long term follow-up.

683. Mishne, Judith Marks. CLINICAL WORK WITH
     ADOLESCENTS. New York: The Free Press, 1086.
     Aims to provide a clear and comprehensive presentation of the fundamentals of clinical assessment and treatment of adolescents. Presents an overview of adolescence and sections on assessment, adolescent pathology, adolescent sexual behavior, selecting a treatment plan, and the treatment process.

684. Nickel, Phyllis Smith, and Holly Delany. WORKING WITH
     TEEN PARENTS: A SURVEY OF PROMISING
     APPROACHES. Chicago: Family Resource Coalition, 1985.
     Describes approximately 40 programs that work with adolescent parents with a focus on identifying successful innovative program strategies.

685. Oettinger, Katherine B., with Elizabeth C. Money. "NOT MY
     DAUGHTER": FACING UP TO ADOLESCENT
     PREGNANCY. Englewood Cliffs, New Jersey: Prentice
     Hall, 1979.
     Discusses the history of concern with the pregnant adolescent, ways of dealing with adolescent sexuality in the home, building programs in the community, and the value of peer counseling. Includes a resource guide listing organizations and program materials.

686. Rains, Prudence Mors. BECOMING AN UNWED MOTHER:
     A SOCIOLOGICAL ACCOUNT. Chicago:
     Aldine/Atherton, 1971.

Describes the process of becoming an unwed mother in two very different groups of girls; a group living in a maternity home and a group of Negro girls who plan to keep their babies. Makes suggestions for services.

687. Rapoport, Robert N. NEW INTERVENTIONS FOR CHILDREN AND YOUTH: ACTION RESEARCH APPROACHES. New York: Cambridge University Press, 1987.

Examines ten projects that represent new approaches to the mental health problems of children and youths. The projects all represent collaborations between an action system operating in the community and researchers. Several of the programs and the research associated with them are concerned with various aspects of adolescent pregnancy and parenting.

688. Worthington, Everett L. COUNSELING FOR UNPLANNED PREGNANCY AND INFERTILITY. Waco, Texas: Word Books, 1987.

Emphasizes the counseling, in Christian contexts, of families experiencing unplanned pregnancies and infertility.

689. Zitner, Rosalind, and Shelby Hayden Miller. OUR YOUNGEST PARENTS. New York: Child Welfare League of American Inc., 1980.

Uses data from 185 adolescent mothers who received services from four Florence Crittenton homes to explore the relation of access to specialized services during pregnancy and immediately after delivery to the young mothers' need for and use of support service. Six major findings are presented. The longer the period of service at the Crittenton agency around the time of pregnancy and delivery, the greater the number of formal services used later. These adolescent mothers made extensive use of informal support networks. The father of the infant provided significant support. The adolescent mothers and their own mothers had different attitudes toward services and different perceptions of unmet needs. A year or more after the birth of their children adolescent mothers still had unmet service needs.

XII. LAWS AND LEGAL ISSUES

A. Articles

690. Monroe, Pamela. "Adolescent Pregnancy Legislation: the Application of An Analytic Framework." FAMILY RELATIONS 36 (January 1987): 15-21.

    Argues that family scientists should be able to read and interpret policies, bills, statutes, committee testimony, and other political documents because they influence our research outputs. Also argues that such skill has the potential to be very beneficial in grant preparation. Presents a framework for analyzing the first phase of policy analysis, the development of the statute. And applies this framework to adolescent pregnancy legislation in order to demonstrate how the framework can be used. Describes the Office of Adolescent Population Affairs.

691. Paul, Eve W., and Harriet F. Pilpel. "Teenagers and Pregnancy: The Law in 1979." FAMILY PLANNING PERSPECTIVES 11 (September/October 1979): 297-302.

    Explains the rulings of the Supreme Court in regard to the reproductive rights of minors. As of 1979 mature minors have the right to consent to their own reproductive health care. All minors must be offered alternatives to parental involvement in such care.

692. Savage, Barbara D. CHILD SUPPORT AND TEEN PARENTS. Washington, D.C.: Children's Defense Fund's Adolescent Pregnancy Prevention Clearing House (November 1987).

    Focuses on ways to increase and improve paternity establishment and other child support enforcement services for the children born to adolescent mothers. Also discusses grandparent liability and the rulings of the Supreme Court in regard to children born out of wedlock.

693. Weinman, Maxine L.; Robinson, Maralyn; Simmons, Jane T.; Schreiber, Nelda B.; and Ben Stafford. "Pregnant Teens: Differential Pregnancy Resolution and Treatment Implications." CHILD WELFARE 68 (January/February): 45-55.

    Points out that there are diverse populations within the universe of adolescent mothers which require different treatment plans.

The profiles of pregnant adolescents in a comprehensive service program identified three different groups of pregnant adolescence in terms of their resolution decisions and adherence to them. The first group was composed of those adolescents who followed through with an initial plan to parent. The second group was composed of those who followed through with an initial plan to adopt. But the third group, comprising as much as one third of the population, was composed of those who changed their minds about putting their children up for adoption. As this last group had not received any of the training or services directed at those who initially planned to parent they fell through what needs to be recognized as a crack in service delivery.

B. Chapters in Books

694. Barkin, Eugene N. "Legal Issues Surrounding Teenage Pregnancy." TEENAGE PARENTS AND THEIR OFFSPRING. Edited by Keith G. Scott, Tiffany Field and Euan G. Robertson. New York: Grune and Stratton, 1981, pp. 55-72.
Reviews decisions of the Supreme Court which have an impact on adolescent pregnancy. Focuses on abortion, birth control, educational regulations and parental and family rights.

695. Dowben, Carla W., and Peggy L. Bunch. "Legal Aspects of Adolescent Pregnancy." ADOLESCENT PREGNANCY: PERSPECTIVES FOR THE HEALTH CARE PROFESSIONAL. Edited by Peggy B. Smith and David M. Mumford. Boston: G.K. Hall, 1980, pp. 173-197.
Treats the legal aspects of the adolescent's right to consent to reproductive health care including contraception and abortion. Discusses the legal views on financial responsibility for such health care, the rights of adolescent fathers, and adolescent family planning legislation.

696. Paul, Eve W., and Paula Schaap. "Legal Rights and Responsibilities of Pregnant Teenagers and Their Children." PREGNANCY IN ADOLESCENCE: NEEDS, Edited by Irving R. Stuart and Carl F. Wells. New York: Van Nostrand Reinhold Company, 1982, pp. 3-26.

Discusses many of the legal problems facing sexually active, pregnant and parenting teens. Discusses the Supreme Court Decisions in regard to abortion and deals with the laws concerned with parental consent and notification. Also talks about the legal distribution of financial rights and obligations and the situations which can result in termination of the teenager's parental rights.

697. Pilpel, Harriet F. "Law Relating to Family Planning Services for Girls Under Eighteen." THE TEENAGE PREGNANT GIRL. Edited by Jack Zackler and Wayne Brandstadt. Springfield, Illinois: Charles C. Thomas, 1975, pp. 231-240.

698. Scharf, Kathleen. "Funding for Pregnant Adolescents: A Legislative History." ADOLESCENT PARENTHOOD. Edited by Max Sugar. New York: SP Medical and Scientific Books, 1984, pp. 197-214.
Outlines the legislative history of the Adolescent Health Services and Pregnancy Prevention Act of 1978. Also discusses changes and attempted changes ushered in by the "New Right" and the Reagan Administration.

699. Steinfels, Margaret O'Brien. "Ethical and Legal Issues in Teenage Pregnancies." TEENAGE PREGNANCY IN A FAMILY CONTEXT. Edited by Theodora Ooms. Philadelphia: Temple University Press, 1981, pp. 277-306.
Discusses the legal and ethical issues surrounding adolescent pregnancy. Examines the rulings of the Supreme Court in this area. Makes recommendations about the type of legal framework which would protect the rights of the adolescent and the role of the family in child rearing.

C. Books

700. Rodman, Hyman; Lewis, Susan; and Saralyn B. Griffith. THE SEXUAL RIGHTS OF ADOLESCENTS. New York: Columbia University Press, 1984.
Focuses on the questions concerned with minors' access to contraception and abortion: Legally, what decisions can minors make and what actions can they take on their own. When must they involve their parents or have their parents' consent? Also reviews the available social science literature on the competence

of minors to make such decisions and that on the contraceptive
and abortion decision making and behavior of adolescents.

XIII. HOLDINGS OF THE DATA ARCHIVE ON ADOLESCENT PREGNANCY AND PREGNANCY PREVENTION (DAAPPP)

701. DAAPPP Data Set 1. 1971 U.S. National Survey of Young Women: Selected Variables (Melvin Zelnik and John Kantner)

702. DAAPPP Data Set 2. 1976 U.S. National Survey of Young Women (John Kantner and Melvin Zelnik)

703. DAAPPP Data Set 3. Project TALENT: Consequences of Adolescent Childbearing for the Young Parents' Future Life, 1960-1974 (J. J. Card)

704. DAAPPP Data Set 4. Detroit Mother-Daughter Communication Patterns: Mother File, 1978 (Greer Fox)

705. DAAPPP Data Set 5. Detroit Mother-Daughter Communication Patterns: Daughter File, 1978 (Greer Fox)

706. DAAPPP Data Set 6. Philadelphia Collaborative Perinatal Project: Economic, Social and Psychological Consequences of Adolescent Childbearing 1959-1965 (Jeanne Marecek)

707. DAAPPP Data Set 7. Nashville General Hospital Comprehensive Child Care Project, 1974-1976: Selected Variables (Howard Sandler)

708. DAAPPP Data Set 8. State Policy Determinants of Teenage Childbearing, 1979 (Kristin Moore)

709. DAAPPP Data Set 9. 1980 U.S. Survey of Services Provided by Adolescent Pregnancy Programs (JRB Associates)

710. DAAPPP Data Set 10. 1982 Evaluation of OAPP Adolescent Pregnancy Programs (Martha Burt)

711. DAAPPP Data Set 11. 1980 Current Population Survey: Selected Variables--Females (U.S. Bureau of the Census)

712. DAAPPP Data Set 12. 1980 Current Population Survey: Selected Variables--Males (U.S. Bureau of the Census)

713. DAAPPP Data Set 13. 1980 Current Population Survey: Selected Variables--Children (U.S. Bureau of the Census)

714. DAAPPP Data Set 14. 1982 Current Population Survey: Selected Variables--Females (U.S. Bureau of the Census)

715. DAAPPP Data Set 15. 1982 Current Population Survey: Selected Variables--Males (U.S. Bureau of the Census)

716. DAAPPP Data Set 16. 1982 Current Population Survey: Selected Variables--Children (U.S. Bureau of the Census)

717. DAAPPP Data Set 17. 1977 Current Population Survey: Selected Variables--Females (U.S. Bureau of the Census)

718. DAAPPP Data Set 18. 1977 Current Population Survey: Selected Variables--Males (U.S. Bureau of the Census)

719. DAAPPP Data Set 19. First U.S. Health and Nutrition Examination Survey (HANES, 1971-1976 (National Center for Health Statistics)

720. DAAPPP Data Set 20-24. National Longitudinal Study of Youth (NLSY), 1979-1982: Selected Variables (Waves 1-4), and Supplementary Variables (Ohio State University)

721. DAAPPP Data Set 25. 1981 U.S. Survey of Title X-Funded Family Planning Clinics (Roberta Herceg-Baron)

722. DAAPPP Data Set 26. 1982 National Survey of Family Growth (NSFG), Cycle III (Women Aged 15-44) (National Center for Health Statistics)

723. DAAPPP Data Set 27. 1982 National Survey of Family Growth (NSFG), Cycle III (Women Aged 15-19) (National Center for Health Statistics)

724. DAAPPP Data Set 28. 1979-1980 U.S. Survey of Unmarried Women under 18 in Family Planning Clinics (Aida Torres)

725. DAAPPP Data Set 29. Effects of Organized Family Planning Programs on U.S. Adolescent Fertility, 1970-1975 (Jacqueline Darroch Forrest)

726. DAAPPP Data Set 30. Johns Hopkins Study of Repeat Adolescent Pregnancy, 1976-1982 (Janet B. Hardy)

727. DAAPPP Data Set 31. 1972-74 Ventura County Survey of Unmarried Pregnant Women Aged 13-20 (Jerome Evans, Winston Chow, and Marvin Eisen)

728. DAAPPP Data Set 32. 1982 San Jose, California Study of Adolescent Perinatal Risk Reduction Behavior (Paul Hensleigh and Nancy Moss)

729. DAAPPP Data Set 33. 1981-1982 Evaluation of OAPP Adolescent Pregnancy Programs: Individual Level Data I (Martha Burt)

730. DAAPPP Data Set 34. 1981-1982 Evaluation of OAPP Adolescent Pregnancy Programs: Individual Level Data II (Martha Burt)

731. DAAPPP Data Set 35. 1979-1981 Philadelphia Study of Psychological Factors Associated with Adolescent Fertility Regulation--Females (Eugenie Walsh Flaherty and Jeanne Marecek)

732. DAAPPP Data Set 36. 1979-1981 Philadelphia Study of Psychological Factors Associated with Adolescent Fertility Regulation--Males (Eugenie Walsh Flaherty and Jeanne Marecek)

733. DAAPPP Data Set 37-38. The National Survey of Children, 1976 (Child Trends, Inc.)

734. DAAPPP Data Set 39. Florida-Puerto Rico Study of Adolescent Pregnancy and Neonatal Behavior, 1978 (Barry M. Lester)

735. DAAPPP Data Set 40. Maricopa County, Arizona Study of Child Maltreatment Risk among Adolescent Mothers, 1978-1978 (Frank G. Bolton, Jr.)

736. DAAPPP Data Set 41. 1955 Growth of American Families: Married Women (Arthur A. Campbell, Pascal K. Whelpton, and John E. Patterson)

737. DAAPPP Data Set 42. 1955 Growth of American Families: Single Women (Arthur A. Campbell, Pascal K. Whelpton, and John E. Patterson)

738. DAAPPP Data Set 43. 1960 Growth of American Families (Arthur A. Campbell, Pascal K. Whelpton and John E. Patterson)

739. DAAPPP Data Set 44. 1979 U.S. National Survey of Young Women (Melvin Zelnik and John F. Kantner)

740. DAAPPP Data Set 45. 1979 U.S. National Survey of Young Men (Melvin Zelnik and John F. Kantner)

741. DAAPPP Data Set 46. Chicago Urban League 1979 Young Chicagoans Survey (Dennis Hogan and Evelyn Kitagawa)

742. DAAPPP Data Set 47. 1972-74 Ventura County Survey of Unmarried Pregnant Women Aged 13-20 Six-Month Follow-up (Jerome Evans, Winston Chow and Marvin Eisen)

743. DAAPPP Data Set 48-49. 1965 U.S. National Fertility Study (Norman Ryder and Charles Westoff)

744. DAAPPP Data Set 50-51. 1970 U.S. National Fertility Study (Charles Westoff and Norman Ryder)

745. DAAPPP Data Set 52. 1975 U.S. National Fertility Study (Charles Westoff and Norman Ryder)

746. DAAPPP Data Set 53-55. National Fertility Study: Married Women Interviewed in 1970 and 1975 (Charles Westoff and Norman Ryder)

747. DAAPPP Data Set 56. 1973 Madison, Wisconsin Study of Premarital Sexuality Among Young People: Students (John DeLamater)

748. DAAPPP Data Set 57. 1973 Madison, Wisconsin Study of Premarital Sexuality Among Young People: Nonstudents (John DeLamater)

749. DAAPPP Data Set 58-60. 1957-1967 Study of American Family Growth--The Princeton Study (Charles F. Westoff, Robert C. Potter, Jr., Philip C. Sagi and Elliott C. Mishler)

750. DAAPPP Data Set 61. 1982 National Survey of Family Growth Cycle III Exposure Interval File (William Grady)

751. DAAPPP Data Set 62. 1968 Study of Family Planning Services and the Distribution of Black Americans (Kenneth C. Kammeyer, Norman R. Yetman and McKee J. McClendon)

752. DAAPPP Data Set 63-66. 1966-1972 Baltimore Study of Unplanned Teen Parenthood (Frank F. Furstenberg)

753. DAAPPP Data Set 67. U.S. National Survey of Teens Seeking Abortion Services, 1979-1980 (Aida Torres)

754. DAAPPP Data Set 68. Parental Notification Policies in U.S. Abortion Facilities, 1979-1980 (Aida Torres)

755. DAAPPP Data Set 69. U.S. Family Planning Clinic Parental Notification Policies, 1979-1980 (Aida Torres)

756. DAAPPP Data Set 70. Fee Policies for U.S. Clinics With and Without Title X Funding (Aida Torres)

757. DAAPPP Data Set 71-72. 1982 and 1983 Surveys of U.S. Family Planning Agencies (Aida Torres)

758. DAAPPP Data Set 73. 1983-85 Pennsylvania Study of Family Planning Discontinuation: Clinic and Community File (Roberta Herceg-Baron)

759. DAAPPP Data Set 74. 1983-85 Pennsylvania Study of Family Planning Discontinuation: Visit File (Roberta Herceg-Baron)

760. DAAPPP Data Set 75. 1983-85 Pennsylvania Study of Family Planning Discontinuation: Patient File (Roberta Herceg-Baron)

761. DAAPPP Data Set 76. 1983-85 Pennsylvania Study of Family Planning Discontinuation: Discontinuer Survey File (Roberta Herceg-Baron)

762. DAAPPP Data Set 77. 1979 U.S.-Mexico Border Survey (Jack C. Smith)

763. DAAPPP Data Set 78. 1980-1982 U.S. National Study of High School and Beyond, Selected Variables: A Longitudinal Study of Female Sophomores (Peter Morrison, Linda Waite, and Allan Abrahamse)

764. DAAPPP Data Set 79-81. 1980-1981 Philadelphia Study of Kinship Support for Adolescents in Family Planning Programs (Roberta Herceg-Baron and Frank F. Furstenberg)

765. DAAPPP Data Set 82-83. 1980 U.S. National Natality Survey (National Center for Health Statistics)

766. DAAPPP Data Set 84-85. 1980 U.S. National Fetal Mortality Study (National Center for Health Statistics)

767. DAAPPP Data Set 86-87. 1981 Child Health Supplement to the National Health Interview Survey (National Center for Health Statistics)

768. DAAPPP Data Set 88-90. The 1981 National Survey of Children (Child Trends, Inc.)

769. DAAPPP Data Set 91-94. Project Redirection, 1980-1983 (Denise Polit)

770. DAAPPP Data Set 95. 1975 Los Angeles County Study of Motivations, Roles, and Family Planning of Women (Linda J. Beckman)

771. DAAPPP Data Set 96-97. 1973-1976 New York City Study of the Social and Demographic Consequences of Teenage Childbearing (Harriet B. Presser)

772. DAAPPP Data Set 98. 1975 National Survey of Physicians' Attitudes Toward Abortion (Leonard LoSciuto)

773. DAAPPP Data Set 99. 1964-1966 U.S. National Infant Mortality Survey (National Center for Health Statistics)

774. DAAPPP Data Set Al-A2. 1983 Cuyohoga County, Ohio Familial Communication and Adolescent Sexual Behavior Project (Janet R. Kahn)

775. DAAPPP Data Set A3. 1964-1966 U.S. National Natality Survey (National Center for Health Statistics)

776. DAAPPP Data Set A4. 1967 U.S. National Natality Survey (National Center for Health Statistics)

777. DAAPPP Data Set A5. 1968 U.S. National Natality Survey (National Center for Health Statistics)

778. DAAPPP Data Set A6. 1969 U.S. National Natality Survey (National Center for Health Statistics)

779. DAAPPP Data Set A7. 1972 U.S. National Natality Survey (National Center for Health Statistics)

780. DAAPPP Data Set A8. 1975-1983 State and Regional Indicators Archive (Murray A. Straus)

781. DAAPPP Data Set A9. U.S. Census County and City Databook, 1983: State Files Plus Washington, D.C. (U.S. Census Bureau)

782. DAAPPP Data Set Bl. U.S. Census County and City Data Book, 1983: City Files (U.S. Census Bureau)

783. DAAPPP Data Set B2. Contemporary American Family Poll, Sept. 18-25, 1981 (Yankelovich, Skelly and White)

784. DAAPPP Data Set B3. Contemporary Views on Sex Education, Nov. 10-12, 1986 (Yankelovich, Clancy and Shulman)

785. DAAPPP Data Set B4. 1983 Survey of Family Relations and Adolescent Sex Behavior in Salt Lake City, Utah, and Albuquerque, New Mexico (Brent C. Miller)

786. DAAPPP Data Set B5. 1984 Survey of Family Relations and Adolescent Sex Behavior in Salt Lake City, Utah, Albuquerque, New Mexico, and San Bernardino County, California (Brent C. Miller)

787. DAAPPP Data Set B6. 1976-1980 Second U.S. National Health and Nutrition Examination Survey: Selected Variables (National Center for Health Statistics)